D0014588

# ERMA BOMBECK
## Giant Economy Size

# ERMA BOMBECK
## Giant Economy Size

**AT WIT'S END**

**"JUST WAIT TILL YOU HAVE CHILDREN OF YOUR OWN!"**

**I LOST EVERYTHING IN THE POST-NATAL DEPRESSION**

DOUBLEDAY & COMPANY, INC.
*Garden City, New York*
1983

*Library of Congress Cataloging in Publication Data*

Bombeck, Erma.
    Erma Bombeck giant economy size.

        Contents: At wit's end—"Just wait till you have children of your own!"
—I lost everything in the post-natal depression.
    I. Title.
PS3552.O59A6  1983    818'.5402    82–45557
ISBN 0-385-18394-1

# AT WIT'S END

*Illustrated by Loretta Vollmuth*

*This isn't a book.*

*It's a group therapy session.*

*It is based on six predictable depression cycles that beset a woman during a twelve-month span.*

*These chapters will not tell you how to overcome these depression cycles.*

*They will not tell you how to cope with them.*

*They will have hit home if they, in some small way, help you to laugh your way through while hanging on to your sweet sanity.*

# WHAT'S A NICE girl like ME

# doing in a dump like THis?

IT HITS on a dull, overcast Monday morning. I awake realizing there is no party in sight for the weekend, I'm out of bread, and I've got a dry skin problem. So I say it aloud to myself, "What's a nice girl like me doing in a dump like this?"

The draperies are dirty (and will disintegrate if laundered), the arms of the sofa are coming through. There is Christmas tinsel growing out of the carpet. And some clown has written in the dust on the coffee table, YANKEE GO HOME.

It's those rotten kids. It's their fault I wake up feeling so depressed. If only they'd let me wake up in my own way. Why do they have to line up along my bed and stare at me like Moby Dick just washed up onto a beach somewhere?

"I think she hears us. Her eyelids fluttered."

"Wait till she turns over, then everybody cough."

"Why don't we just punch her and ask her what we want to know."

"*Get him out of here.*"

"She's pulling the covers over her ears. Start coughing."

I don't know how long it will be before one of them discovers that by taking my pulse they will be able to figure out by its rapid beat if I am faking or not, but it will come. When they were smaller, it was worse. They'd stick their wet fingers into the opening of my face and whisper, "You awake yet?" Or good old Daddy would simply heave a flannel-wrapped bundle at me and say, "Here's Mommy's little boy." (Any mother with half a skull knows that when Daddy's little boy becomes Mommy's little boy, the kid is so wet he's treading water!) Their imagination is straight from the pages of Edgar Allan Poe. Once they put a hamster on my chest and when I bolted upright (my throat muscles paralyzed with fright) they asked, "Do you have any alcohol for the chemistry set?"

I suppose that's better than having them kick the wall until Daddy becomes conscious, then ask, "Do you want the cardboards that the laundry puts in your shirts?" Any wrath beats waking Daddy. There has to be something wrong with a man who keeps resetting his alarm clock in the morning and each time it blasts off smacks it silent and yells, "No one tells me what to do, Buddy."

Personally I couldn't care less what little games my husband plays with his alarm clock, but when I am awakened at 5:30, 6:00, 6:15, and 6:30 every morning, I soon react to bells like a punchy fighter. That's what I get for marrying a nocturnal animal. In the daylight, he's nothing. He has to have help with his shoelaces. In all the years we've been married he only got up once of his own accord before 9:30. And then his mattress was on fire. He can't seem to cope with daytime noises like flies with noisy chest colds, the crash of marshmallows as they hit the hot chocolate, the earsplitting noises milk makes when you pour it over the cereal.

The truth of it is, he's just not geared to function in an eight-to-five society. Once he even fell out of his filing cabinet.

Around eleven at night a transformation takes place. He stretches and yawns, then his eyes pop open and he kicks me in the foot and says, "What kind of a day did you have?"

"You mean we're still on the same one?" I yawn.

"You're not going to bed already, are you?"

"Yes."

"Would it bother you if I played the guitar?"

"Yes."

"Well, then maybe I'll read a little before I go to sleep."

"Why not? I have the only eyelids in the neighborhood with a tan."

No doubt about it, if I could arise in a graceful manner, I could cope.

It's starting to snow. Thanks a lot up there.

Before moving to the suburbs, I always thought an "Act of God" was a flash of lightning at Mt. Sinai or forty days and forty nights of rain. Out here, they call a snowfall an "Act of God" and they close the schools.

The first time it happened I experienced a warm, maternal glow, a feeling of confidence that I lived in a community which would put its children above inclement weather. The second time, that same week, I experienced a not-so-warm glow, but began to wonder if perhaps the kids could wear tennis rackets on their feet and a tow rope around their waists to guide them. On the third day school was canceled within a two-week period, I was organizing a dog-sled pool.

We racked up fifteen Acts of God that year and it became apparent to the women in our neighborhood that "somebody up there" was out to get us.

It got to be a winter morning ritual. We'd all sit around the radio like an underground movement in touch with the free world. When the announcer read the names of the schools closed, a rousing cheer would go up and the kids would scatter. I'd cry a little in the dishtowel, then announce sullenly, "All right, don't sweat in the school clothes. RE-PEAT. Don't sweat in the school clothes. Hang them up. Maybe tomorrow you'll visit school. And stay out of those lunch boxes. It's only eight-thirty." My words would fall on deaf ears. Within minutes they were in full snow gear ready to whip over to the school and play on the hill.

Little things began to bother me about these unscheduled closings. For example, we'd drive by the school and our second-grader would point and ask, "What's that building, Daddy?" Also, it was March and they hadn't had their Christmas exchange yet. Our ten-year-old had to be prompted with his alphabet. And the neighborhood "Love and Devotion to Child Study" group had to postpone their meetings three times because they couldn't get the rotten kids out from under foot.

"We might as well be living in Fort Apache," said one mother. "If this snow doesn't melt soon, my kid will outgrow his school desk."

We all agreed something had to be done.

This year, a curious thing happened. In the newspaper it was stated that snow was no longer to be considered an Act of God by the state board of education. Their concern was that the children spend a minimum number of hours in school each week and that the buses would roll come yells or high water.

Snow is a beautiful, graceful thing as it floats downward to the earth, and is enhanced greatly by the breathtaking indentation of school bus snow tires. Snow is now considered an Act of Nature in the suburbs. And everyone knows she's a Mother and understands these things.

"Whip it up, group. Everyone to the boots!"

"What do you mean you're a participle in the school play and you need a costume? You be careful in that attic, do you hear? If you fall through and break your neck, you're going to be late for school!"

A drudge. That's all I am. They'll all be sorry when I'm not around to run and fetch.

"So you swallowed the plastic dinosaur out of the cereal box. What do you want me to do, call a vet?"

Lunches. Better pack the lunches. Listen to them bicker. What do they care what I pack? They'd trade their own grandmother for a cough drop and a Holy picture.

Of course, none of these things would bother me if I had an understanding husband. Mother was right. I should have married that little literature major who broke out in a rash every time he read Thoreau. But no, I had to pick the nut standing out in the driveway yelling at the top of his voice, "I am thirty-nine years old. I make fifteen thousand dollars a year. I will not carry a Donald Duck thermos to the office!" Boy, he wouldn't yell at me if my upper arms weren't flabby. He never used to yell at me like that. *He* should worry. He doesn't have to throw himself across the washer during "spin" to keep it from walking out of the utility room. He doesn't have to flirt with a hernia making bunk beds. He doesn't have to shuffle through encyclopedias before the school bus leaves to find out which United States president invented the folding chair.

It's probably the weather. "Everybody out!"

Look at 'em stumbling around the driveway like newborn field mice. It's the weather all right. No leaves on the trees. No flowers. No green grass. Just a big picture window with nothing to look at but . . . *a new bride moving into the cul-de-sac!* Well, there goes the neighborhood. Would you look at her standing at her husband's elbow as he stencils their marvy new name on their marvy new garbage cans? I suppose tomorrow she'll be out waxing her driveway. So give her a few years, and she'll be like the rest of us sifting through the coffee grounds looking for baby's pacifier.

What am I saying? Give her a few years of suburban living and she'll misplace the baby! What was it I was supposed to look for this morning? Maybe I'll think of it. I wonder how much time I waste each day looking for lost things. Let's see, I spent at least two hours yesterday looking for the bananas and enough straight pins to pin up a hem. Lucky the kids came up with the idea of walking across the floor in my bare feet or I'd be looking for pins yet. I suppose I could've uncovered the bananas by smelling breaths, but you have to trust someone sometime when they say no.

The day before that I misplaced the car keys. Of course, that's not my fault. That was the fault of the clown who left them in the ignition. You'd certainly never think to look there for them. Just say I spend about two hours a day looking for stuff. That amounts to 730 hours a year, not counting the entire months of November and December when I look for the Christmas cards I buy half price the preceding January.

I'd have a child growing up on the Pennsylvania Turnpike today if a group of picnickers hadn't noticed her sifting through trash barrels in the roadside park and become curious about how she got there. I wonder if other women piff away all that time looking for nail files and scotch tape.

I knew a woman once who always said, "Have a place for everything and everything in its place." I hated her. I wonder what she would say if she knew I rolled out of bed each morning and walked to the kitchen on my knees hoping to catch sight of a lost coin, a single sock, an overdue library book or a boot that could later inspire total recall.

I remember what I was going to look for . . . my glasses! But that was only if I wanted to see something during the day. So what do I have to see today that I couldn't put off until tomorrow? One of the kids said there was something strange in the oven. Probably a tray of hors d'oeuvres left over from the New Year's party. I'll look for the glasses tomorrow.

In the meantime, maybe I'll call Phyllis and tell her about the new bride. Better not chance it. Phyllis might be feeling great today and then I'd feel twice as crumby as I feel now.

This place will have to be cleaned before they can condemn it. Wouldn't be at all surprised if I ended up like my Aunt Lydia. Funny, I haven't thought about her in years. Grandma always said she ran away with a vanilla salesman. Lay you odds she made her move right after the holidays. Her kids probably hid the Christmas candy in the bedroom closet and the ants were coming out of the woodwork like a Hessian drill team. One child was going through the dirty clothes hamper trying to retrieve her "favorite" underwear to wear to school.

Lydia spotted her nine-year-old dog (with the Christmas puppy plumbing) and ran after it with a piece of newspaper. The dog read a few of the comics, laughed out loud, then wet on the carpet.

Uncle Wally probably pecked her on the cheek with all the affection of a sex-starved cobra and said he wanted to talk about the Christmas bills when he came home.

She passed a mirror and noticed a permanent crease on her face where the brush roller had slipped. Her skirt felt tight. She sucked in her breath. Nothing moved. Her best friend called to tell her the sequin dress she bought for New Year's Eve had been reduced to half price.

Speculating on her future she could see only a long winter in a house with four blaring transistor radios, a spastic washer, and the ultimate desperation of trying to converse with the tropical fish.

You know something. The odds are Aunt Lydia didn't even know the vanilla salesman. When he knocked on the door, smiled and said, "Good morning, madam, I'm traveling through your territory on my way to Forked Tongue, Iowa," Aunt Lydia grabbed her satchel, her birdcage, and her nerve elixir, closed the door softly behind her and said quietly, "You'll do."

Each woman fights the doldrums in her own way. This illustrated guide, *What to Do Until the Therapist Arrives with the Volleyball,* is not unique. Its suggestions may, however, keep you from regressing into a corner in a foetal position with your hands over your ears.

A: KNIT.   Learning how to knit was a snap. It was learning how to stop that nearly destroyed me. Everyone in the house agreed I was tense and needed to unwind. So, I enrolled in an informal class in knitting.

The first week I turned out thirty-six pot holders. I was so intent on an afghan you'd have thought I was competing with an assembly line of back-scratcher makers from Hong Kong.

I couldn't seem to stop myself. By the end of the first month of knitting, I was sick from relaxation. There were deep, dark circles under my eyes. My upper lip twitched uncontrollably. There were calluses on both my thumbs and forefingers. I cried a lot from exhaustion. But I was driven by some mad, inner desire to knit fifteen toilet tissue covers shaped like little men's hats by the end of the week.

In the mornings I could hardly wait until the children were out of the house so I could haul out my knitting bag full of yarn and begin clicking away. "All right, group, let's snap it up," I'd yell. "Last one out of the house gets underwear for Christmas."

"It's only six-thirty," they'd yawn sleepily.

"So you're a little early," I snapped impatiently.

"BUT IT'S SATURDAY!" they chorused.

My husband was the first one to suggest I needed professional help. "You've gone beyond the social aspect of knitting," he said. "Let's face it. You have a problem and you're going to have to taper off. From here on in no more yarn." I promised, but I knew I wouldn't keep my word.

My addiction eventually led to dishonesty, lying, cheating, and selling various and sundry items to support my habit. I was always being discovered. The family unearthed a skein of mohair in a cereal box and an argyle kit hidden in the chandelier, and one afternoon I was found feverishly unraveling an old ski cap just to knit it over again. One night when the clicking of the needles in the darkness awakened my husband, he bolted up in bed, snapped on the light, and said quietly, "Tomorrow, I'm enrolling you in 'Knitters Anonymous.' Can't you see what's happening to you? To us? To the children? You can't do this by yourself."

He was right, of course. "Knitters Anonymous" pointed out the foolishness of my compulsion to knit all the time. They eventually weaned me off yarn and interested me in another hobby—painting.

Would you believe it? I did eight watercolors the first week, fifteen charcoal sketches the second and by the end of the month I will have racked up twenty-three oils . . . all on stretched canvasses!

B: DRINK. A while back some overzealous girl watcher noted a mass migration of the Red-Beaked Female Lush to split-levels in the suburbs.

That a total of 68 percent of the women today drink, there is no quarrel. But that they've all settled in the suburbs is questionable. Following this announcement, we in the suburbs called an emergency meeting of the "Help Stamp Out Ugly Suburban Rumors" committee. We decided to dispel the stigma once and for all by conducting a sobriety test among women at 8 A.M. Monday morning in the town hall.

We uncorked—rather, uncovered—only three sherry breaths, a cognac suspect, and one woman who wasn't sauced at all but who said she always shook that way after getting her four kids onto the school bus in the mornings.

A few of them admitted to nipping away at a bottle of vanilla in the broom closet or getting a little high sniffing laundry bleach, but most of them confessed drinking in the suburbs is not feasible. They cited the following reasons.

*Privacy:* "You show me a mother who slips into the bathroom to slug down a drink and I'll show you seven children hidden in the bathtub flashing a Popeye home movie on her chest."

*Discretion:* "To children, drinking means an occasion.

When not given a satisfactory occasion to tout, they will spread it all over the neighborhood that Mama is toasting another 'No Baby Month.' "

*Guilt:* "With the entire block of my friends feeling trapped, bored, neurotic, and unfulfilled, why should I feel good and alienate myself?"

One woman did confess her system of rewarding herself with a drink had gotten a bit out of hand. At first she rewarded herself with a drink for washing down the kitchen walls or defrosting the refrigerator. Now she was treating herself to a drink for bringing in the milk or opening the can of asparagus at the right end.

Undoubtedly the girl watcher was tabulating the many gourmet clubs that have sprouted up in the suburbs. They are the harmless little luncheons where a light wine is served before the luncheon and gourmet foods using brandies and wines are served to stimulate women's interest in cookery.

Some of these are held on a monthly basis to observe some special occasion such as a birthday or an anniversary of a member. In our group, we also observe Mao Tse-tung's backstroke victory, the anniversary of the escape of Winnie Ruth Judd, the January White Sale at Penguin's Department Store, the introduction of soy beans to Latin America, and the arrival and departure dates of the *Queen Mary*. Each month we present an award to the most unique dish served. Last month's prize was copped by my neighbor for a wonderful dessert which consisted of a peach seed floating recklessly in a snifter of brandy.

Frankly I think the girl watchers owe the women of the suburbs an apology for their accusations. Anyone here want to drink to that?

c: READ. One of the occupational hazards of housewifery and motherhood is that you never get the time to sit down and read an entire book from cover to cover.

A spot check of my most erudite friends revealed that the

last books they read were: *Guadalcanal Diary, The Cat in the Hat Dictionary, The Picture of Dorian Gray,* and *First Aid.* (The fifth fell asleep over her "Know Your Steam Iron Warranty and Manual," but we counted it anyway.)

This is a sad commentary on the women who are going to be the mothers of all these scientists and skilled technicians of tomorrow. As I always say, "What doth it profiteth a woman to have a clean house if she thinks anthropologist Margaret Mead is a foot doctor!" (I recommended her to three of my friends.)

First, to find the right book. When you live in a small town you have to be pretty discreet about the books you check out. I, for one, don't want to be known behind the stalls as "Old Smutty Tongue." On the other hand, I don't want to spend my precious time plowing through *Little Goodie Miss Two Shoes and Her Adventures on Bass Island.*

"You know me pretty well, Miss Hathcock," I said to the librarian. "What book would you suggest for me?"

"*Sex and the Senior Citizen* with a glossary in the front listing all the pages with the dirty parts in boldface type," she answered crisply.

"Now, now, Miss Hathcock. We will have our little humor, won't we? Keep in mind I have very little time for reading and I want a book I can talk about in mixed company."

"If I were you," she said slowly, "I'd check out *Come Speed Read with Me* by M. Fletcher. It guarantees that in three days it will increase your reading speed enormously. You will be literally digesting an entire newspaper in nineteen minutes, novels in thirty minutes, and anthologies in an hour."

I tested myself the minute I got home. It took me forty-five minutes to read one paragraph. Maybe it was possible I had lost my old power of concentration. According to the contents of the first chapter, my diagnosis was a simple one. My eyes jerked and stopped at every word. I read each word, not sentences or images. That would take work.

Whenever I got the chance I picked up my *Come Speed Read with Me* book and spent an hour or two in diligent application.

Yesterday I approached Miss Hathcock at the return desk.

"Well, how did your speed reading go?" she smiled. "Are you ready for the complete works of Churchill? How about *Hawaii*? Or Ted Sorensen's *Kennedy*?"

"Actually," I giggled, "I kept drowsing over chapter two. That's the 'Lack of Attention' chapter. Once I hurdle that, I feel I can whip through the entire thing in no time at all. How about an additional twenty-one days renewal on it?"

"How about *Sex and the Senior Citizen*?" she sighed wearily. "And I'll wrap it in a plain piece of brown paper."

D: TELEPHONE. A noted heart specialist has openly attacked women's use of the extension phone. He has charged these convenient outlets will (a) broaden hips, (b) cause sluggish circulation, and (c) eventually take away her lead over men in life expectancy.

Doctor, you are either naïve on the subject of telephone conditioning or you are pulling our fat, muscular legs.

At the first ring of the telephone, there is an immediate conditioned response that has every kid in the house galloping to the instrument to answer it. You show me a woman who is alert and who wears deep-tread sneakers and I'll show you a woman who gets to answer her own telephone.

Once Mama is settled comfortably on the phone, the children swing into action like a highly organized army on maneuvers, each marching to his favorite "No, No, Burn Burn" or whatever. Refrigerator doors pop open, cupboards bang back and forth, makeshift ropes carry kids sailing through the air, razor blades appear, strange children come filing through the doors and windows, the aromas of nail polish and gasoline permeate the air, and through it all one child will crawl up on the television set and take off his clothes! There is nothing like it to pep up tired blood.

Some mothers are clickers—that is, rather than interrupt a telephone conversation they will click fingers and point, pound on the table and point, whistle through their fingers and point, or pick up a club and point. So much for circulation.

Other mothers resort to muffled. cries as they hold their hands over the receivers. They can't fake it. They've got to administer the whack, clean up the sugar, blow up a balloon, put out the fire, mop up the water *right now!* So much for hip exercises.

A few telephone exponents are a study in pantomime. I used to be mesmerized by a woman who formed the words, "I'm going to give you kids one in a minute," followed shortly by, "I'm going to give you kids two in a minute." She alone knew the magic number whereby she would stop and give them a belt.

Some mothers have even attempted to put a busy box, filled with toys, near their telephones. Of course, kids are too bright to fall for that. You could have Mary Poppins hanging by her umbrella whistling "Dixie" and kids would still roll the onions across the floor and gargle the laundry bleach.

I don't think women outlive men, Doctor. It only seems longer.


*Shape Up Before You Ship Out*

IN THE throes of a winter depression cycle, there is nothing that will set you off like a group of fashion authorities who want to know, "Is your figure ready for a bikini this summer?"

I got a flash for you, Charlie. My figure wasn't ready for a bikini last summer. Very frankly, I've hit a few snags.

You see, for years I have built my figure on the premise that "fat people are jolly." I have eaten my way through: pleasant, cheery, sunny, smiling, gay, spirited, chipper, vivacious, sparkling, happy, and sportive and was well on my way to becoming hysterical. Now I find that a group of experts say this is a myth. "Fat people aren't jolly at all. They're just

frustrated and fat." You'd have thought they would have said something while I was back on pleasant.

There was a time when I had a twenty-three-inch waist. I was ten years old at the time. As I recall, my measurements were 23-23-23. I'm no fool. Even at ten years, I knew I could never be too jolly with those figures so I started to eat.

In high school I used to reward myself with after-school snacks for (a) not stepping on a crack in the sidewalk, (b) spelling Ohio backwards, (c) remembering my locker combination.

After marriage, I added thirty pounds in nine months, which seemed to indicate I was either pregnant or going a little heavy on the gravy. It was the former. I am listed in the medical records as the only woman who ever gained weight *during* delivery.

My husband, of course, used to try to shame me by pasting a picture of Ann-Margret on the refrigerator door with a terse note, "Count Calories."

He hasn't tried that routine, however, since our trip to the shopping center last spring that coincided with a personal appearance by Mr. Universe.

"I thought we came here to look at a bedroom rug," he snapped. "You see one muscle, you've seen them all," he snorted.

"I've been married eighteen years and I've yet to see my first one," I said standing on my tiptoes. "Just let me see what he looks like."

Mr. Universe worked in a fitted black T-shirt and shorts. If muscles ever go out of style he could always get a job on the beach kicking sand in the faces of ninety-seven-pound weaklings and yelling, "Yea, skinny!" He thumped onto the platform and my jaw dropped.

"For crying out loud, close your mouth," whispered my husband. "You look like someone just dropped a bar bell on your foot."

"Did you ever see so many muscles in your life?" I gasped. "That T-shirt is living on borrowed time. And listen to that. He says it just takes a few minutes a day to build a body like his. Hey, now he's touching his ear to his knees. Can you touch your ear to your knee?"

"What in heaven's name for?" he sighed. "There's nothing to hear down there. Besides, I'd be embarrassed to look like that. My suits wouldn't fit right. And I couldn't bear having all those people staring."

"You're really sensitive about all this, aren't you?"

"I certainly am not," he said emphatically. "It's just that I'm not a beach boy."

"I'll say you're not a beach boy. Remember when that kid wanted to borrow your inner-tube last summer at the pool and you weren't wearing one?"

"Are we going to look at that bedroom rug or aren't we?" he growled.

"Not until you admit that you can't kick seven feet high,

throw a football seventy-five yards and jump over an arrow you're holding in both hands."

"Okay, so I'm not Mr. Universe."

"Then you'll take that picture of Ann-Margret off my refrigerator door?"

"Yes. You know, in my day I used to have a set of pretty good arm muscles. Here, look at this. I'm flexing. Hurry up! See it? How's that for muscle?"

Personally I've seen bigger lumps in my cheese sauce, but when you've won a war, why mess around with a small skirmish?

I think the trouble with most women dieters is that they can't get from Monday to Tuesday without becoming discouraged. I am a typical Monday dieter. Motivated by some small incident that happens on a Sunday ("Mama's outgrown her seat belt. We'll have to staple her to the seat covers, won't we?") I start in earnest on a Monday morning to record my era of suffering.

### Diary of a Monday Dieter

8:00 A.M.: This is it. Operation twenty pounds. Called Edith and told her what I had for breakfast. Reminded her to read a story in this month's *Mother's Digest*, "How Mrs. M., St. Louis, ate 25 Hungarian Cabbage Rolls a Day and Belched Her Way to a Size 10."

12:30 P.M.: Forced myself to drink a cup of bouillon. Called Edith and told her I noticed a difference already. I don't have that stuffed feeling around my waist. I have more energy and my clothes fit better. Promised her my gray suit. After this week, it will probably hang on me like a sack.

4:00 P.M.: An article in *Calorie* (the magazine for people who devour everything in sight) offers a series of wonderful dinner menus for weight-watchers.

As I was telling Edith a few minutes ago, we mothers have an obligation to our families to feed them nutritious, slimming meals. Tonight we are having lean meat, fresh garden peas, Melba thins in a basket, and fresh fruit.

4:30 P.M.: Husband called to say he'd be late for dinner. Fresh garden peas looked a little nude, so added a few sauteed mushrooms and a dab of cream sauce. After all, why should the children be sick and suffer because they have a strong-willed mother?

4:45 P.M.: I ate the Melba toast—every dry, tasteless crumb of it! (Come to think of it the basket is missing.) Luckily I had a biscuit mix in the refrigerator and jazzed it up with a little shredded cheese and butter. The magazine said when you begin licking wax from the furniture you should supplement your diet with a snack.

5:00 P.M.: Well, maybe that lousy fruit in the bowl would look pretty good to Robinson Crusoe, but I put it under a pie crust where it belongs. In fifty minutes I'll have a warm cobbler, swimming in rich, thick cream. Who does my husband think he is? Paul Newman?

5:30 P.M.: The kids just asked what I am doing. I'm putting on a few potatoes to go with the gravy, that's what I'm doing. That's the trouble with kids today. Half of the world goes to bed hungry and they expect me to pour good meat drippings down the drain. Kids are rotten. They really are.

6:00 P.M.: Blood pressure has dropped. Stomach is beginning to bloat. Vision is impaired. I've added two more vegetables and a large pizza with everything to the menu. That fink Edith had the nerve to call and ask if she could have the blouse to the gray suit. Edith's a nice girl, but she's a pushy individual who drives you crazy phoning all the time. I told the kids to tell her I couldn't talk. I was listening to my Bonnie Prudden records.

6:30 P.M.: Husband arrived home. I met him at the door and let him have it. If it weren't for his rotten working hours, I could be the slip of the girl he married. He had the gall to act like he didn't know what I was talking about.

No, I don't think I'm ready for a bikini again this year. Heaven knows I try to bend to the dictates of fashion, but let's face it, I'm a loser. When I grew my own bustle, they went out of style. When my hips reached saddlebag proportions, the "long, lean look" came in. When I ultimately discovered a waistline, the straight skirt came into being. I had a few bright moments when they were exploiting the flat chest as denoting women with high I.Q.'s, but then someone revealed a certain clearly unflat movie star's 135 (I.Q. that is) and shot *that* theory down.

Here's my basic equipment, if you fashion moguls care to check it out, but frankly it doesn't look too encouraging.

*Shoulders:* Two of them. Unfortunately they don't match. One hooks up higher than the other, which they tell me is quite common among housewives who carry fat babies, heavy grocery bags, and car chains.

*Midriff:* If I can't tighten up the muscles in time for beach exposure perhaps I can use it for a snack tray.

*Eyes:* Some people with myopic vision look sexy. I look like I have myopic vision. Don't tell me what to do with my eyebrows. I tried several things and either look like Milton Berle or Bela Lugosi with a sick headache.

*Waist:* It's here somewhere. Probably misfiled.

*Hips:* Here. They weren't built in a day, friend, so don't expect miracles. Right now, they couldn't get a rise out of a factory whistle.

*Knees:* Let me put it this way. A poet at a neighborhood cocktail party once described them as "divining rods that could get water out of the Mojave Desert."

*Legs:* Ever wonder who got what Phyllis Diller discarded?

*Guts:* Hardly any.

Tell you what. If I don't "shape up" by June, go on to the beach without me. Stop on the way back and I'll serve you a dish of homemade shortcake, topped with fresh strawberries crusted in powdered sugar and wallowing in a soft mound of freshly whipped cream.

MARCH 5 — MAY 6

# i want to be more than

# just another pretty face ...

TALENT is a big thing.

Most of us can't be like the optimist who was given a barn full of fertilizer and ran through it pell mell shouting, "I know there's a pony here somewhere." We wonder where we were when talent was passed out. Making Jockey shorts for Ken dolls? Fashioning angels out of toilet tissue rolls? Baking no-cal cupcakes for fat Girl Scouts?

Why do we feel so dumb? So out of touch with the world? So lacking in self-confidence? As you look at the reflection in the mirror, your brush rollers towering high above you, your cold sore shimmering from ointment, you mumble to yourself, "I want to be more than just another pretty face. I want to make some difference in this world. Just once I want to stand up at a PTA meeting and say, 'I entertain a motion that we adjourn until we have business more pressing than the cafeteria's surplus of canned tomatoes, and more entertaining than a film on *How Your Gas Company Works for*

*You.*'" Just once I'd like to have a tall, dark stranger look at me like I wasn't on the sixth day of a five-day deodorant pad. Just once I'd like to have a real fur coat that I could drag behind me on the floor. (Not those 218 hamsters with tranquilizers that I wear to club.)

But me? I couldn't even carry off a trip to Mr. Miriam's Hair Palace. There I stood surrounded by elegance in my simple, peasant headscarf, my wrap-around skirt, my summer tennis shoes, and, my God! *Not Girl Scout socks!*

"Are you a standing?" asked the receptionist.

"A standing what?" I asked.

"Do you have a standing appointment?"

I shook my head.

"I say, you didn't cut your bangs at home with pinking shears or anything, did you?" she asked suspiciously. "Or turn your hair orange with bleach over bleach? Or fall asleep and forget to turn your home permanent off?"

"Oh no," I said. "I just want my hair done because I've been a little depressed since the baby was born."

"Oh," she said softly, "how old is your baby?"

"Twenty-four," I answered.

Because I was unknown to the shop, I drew Miss Lelanie, who had been out of beauty school three days—this time. (The lawsuit with the nasty bald woman is still pending.) With Miss Lelanie, I felt as relaxed as a cat in a roomful of rocking chairs. She didn't say anything, really. She just flipped through my hair like she was tossing a wilted salad. Finally she called in Mr. Miriam to show him what she had found. Both concurred that my ends were split, my scalp diseased, and I was too far over the hill to manufacture a decent supply of hair oil.

"It's all that dry?" I asked incredulously.

"I'd stay away from careless smokers," said Miss Lelanie without smiling.

Miss Lelanie massaged, combed, conditioned, rolled,

brushed, teased, and sprayed for the better part of two hours. Then she whirled me around to look into the mirror. "Why fight it?" I said, pinching the reflection's cheek, "You're a sex symbol." Miss Lelanie closed her eyes as if asking for divine guidance.

I don't mind admitting I felt like a new woman as I walked across the plush carpet, my shoulders squared, my head held high. I could feel every pair of eyes in the room following me.

"Pardon me, honey," said Miss Lelanie, "you're dragging a piece of bathroom tissue on your heel. Want me to throw it away?"

I could have been a standing and I blew it. That's the way it is with me.

Even my own children know I'm a no-talent. There was a time when I could tell them anything and they would believe me. I had all the answers. "Mama, what does the tooth fairy do with all those teeth she collects?" I'd smile wisely and say, "Why she makes them into necklaces and sells them at Tiffany's for a bundle." "What's a bundle, Mama?" "Please, dear," I would say, feigning dizziness, "how much brilliance can Mommy pour into your small head in one day." And so it went. I was their authority on the solar system, the Bible, history, mathematics, languages, fine arts, the St. Lawrence Seaway, air brakes, and turbojets. I even had them believing the traffic lights changed colors when I blew hard and commanded them to "turn green." (So, my kids were a little slow.)

Then one day recently my daughter asked, "Do you know the capital of Mozambique?" "No, but hum a few bars and I'll fake it," I grinned. "Mother," she announced flatly, "you don't know anything!"

That was the beginning. Day by day they chipped away at my veneer of ignorance. I didn't know how to say in French, "Pardon me, sir, but you are standing on my alligator's paw." I didn't know how to find the expanding notation of a number in modern math. (I didn't even know it was missing.) I didn't know the make of the sports car parked across the street, or the exact height of Oscar Robertson. I had never read *Smokey, the Cow Horse.* I didn't even know General Stonewall Jackson always ate standing up so his food would digest better.

In desperation I wrote to Bennington College in Vermont, which, I understood, was offering a course just meant for me.

Sirs:

I read with great interest the possibility of a new course being added to your curriculum, "Boredom of Housewifery." Knowing there will be several million housewives who will invade your city riding trucks, tanks, cars, planes, trains, pogo sticks, rickshaws, bicycles, and skateboards, I hasten to be considered for enrollment.

My background would seem to qualify me. I have three children who are hostile and superior to me mentally, a husband who loves his work and plays the guitar, and a house that depresses me. I cry a lot.

I don't seem to know what to do with my time. I think I waste a lot of it. When I am in the car waiting for the children at school I have taken to writing down the car mileage, multiplying it by my age, subtracting the number of lost mittens behind the seat, and dividing it by my passengers. Whatever number I come up with, is the number of cookies I allow myself before dinner.

I am not stimulated by housework as are other women I know. They are always doing clever things with old nylon hose and egg cartons. Last month I stuck a four-inch nail into the wall above my sink to hold the unpaid bills. When I tried to share my idea with my friends they said I needed to get out more. Sometimes I think the winter has fifteen months in it.

I have also tried joining various organizations, but this does not seem to solve my problem. Last school year I was Sunshine Chairman of the PTA. It seems I spread more sunshine than the treasury was prepared to spread. They dismissed me with a polite note that read, "It is nice to make people happy, but you don't have to tickle them to death."

You stated that the program at Bennington would be designed to aid wives "whose vital intellectual capacity is sapped by what seems to them like endless hours during which they serve as combination caretakers, nurses, policewomen, and kitchen helpers." I like that.

The announcement did not deal specifically with any of the topics to be discussed, but I am hopeful they will cover "Lies and Other Provocative Sayings" for dinner parties, outings, and class reunions. I'd also like a class in "Conversational Hobbies." I passed up the chance to take "Auto Harp Lessons" because I thought I hadn't been driving long enough.

Sincerely,
Desperate

Needless to say the class was filled before they received my application and I continue to feel inadequate and unsure of myself. Why is this? I can see it in my husband's attitude toward me. The other night he took me to dinner. We were having a wonderful time when he remarked, "You can certainly tell the wives from the sweethearts."

I stopped licking the stream of butter dripping down my elbow and replied, "What kind of a crack is that?"

"Just look around you," he said. "See that sweet young thing staring into her young man's eyes? She's single. Now look at the table next to them. That woman has buttered six pieces of bread and is passing them clockwise around the table. Soon she will cut up everyone's meat within a six-table radius and begin collecting swizzle sticks to take home to the kids. She's obviously married. You can always tell. Married women rarely dance. They just sit there and throw appetizers down their throats like the main course just went out of style. Single women go out to 'dine.' Married women go out to 'eat.'"

All the way home, holding the doggy bag filled with tossed salad out the no-draft so it wouldn't drip through on my coat, I thought about what he said. It was true. Women were in a rut. At parties all the women retired to the living room to relive their birth pains and exchange tuna recipes while the men hovered around the kitchen and attacked the big stuff like strikes, racial differences, and wars.

"Why don't you ever talk with us about those things?" I asked.

"What things?"

"Like wars and economics and the UN?"

He grimaced. "Remember the last time at a party I mentioned Taylor was in Vietnam?" (I nodded.) "And you asked if Burton was there with her?" (I nodded.) "That's why."

"That's not fair," I shouted. "You know I'm nothing at parties. I'm just not large on small talk."

"I noticed that," he retorted, "you spring into the first

chair you see like there are magnets in your garters and you never leave it. You just sit there and watch your feet swell."

"It all seems so ridiculous," I snapped. "The other night at that dreary party, one of your friends, whom I shall call Mr. Teeth for want of a better description, said to me, 'I've been looking for you all evening. What have you been reading lately?' "

"What's wrong with that?"

"Nothing. Only he wasn't even looking at me. His head was pivoting like a red light on a police cruiser all the while. I told him I had read 'The Causes and Effects of Diaper Rash' and he said, 'Good show! The critics in the East raved about it.' He hugged me and left."

"What about Larry Blagley. I saw him talking with you."

"You mean 'Mr. Sincere'?"

"I wish you'd stop tagging my friends those goofy names."

"I was enjoying a good, stiff drink when he said, 'Doesn't water pollution bother you at all?' I nearly choked to death. 'Am I drinking it?' I asked. He said, 'Why I have samples in my lab of that stinking, slimy glob of bilge and garbage that looks like so much sticky, clotted, ropey yuuuuuck. It infiltrates your drinking water and mine. If you saw it, it would make your hair stand on end.' 'Just hearing about it isn't doing much for the liver paste that's stuck in my throat either,' I told him."

"The trouble with you," said my husband, "is you're just too cute for words. Coming over and grabbing my sleeve and insisting we leave this deathly dull group!"

"So, I forgot we were the host and hostess. It's a perfectly natural mistake."

"You ought to get out more. Do something to make your day important. Give you something to talk about in the evening."

He had a point. What did I do all day? The only big thing that had happened was I used the wrong aerosol can for my deodorant and I didn't have to worry about clogged-up nasal passages in my armpits for twenty-four hours. No wonder he never talked to me. Out loud I said defensively, "Women would have more confidence if there were more Viktor Syomins in the world!"

"Who is Viktor Syomin?" he asked.

He was paying attention. "Viktor," I explained "is a little-known Russian whose wife was attending Moscow University until one grim day her professor told her, 'In four years you have failed sixteen courses and you don't know anything.' Now any normal American husband would have looked at his wife and said, 'Face it, Luvie, you're a dum dum,' but not Viktor.

"Viktor stomped into the professor's office and demanded, 'You pass my wife or else.' The professor retorted, '*Chepuka*,' which I think means 'And-so's-your-amoeba-brained-wife.' At any rate, Viktor said, 'You have insulted my wife's intelligence,' and broke the professor's nose.

"It's not important that Viktor's assault and battery case comes up in three months," I concluded angrily. "What is important is that he regards his wife as more than a pretty face. He regards her as a mental equal. You hear that? A mental equal! Now, do you want to hear my hilarious story about the aerosol nasal spray I pffted away under my arms or not?"

After a moment's silence, he grinned. "You've got a big mouth."

It's not much of a talent to go on, but I think I just found a pony in my barn.

## The Rocky Road to Self-Improvement

AT SOME POINT in her life a woman will go the "self-improvement" route.

This could mean a $3.95 investment in a Bonnie Prudden exercise record, a short course in Conversational Hebrew, Contract Bridge for Blood and Revenge, Mau Mau Flower Arrangements, or a trip back through time to an ivy-covered university.

These courses do what they are supposed to do. They get a woman out of the house, give her a goal or a dream to hang onto, and focus a little attention on herself for a change. It gives her something to contribute to the conversation at dinner. ("You'll never guess who almost fell into the ceramic kiln and made an ashtray of herself!") In short, it gets her out of the proverbial rut.

You take my neighbor Marty. Marty is what we always called a "child-geared" woman. When her pediatrician recommended she use baby talk to communicate with her youngsters, Marty was the first to crawl around on all fours slobbering uncontrollably and gurgling, "No, nee, now, noo, noo."

We wondered about it, but Marty said it was a new theory, and she owed it to her kids to try it. That was ten years ago. Today Marty's children talk like Fulbright Scholarship winners. It's Marty who can't kick the baby-talk habit. For example, the other night she said to her husband, "I've laid out your jammies and your bow wow. As soon as you drink your moo cow, you can give Mama a sugar and go upsie-daisy to beddie-bye." Sterling (Marty's husband) just looked at her and said quietly, "I've been thinking, Marty, maybe you oughta have your tongue fixed. I think you're regressing. Have you considered a self-improvement speech course to enlarge your vocabulary?"

Marty was hurt and shocked. She hadn't realized her speaking habits were that bad. Thus was born Marty's "Word a Day" improvement course. It worked very simply. Every morning Marty would get down the large dictionary to her encyclopedia set and flip through it at random. With eyes closed she would point to a word on a page. That was her word for the day. By her own rules she would be compelled to use the word in a sentence at least five times before the sun went down.

We bled for poor Marty. We really did. Her word-for-the-day was sometimes impossible to work into everyday conversation. Like tse-tse fly. At a woman's luncheon Marty threw it out. "Oh, is that a tse-tse fly?" "No," said her hostess coldly, "that is a raisin and I'll thank you to keep your voice down while I am serving it." Or at a cocktail party when she was telling her husband's boss, "I was lying around 'supine' all morning until the mailman came." At his shocked reaction she added quickly, "That's not a dirty word. It's an adjective meaning lying down, lethargic."

Usually it wasn't too tricky to pick out her word-for-the-day by the number of times she used it. We recorded one sentence as follows: "My problems have been infinitesimal lately, but then I say to myself every morning, 'Marty, you are too young to let infinitesimal things bother you. At this rate you'll end up with infinitesimal flu!'" (Three down and two to go.)

As the pressures of home and family increased it became apparent that poor Marty often had no time to look up the meanings of her words. Thus, we would hear her lament, "I have always wanted to play the clavicle." Or, "I never win at Monotony. The kids buy up all the railroads and fertilities and where does that leave me?"

We heard her self-improvement route ended one night when she asked her husband, "Did Fred pass his civil service elimination or was he having one of those days?"

Marty told us her husband said to her, "Martykins, let's find our way back to snookums, horthies, and moo cows. I liked you better when I couldn't understand a word you were saying."

That's one of the hazards of self-improvement. People overdo, and before you know it, they're taking themselves seriously.

We've often said that's what happened to poor Myrtle Flub. Myrtle was a real golf enthusiast. We met her in a six-week golf clinic at the YWCA. To the rest of us, golf was something to do with your hands while you talked. (Unless you smoked. Then, you never had to leave the clubhouse.) With Myrtle it was different. Whenever we got a foursome together, it was always Myrtle who insisted on keeping the scores in ink. Her clubs were never rusted or dulled by wads of bubble gum. (She was horrified the day I found a pair of child's training pants in my golf bag.)

She always played by the book. This was upsetting. We used to try to jazz up the game a bit. For example, if you forgot to say, "Mother, may I?" before you teed off, you had to add a stroke. If you clipped the duck on the pond and made him quack, you didn't have to play the sixteenth hole at all, and if you had more than fifteen strokes on one hole, you didn't have to putt out. This used to drive Myrtle crazy. She never understood why we allowed each other five "I didn't see you swings" in one game.

Then one day she arrived at the course, bubbling with excitement. "I've found a way to take points off my score," she said. (At last, we thought, she's going to cheat like the rest of us.)

"I have just read this article by a British obstetrician who says pregnant women play better golf than women who are not pregnant. He conducted this extensive survey and discovered golf scores were bettered by ten and fifteen strokes."

"But surely," we gasped, "you're not seriously considering . . ."

"If the road to motherhood is paved with birdies, pars, and eagles," she answered, "call me Mom."

The first few months of pregnancy, Myrtle wasn't too sensational on the golf course. She was nauseous. Her normally neat golf bag was a mass of soda cracker crumbs and once when I offered her a piece of cold pizza, she quit playing. Right there on the fifth hole, she quit.

During the early fall, she had a bit of trouble with swollen ankles, so her salt intake and her golf games were kept at a minimum. "Just wait until spring," she said. "I'll be the talk of the club." She was. When Myrtle tried to tee off it was like trying to land on an aircraft carrier without radar. She couldn't see her feet, let alone her ball. To be blunt, she was too pregnant to putt.

Last week we dropped by Myrtle's house en route to the golf course. (She'll resume play when the baby is older.) We talked about the good doctor's survey. "Who is this man?" asked one of the girls. "A medical doctor," Myrtle insisted, "who has done extensive research on women golfers. Here is the picture and the clipping."

We looked in disbelief. There was no doubt in our minds. He was the same man who played behind us the day we dodged the sprinkling system and made the rule that if you got wet, you had to drive the golf cart in reverse back to the clubhouse.

Boy, men sure are bad sports.

I have traveled the self-improvement route on a few occasions myself. A few years back, I found myself not only talking to a fishbowl of turtles, I started to quarrel and disagree with them.

As I told the registrar who was conducting some informal evening classes in the high school, "I want to acquire some skills and the self-confidence to go with them. I don't want to leave this world without some important contribution that will show I've been here. Is the '500 Ways with Hamburger' class filled yet?" It was.

She suggested a class called "Let's Paint." I explained to her I was a beginner. She assured me that "Let's Paint" was a class for amateur artists who had never before held a paintbrush in their hands. She should have added "between their toes or stuck in their ears," because they most certainly wielded them from every other point.

My first table partner was a slim blonde who sprung open her fishing-tackle box and ninety dollars worth of oil paints fell out. She hoisted her canvas on a board like a mast on a sailboat and in twenty minutes had sketched and shaded an impressionistic view of the Grand Canyon in eight shades of purple.

"What are you working on?" she asked, not taking her eyes from her work.

"It's nothing really," I said. "Just a little something I felt like doing today."

She grabbed my sketchbook. "You're tracing a snowman from a Christmas card?"

My next table partner was an elderly woman who confessed she hadn't had a canvas in front of her for years. I'm no fool. She had her own dirty smock and, I suspect, her own scaffold from which she retouched the ceiling of the Sistine Chapel on weekends.

"What have we here?" she bubbled, grabbing my sketch pad. "It's a kitchen window, isn't it? You don't have to label things, my dear. It detracts from the work. Of course, if you don't mind a suggestion, your curtains are a little stiff and stilted. Curtains billow softly."

"Well, ordinarily mine would too," I said, "but I put too much starch in them the last time. You can crack your shins on them."

My next table partner was a young wife awaiting the arrival of her first child. "Did you have any trouble with your still life of the fruit and the pitcher?" she asked shyly.

"Not really," I said, pulling out a sheet of sketch paper with only a few scattered dots on it.

"But the grapes, bananas, and apples?"

"My kids ate them."

"And the pitcher?"

"Dog knocked it off the table."

"And the little dots?"

"Fruit flies."

I like having a table to myself. Talking distracts me from my serious work.


*Diseases I'd Tell My Doctor About If It Weren't Wednesday Afternoon*

A: ACUTE POSSESSIONITIS. "I've got this problem, Doctor. Lately I've been experiencing a fierce sense of possession. I want to have a closet all my own, a dresser drawer that is all mine and no one else's and personal things that belong only to me. I want to share my life with my family, mind you, but not my roll of scotch tape. Can you understand that?"

He smiled. "I think so. Why don't you tell me about it?"

"I guess I first noticed it one night at the dinner table. I took a bite out of this fig newton and set it down. When I went to pick it up again one of the children was popping it into his mouth. 'That's my fig newton,' I said, my lip beginning to quiver. 'You can get another one,' he grinned. 'I don't want another one,' I insisted. 'That was *my* fig newton and you had no right to take it!' He giggled, 'I knew it was your fig newton.' 'Then why did you take it?' I shouted. 'Because I'm nasty and maladjusted,' he shouted back.

"From then on, Doctor, I became terribly conscious of personal items of mine that were being used without my permission. I discovered the family was using my eyebrow pencils to write down messages by the telephone. My Sunday black earrings were the eyes of a snowman. My lace headscarf was the stole of a Barbie doll. My eyebrow tweezers were dissecting a frog. Even my chin strap was filled with buckshot and was on maneuvers in the back yard.

"I can't begin to describe the resentment that began to

build. I finally bought a very large old desk that would house all my personal belongings. It was marvelous. It had forty-five pigeonholes, secret drawers, and sliding panels, and if you didn't hold the lid just right it would fall down and snap your arm off. I transferred all my valuables to the desk like a pack rat anticipating a long winter.

"For a while, things went well. Then things began to slip away from me. My paper clips one by one. My cotton balls. And my rubber bands. (I even disguised them in an old laxative box.) But I'm tired, Doctor. I can't fight anymore."

He smiled. "You're suffering from an old 'return-to-your-single-status' psychosis where you enjoyed some rights and independence. It can happen in an eighteen-year-old marriage. Let me give you a prescription." He stood up, removed the pillow from his chair, unzipped the cover and removed the key. He proceeded to the sixth brick in the fireplace, where he extracted a small box and unlocked it. "My prescription blanks," he laughed nervously. "If I don't hide them from my nurse she uses them for scratch pads."

"I understand," I said.

B: DRAGGING POSTERIER. "Doctor, according to national statistics, I make a dollar fifty-nine an hour. My fringe benefits are few. I get bed and board, a weekly trip to the discount house to listen to the piped-in music, and all the aspirin I can throw down.

"My problem is Sunday work. I am the only one in the house who works on Sundays. It's the same old saw. Everyone pads around all morning in pajamas, running through the comics in their bare feet, and lolling around on the beds like a group of tired Romans waiting for Yvonne deCarlo to appear with a trayful of tropical fruit."

"While you?"

"While I whip around the house getting meals, making beds, finding mates to white gloves, and keeping the fire exits clear of debris."

"And they do nothing?"

"Nothing is right. They eat and watch television. One morning I found them watching test patterns on television. They thought it was a golf show with a diagram pointing out the yardage to the cup."

"What happens when you sit down to relax?"

"One gets a bee caught in his nose. They rub poison oak into their pores. Sometimes they nip away at the paint thinner. Nine out of our last ten emergencies happened on Sunday. Once I almost got a nap. Then my husband said, 'You look bored. Let's clean the garage.'"

"What about the evenings?"

"Evenings are memory time. They remember they need an American flag out of the attic for a school play. One can't take a bath because his toenail is falling off, and somewhere along the line I must give birth to twenty-four pink cupcakes. It's my attitude that bothers me. Last Sunday I did a mean thing, Doctor. I flushed them out of their beds at 7 A.M. yelling, 'You're all going to be late for school.' They staggered around the driveway in the final stages of shock."

"There's no reason for you to have a guilt complex," he explained. "We all have our threshold of endurance. Just put it out of your mind."

"I can't, Doctor. You should hear what I've got planned for next Sunday!"

c: GLUE-BREATH. "It happened the other morning, Doctor. My cleaning woman approached me and said, 'You may fire me for this, but you've got glue-breath.'

" 'But I use a mouthwash,' I insisted. She backed up, weaving unsteadily and said, 'That soda pop isn't doing the job.' In my heart I knew she was right, but I can't help myself. Like most other housewives in America, I succumbed a few years ago to the lure of trading stamps. At first, it was innocent enough. We saved a couple of books and got a croquet

set for the kids . . . then a few more books for a lawn trim-
mer for Dad . . . and finally eight or so books for a leg
shaver for me . . . things we really needed.

"Then one day we read a story in the newspaper about a
New York zoo that bought a gorilla for 5,400,000 trading
stamps. Just reading about all those stamps gave our family
a case of redemption fever. We gathered around the dining
room table after dinner and began to speculate on what would
happen if we upped our consumption of gasoline, oil, tires,
windshield wipers, and sunglasses from Bernie's Service Station. 'In three years,' my husband shouted, 'we could buy
the New York Mets!'

"Our son figured out if we could get doctors, lawyers, and
the sanitary department to issue trading stamps we might
even amass enough to earn a Rhino hunt weekend for two in
scenic Kenya. We went half crazed with desire. One of the
children vowed to start saving for Rhode Island, another for
Richard Nixon's older daughter . . . another for a do-it-yourself missile site for the back yard. I personally wanted to visit
the Senior Citizen Center to which Cary Grant belonged.
The possibilities were crazy and without limits.

"From that day on, our entire buying habits changed. We
often ran out of gas looking for a station with our brand of
stamps. We bought food we hated to get bonus stamps. In
desperation, we even switched to a newly-formed church
across town that gave one hundred and twenty trading stamps
each time we attended. (We now worship a brown and
white chicken with a sunburst on its chest.)

"I know it sounds ridiculous, but I have pasted stamps in
1563 books. I'll match that against J. Paul Getty's stamp
books any day of the week! Someone in the family guards
them twenty-four hours a day and we count them once a
week. We stage mock fire drills from time to time so we
can evacuate them quickly in case of fire. In the event of a
nuclear attack, we have instructions to empty out the drink-

ing water and save the stamp books. Trading stamps have possessed me, Doctor. What do you think?"

The doctor tapped his pencil slowly on the desk. "I personally think you are some kind of a nut with fuzzy breath, that's what I think. What in the world are you going to buy with 1563 books?"

"When I fill five more pages, Doctor," I said stiffly, "I will own this office building. And if I were you, I wouldn't have any more magazines sent to this address!"

D: CAR POOL ALLERGY.  "You see, Doctor, children see their mothers as symbols of some kind—hot apple pie, delicate perfume, a soft kiss to heal a scraped knee.

"My children see me as four wheels, a motor, and a drive shaft. I am Snow White with a set of car keys. Peter Pan off in a cloud of blue exhaust. Mary Poppins with fifteen gasoline credit cards.

"People are always talking about men who commute. I don't feel sorry for them. At least they drive on designated roads where their only annoyances are a few bad drivers and a few dozen police cars camouflaged as spirea bushes.

"But women in car pools! Women get cuffed with lunch boxes while they're driving. Women have to cut bubble gum out of their hair with scissors. Women have to charter new routes over barren fields and swamplands looking for the 'Blue team on Diamond 12.'

"Frankly, Doctor, I've been involved in so many car pools I'm beginning to walk like Groucho Marx. This business of chauffeuring really began to bother me about two weeks ago. I pulled up in front of a traffic light and five girls piled in. One said, 'Carol, tell your mother to turn right at the next street.' A girl called Carol said, 'She's not my mother. I thought she was your mother.' 'No,' said the other voice, 'My mother wears glasses. Or is it my father who wears glasses? Hey, gang, is this anyone's mother?'

" 'The back of the head does look familiar,' said one. 'Did you take a group of girls on school patrol on a tour of bus station restrooms recently?' I shook my head no.

" 'I got it,' said another. 'You brought the garbage home from Girl Scout Camp! I remember now. It was out-of-season so we couldn't bury it. When she came to pick up her group she got stuck with bringing the garbage home. Sorry, but I didn't recognize you without all those fruit flies.'

"I nodded affirmatively. How long ago was it when I begged for wheels of my own? A car was going to restore independence to my dreary life, open up lines of communication to a whole new world of culture and entertainment. It was going to free me from the bonds of my daily routine. What happened?

"When I left the girls off, I ended up with two small passengers, my Wednesday afternoon kindergarten drop-offs. 'I'm five years old,' one of them announced to the other. 'I wonder how old she is.' (Note: Small children always refer to the driver in the third person, never directly. This destroys the impersonal driver-passenger relationship.) 'I'm eight years old!' I yelled back impulsively.

" 'Do you think she's really eight years old?' asked the other one.

" 'I'm big for my age,' I added.

" 'My mother is that big and she's thirty-two,' said the first one.

" 'Big people act funny sometimes,' said the second child.

" 'Yeah,' said the first child, 'but it beats walkin'.' "

E: IDENTITY PAINS. "I might as well confess it before you hear it from someone else, Doctor. I've found my identity.

"You can't imagine what this means. People who have considered me a friend for years shout, 'Fraud, fake, and traitor.' Some of them have burned copies of *Hints from Heloise* on my front yard. I know I will be asked to turn in my Betty Friedan signet ring. Nevertheless it is true.

"I wasn't real took with the movement for women's equality in the first place. What with carrying out the trash, changing fuses, cutting the grass, and fertilizing the shrubbery, any more equality would kill me. You have to know I'm the type if Carrie Nation had called and said, 'Would you like to make a contribution to your sex?' I'd probably have said, 'My husband gives at the office.'

"I don't know. I tried to have a real mystique going for me, but I didn't get too much mileage out of it. I used to shuffle through the house saying, 'Who am I? Where am I? Where am I going?' All I did was scare the Avon lady half to death. I even said to my husband one night, 'You know, I think I've lost my identity,' and without looking up he said, 'It's probably with your car keys . . . wherever they are.'

"When I told my mother about my 'Oedipus conflict and sibling rivalry that had embedded themselves into my personality,' she said, 'What kind of language is that for a mother?'

"Well, the first clue to my identity came one day when the phone rang and someone said, 'Hello, Erma.' I tell you my eyes misted up like Ben Cartwright on *Bonanza* when his horse goes lame. 'What did you call me?' I asked slowly. The voice repeated the name. That was it. That must be my identity. Feverishly I went through my billfold in my purse and emptied out a stack of credit cards, a YWCA membership, a library card, and a driver's license. They all bore the same name.

"I raced to the bedroom and began rummaging through drawers. There were old report cards signed by me, monogrammed handkerchiefs, and autographed copies of books scrawled, 'To Erma.' At last I knew my real identity.

"Then a card fell to the floor. It was addressed to Mrs. Erma Bombeck, Girl Scout cookie captain. My first real breakthrough. I not only knew who I was but what I was. *I was a commissioned officer in the cookie corps!*

"I felt wonderful and proud, Doctor. My mystique had been solved. My problem now is I can't remember where I put the cookies."

## Parting with Money Is Taxing

THERE WERE REALLY ONLY two men I knew who ever got a laugh out of paying their income taxes. One was cheating the government and getting away with it. The other had a sick sense of humor and would probably have set up a concession stand at the Boston Tea Party and sold sugar cubes and lemon slices.

Sitting up with a sick taxpayer is no picnic. At best "How to live with your husband until his W-2 forms are filed" is pure agony. I have done it for years and these are the lessons I've reaped:

1. Never try to talk your husband out of his depression over his taxes. The last woman I heard who stood at her husband's elbow waving a flag and chanting, "Be thankful for

Mom and apple pie," is now living with her mother and working in a bakery. This is no time to fool around.

2. Never suggest that he file his tax return early. There is
nothing that will unsettle a man more than being jammed in
a post office with a group of New Year's revelers who are filing early only because they are getting a refund. Better to have
him in the cortege of cars that slowly inch their way to the
mailbox at midnight of the April deadline, while a sullen
group on the post-office steps chants, "We shall overcome."

3. Keep the children out of his path. From January through
April they cease to have names. They become Deduction A,
Deduction B, and Deduction C. Mentally he begins to add up
what he has invested in their teeth, arches, sports program,
fine arts, education, clothes, food, lodging, entertainment,
vitamins, and social welfare. Once he has figured out that
$600 wouldn't keep them in catsup and breakfast cereal,
his resentment reaches a danger point.

4. Anticipate his low days. When he is virtually drowning
in a sea of canceled checks, receipts, memos, and statements
of interest and income, offer enthusiastically to have your gall
bladder taken out next year to increase his medical deduction. Promise to adopt an orphan Parisian chorus girl, make
a large donation to the indigent at the Polo Club, invest
unwisely, lose heavily at Chinese checkers, buy an office
building on credit.

Above all, be ready to produce explanations or at least to
discuss any expenditure from a cold capsule to a major purchase like swimming lessons for your daughter.

"How in the name of all that is sane did you spend $175
for swimming lessons?" he shouted, the veins standing erect
in his neck. "I could have gotten Flipper to tutor her in our
own bathtub for $50."

"Actually the swimming lessons were only $4 for ten weeks
at the 'Y,' but I encountered some extras."

"What extras?"

"Extras! There was 49 cents for a nose plug."

"That leaves $170.51."

"And the parking. I think that amounted to $35."

"$35?"

"I parked in a towaway zone. Then one night we stayed downtown and had dinner and went to a movie. That amounted to about $10."

"That narrows it down to $125.51."

"Of course, $12 or so went for bribes."

"Another towaway zone?"

"No, to keep our boys from playing with the paper towels in the restroom and skating on the lobby floors. I had to bribe them with food and things. After all, my pride is worth something."

"That's 'Pride: $12,'" he mused.

"Yes and don't forget the bedspreads. I get to town so rarely I felt I had to run over and look at the bedspreads on sale. I bought two. Take away $24.73."

"That leaves $88.78."

"Well, about $15 went for medication when she forgot to

dry her hair and caught cold. If you're concerned about the waste of pills, I could pack them in her lunch."

"Don't be cute," he said. "What happened to the other $73.78?"

"My goodness, there were a lot of things. Name tapes for the towels, new swimming bag, new headlight for the mail truck I hit, and don't forget the nose plug."

"That was 49 cents, wasn't it?" he asked, unconsciously moistening his ballpoint pen on his tongue.

Laugh at income tax? My dear, I would sooner put out my foot and trip Tiny Tim.

*Sick . . . Sick . . . Sick . . .*

HER STORY:

Actually I was looking forward to Leonard's being home, even if he was recuperating from minor surgery. We were going to have leisure breakfasts, giddy coffee breaks, pore over old picture albums and maybe even harmonize on a few reckless choruses of "Mexicali Rose."

I don't know what went wrong. I ran trays like I was working the dark corner of a drive-in. I fluffed pillows, rubbed his back, delivered papers, smoothed sheets, and was summoned from every room in the house. Of course, Leonard was never able to stand pain. When he suffered a paper cut in '59, I never left his bedside. The doctor said it was my strength that pulled him through.

"Did I tell you I was awake during the entire operation?" he yelled down the hallway.

"Yes!"

"Did I tell you about that herd of vampires who drew blood from me every hour of the day and night?"

"Yes!"

By the second week he had me looking up phone numbers

of all his old Army buddies at Ft. Dix, digging out the ouija board, finding out how much insurance he had on his car (among other research projects), and nursing his pothus plant back to life. ("All right then, *you* tell Miss Cartwright her gift pothus died because it was pot-bound. Go ahead! Break an old woman's heart!")

"You hear me out there?" he'd shout. "While you're flitting around the countryside, stop off at the library and get us a book on playwriting. You hear? We could write a hit play together, you and I."

By the third week he was approaching full strength. He toured the house and discovered the kitchen cupboards were ill-planned, something strange had died in the utility room, and what this family really needed was a well-organized, well-planned duty roster.

His final week was probably his finest hour. He was in his "communications" syndrome, or as we called it, "Chopping Off at the Mouth."

"You tell Ed at the garage I said if he doesn't set that motor up he can jolly well push it all the way to Detroit with the broken nose I am going to give him when I get out of this bed. Got that? As for Clark at the office, you just tell him for me that I've dealt with his kind before and if he thinks he can pull this off while I am flat on my back he's got another thought coming. Remind him what happened in '48."

"What happened in '48?" I asked intently.

"Nothing, but Clark won't remember either. And another thing. You collar that grass cutter you hired and tell him for me to set that mower back where I had it. I don't want a putting green, just some front yard grass left."

I guess I know why the Good Lord had women bear the children. Men would have delegated the job!

HIS STORY:

Actually I was looking forward to staying home with Doris to help her over her bout with the flu. If a man can't pitch in and manage his own kids and his own house, I always say, what's he good for?

I don't know what went wrong. Lord knows I was doing the best I could under the circumstances. I tried to bring a little order to her kitchen, but when I flung open the cabinet doors and read the headlines on the shelf paper, DEWEY CONCEDES TO TRUMAN, I knew I was in for it. I lined up the kids and put them to work. Doris lets them get away with too much.

"Why in heaven's name does your mother keep the marsh-mallows in the oven?" I asked.

"She hides them," they said.

"Now you kids hike this turkey roaster up to the attic. She only uses it on state occasions. Give me those cocktail onions so I can put them on a lower shelf where they'll be within easy reach. Now, where's the coffee?"

"In the stove drawer, Daddy."

"What's wrong with keeping it in the canister marked C-O-F-F-E-E?"

"Because she hides the P-O-P-C-O-R-N there."

We were doing just fine, mind you, when she yells from the bedroom, "Why don't all of you go out and rotate the tires on the car or make lamps out of old bowling pins or something?" That's gratitude for you. Doris is a bit of Mama's girl. Faints when she has to remove a corn pad. I don't like to criticize her while she's flat on her back, but there was stuff in her refrigerator so old that a casserole actually attacked me and drew blood. "If you don't keep those left-overs moving," I warned her, "you're going to have to open a pharmaceutical house."

"Who was on the phone?" she yelled.

"Just the principal. Don't worry."

"What did he want?" she persisted.

"Nothing. He was just explaining the school's policy on bedroom slippers."

She groaned. "Why are the kids wearing bedroom slippers?"

"Because we can't find their shoes. They're probably on the washer, but we can't get to the washer until after seven. I figure the water from the washer should crest at that hour and then begin to recede."

"You mean the washer overflowed?"

How's that for innocence. If I've told her once, I've told her fifty times to put the little socks and underwear in a bag and then the pump wouldn't get stopped up, but she never listens. I didn't get so much as a "Thank you" for going door to door collecting for her "Research for Sweating Feet" drive, or for driving fifteen Cub Scouts on a tour of a frozen food locker.

If Doris only ran a home like men ran their offices, I wouldn't have to take up so much time in organization. All I did was slip a little note on her night stand asking her to fill in her reply on the following:

1. How do you turn on the garbage disposal?

2. How do you turn off the milkman?

3. How do you remove a Confederate flag tattooed in ink on the forehead of a small boy?

4. Where is the anise for the chili?

5. What is your mother's phone number?

That was certainly no reason for her to groan and start getting dressed. Sometimes I wonder why the Good Lord gave the job of having children to women, when men could organize the process and turn them out in triplicate in half the time.

MAY 7 — JULY 9

how do you GET OUT of
this chickEN outfit?

"PARDON ME," said the milkman politely tipping his hat, "but I think you put the wrong note in the bottle this morning. This one reads, 'HELP! I'm being held a prisoner by an idiot with a set of wrenches in a house that has been without running water for three days. How do you get out of this chicken outfit?'"

"You're new on the route, aren't you?" I asked.

"Yes, ma'am," he said, his eyes looking for an escape hatch through the taxus. "This sounds like a call for help," he hesitated. "I just take these bottles back to the plant to be sterilized and filled with milk again. I don't drop them in Lake Erie or anything."

"I know that!" I said irritably. "It's just that I'm married to this home-improvement drop-out and every once in a while I just have to try something!"

He didn't understand about modern marriages. I could tell that by the way he bolted to the truck. Some marriages are made in heaven with stardust in the eyes. Others are made in haste with piles of sawdust whipping around the feet.

Mine was the latter, which I discovered less than two weeks after I was married. My husband came home from the drugstore ecstatic with two cigar boxes under his arm. He rushed to the basement, nailed them together, painted them dark green and called them "shadow boxes."

Despite the fact they looked like two cigar boxes nailed together with "King Edward" bleeding through, I avowed they belonged in the Metropolitan. While showing guests through the apartment I would chin myself on them to prove their strength and exclaim that if I had known what a clever dog he was I would have married him in his playpen.

As usual, I overacted.

How was I to know that later he would saw an opening in our back door to let the dog *in*, then consider how to keep the snow *out*? How could I suspect that he would enclose our garbage cans with a fence so high you had to catapult the garbage and hope for the best? How could I imagine his fifth-grade practical arts course would become a way of life?

For a while he went through his built-in period. Everything in the house had to be contained, stacked, attached, enclosed and out of sight. The garage had shelf units to the ceiling that held all the dried-up cans of paint, old coffee cans, and discarded license plates. He enclosed the television set, the bookcases, the stereo, washer, dryer, 'bar, clothes, blankets, linens, sewing machine, and cleaning supplies. I climbed out of bed one morning and proceeded to stretch my arms and yawn. Before I could get my arms to my sides, I was supporting five shelves of cookbooks and a collection of glass elephants.

Later I was to discover he never went to bed on a finished project. Fired with enthusiasm over a plan for improvement, he would spread the room with wall-to-wall ladders, open a myriad of paint cans (ready for spilling), and roll up the draperies into a ball on the sofa. Then he would smile, climb into his coat, and say, "I am off to study the blister beetle in South America. Don't touch a thing until I get back."

On other occasions, he was not as inventive. He'd simply pull the stove out from the wall, remove the oven door, put the bathroom hardware to soak in a kitchen sink full of vinegar, then announce, "I don't have tools like the rest of the fellas. I do the best I can with a Boy Scout ax and crude tools I've been able to fashion out of boulders and buffalo hide. But when you don't have the right tool for the right job, you can't turn out the work of a craftsman."

Eventually the news that I was supporting a home-improvement drop-out was no secret. We were the couple with the screens in all winter and the storm windows in all summer.

We spread grass seed in the snow and put up our TV antennae in an electrical storm.

Even the simple jobs, he attacked with all the grace of a herd of buffalo under fire.

"I was wondering if you could reach behind the washer and put that simple plug into that simple outlet?" I inquired one evening.

"Let's see now," he said surveying the situation. "First, I'll need my Home Workshop Encyclopedia, Volume VIII. Dig that out for me, will you? Get the chapter on 'Outlets: Electrical.' Now, get my utility belt, my insulated gloves, and hard safety hat with the light attachment. They make these utility rooms for pygmies, you know. And with a running jump I'll hoist myself to the top of the washing machine where I'll—"

"Break the washer cycle dial with your big foot," I said dryly. "Look, maybe I'd better do it," I said. "I'm smaller than you and I can just reach over and—"

"This is man's work," he said firmly. "You go finish shoveling the snow off your driveway and leave me to my job at hand."

"No, I'll just stick around in case your eyeballs flash for help."

He lowered himself behind the appliance and inserted the plug—halfway—blowing out all the power on the kitchen circuit. Shocked (but literally), he backed into the dryer vent, disconnecting it. Simultaneously he dropped his flashlight from his helmet into an opening between the walls. For his "big finish" he rapped his head on the utility shelf and opened a hissing valve on the hot water heater with his belt buckle.

I folded my hands and closed my eyes in prayer. "May he never retire."

Ironically, most women envy me my do-it-yourself husband. "At least he does *something!*" said our new neighbor. "You should be thankful for that."

I smiled. "Would you mind sitting in this chair? I wouldn't ask you to move but my husband's leg is coming through the living room ceiling and I wouldn't want him to fall in your lap. Basically he's shy."

She looked rather alarmed as he yelled down through the opening, "Erma! Put an X on what's left of the ceiling so the next time I'll know there's no stud here!"

"I still think it's wonderful," the neighbor persisted, "how you two tackle all kinds of home projects together. I see you out there cutting grass while he trims the hedge and washing the car while he's cleaning out the glove compartment. It's just wonderful."

I was silent a moment, then I pulled my chair closer. "Let me tell you a secret. I have always resented the helpless female. I resent her because I am secretly jealous of her ability to train grown men to 'heel' and sick and tired of having her feel my flexed muscles at parties.

"If I had it to do all over again, I would be one of those helpless females who faints at the sight of antifreeze. But I was the big mouth who, early in marriage, watched my husband try to start the power mower and said, 'If you are trying to start that power mower, Duckey, you had better attach the spark plug, open the gas line so you can get fuel to the distributor, and pull the choke all the way over. Also, if you don't stand on the other side of the mower, you'd better lean against that tree for balance because you are going to lose your right foot.' "

"How masterful," she said, dabbing her forehead with a lace handkerchief.

"Not so masterful," I said. "From that day forward I was awarded custody of the mower. I also had to repair spoutings, clean out the dryer vent, repair the clothesline, build the rock garden, drain and store the antifreeze, and wash the car."

"My goodness," she whispered, "I'm so addle-brained

about cars I scarcely know how to turn on those little globes in the front . . . the . . ."

"Lights," I prompted. "Incidentally, what's that pet name your husband calls you?"

"You mean, 'Satin Pussy Cat'?"

"That's the one. My husband calls me 'Army,' after a pack mule he had in Korea. You're the one who's got it made. I'll bet you never fertilized a lawn, changed a fuse, plunged a sink, hosed out a garbage can, or hung curtain brackets."

She threw back her head, revealing her slim, white throat, and laughed. "Why I get lightheaded whenever I step up on a curb."

"Take today. I've got this clogged-up washer. I can either ring for Rube Goldberg and his wonder-wrenches, or I can try to fix the thing myself."

She smiled slyly. "I'll bet it's your turbo pump that's clogged. All you have to do is remove the back panel, take out the pulsator, disconnect the thermoschnook, and use a spreckentube to force out the glunk. Then put on a new cyclocylinder, using a No. four pneusonic wrench, and you're back in the laundry business."

"Why you helpless little broad—er fraud! You could run General Motors from a phone booth. You're faking it, aren't you? That helpless routine is all show. And what does it get you? Nothing but dinner rings, vacations out of season, small fur jackets, and a husband standing breathless at your elbow. Do you know the last time my husband stood breathless at my elbow I had a chicken bone caught in my throat? Is it too late for me? Do you suppose a woman over thirty-five could learn to be helpless?"

She smiled. "Of course. And you can start by asking that nice milkman if he'd be a dear and drop your note in the bottle into Lake Erie, if it isn't too much trouble . . ."


## The Outdoor Nut

I HAVE ALWAYS BEEN led to believe a good marriage was based on things a couple had in common.

A while back I read where Liz Taylor, commenting on one of her earlier marriages, said the common bond between her and her husband was that they wore the same sweater size. The obvious conclusion must be: They just don't make sweaters anymore like they used to. In reality, it's what you *don't* have in common that holds a marriage together.

Early in my marriage (my honeymoon, to be exact) I discovered I was married to an outdoor nut. As I sat there in a cabin on Rainbow Trout Lake fingering my nosegay, I said, "What do you want? Me? Or a great northern pike?" Friends have since told me I would have fared better in the competition had I picked a smaller fish. I was pushing.

Through the years the condition has only worsened. All

winter long my husband has what is commonly referred to in fishing circles as the fever. He sharpens his hooks, teases the feathers on his lures, reads articles on "Backlash Lake" and "Angler's Paradise," and follows me around the kitchen inviting me to watch his wrist action.

His wading boots (boots that extend up to the armpits so that when the water pours in, you are assured of drowning instantly) hang on a hook in the garage with all the readiness of a fireman's hat. Whenever a fellow fisherman gives the hysterical cry "The white bass are running!" he grabs his boots and does the same.

Actually I have never known the white bass to do anything else but run. They certainly never stop long enough to nibble at the bait. Theoretically the bass are always on a "hot lake." Now a "hot lake," I discovered, is where all the "hot liars" hang out. The reasons they give for the fish not biting are enough to stagger the imagination.

1. The fish aren't biting because the water is too cold.
2. The water is too hot.
3. The fish are too deep.
4. It is too early.
5. It is too late.
6. They haven't stocked it yet.
7. They're up the river spawning.
8. The water skiers and motorboats have them stirred up.
9. They've been poisoned by pollution.
10. They just lowered the lake level.
11. They're only biting on bubble gum and bent nails.
12. Some novice has just dumped his bait into the water and they're stuffed to the gills and can't eat another bite.
13. They haven't been biting since the Democrats have been in power.

When outdoor camping became the symbol of togetherness, I knew my husband wouldn't rest until he had me reeking of insect repellent and zipped into a sleeping bag out where the deer and the antelope play.

I've relived that first camping trip in my mind a thousand times. (They tell me only shock treatments could erase it permanently.) I've tried to analyze why we failed. First, I think we had seen too many Walt Disney films and expected more help from the animals than we got. Second, unlike other families, our family does not have the necessary primitive instincts for survival. We are lucky to get the car windows rolled down to keep from suffocating.

I personally opposed erecting our tent in a driving rain. I thought it would put us all in a bad humor. As it was, no sooner had we driven the last peg when a passerby remarked to his companion, "Look at that, Lucille. It's listing worse than the *Titanic* just before she went down." Then my husband poked his head out of the flap and retaliated, "Same to you, fella," and I don't mind telling you it took two stanzas of "Nearer My God to Thee" to quiet them down. From that moment on, the bathhouse set referred to us as "Old Crazy Tent."

The rain presented a bit of a problem—all fifteen days of it. This took a lot of ingenuity. "I don't like to mention it," I said one afternoon, "but I think this weather and this tent are beginning to get on my nerves."

"Why do you say that?" asked my husband.

"Because I spent an entire morning counting the grains of sand in the butter."

"The kids keep busy enough," he said.

He was right. They examined their hair follicles under a flashlight, clipped toenails, ate crackers in someone else's sleeping bag, took the labels off the canned goods, kept a rather complete log of frequent visitors to the bathhouse, and wrote postcards home telling everyone what a "blast" they were having.

On the sixteenth day good fortune struck. A hysterical

woman from the next tent heard via her transistor that we were in for a tornado. I combed my hair and put on a trace of lipstick. It was the first time I'd been out of the tent in two weeks.

Sitting in the car, with the thorny feet of one of the kids in my ribs, I heard someone from the back seat say, "We'll survive all right." He had thought to grab two cans without labels on his way out. One was a small tin of cocktail weiners, the other was a can of cleanser.

On the eighteenth day it became apparent we had three choices to make: (a) Fix the tent so we could stand up in it, (b) Have our legs fixed so they would measure no more than one-fourth the length of our bodies, (c) Get into the car and make a side trip.

The children voted for a visit to a deer farm about twenty miles from the campsite. It was one of those commercial little ventures where you pay a price and enter the compound and the deer are roaming free among the visitors. There's also a souvenir shop that sells mother-of-pearl ashtrays, a rocking plane ride that costs a dime and makes the kids throw up, and a popcorn stand. We each bought a box of popcorn and set out to spend a quiet afternoon among these gentle animals with the large trusting eyes.

When I first felt a sharp pinch on my backside, I whispered to my husband, "You devil you." The second time it happened I became quite irritated and turned sharply to face a pair of large, brown trusting eyes and two hoofs on my coat lapels. It seemed popcorn drove the deer half out of their skulls with mad desire. The entire herd charged us, pushing, shoving, nipping. They had one child cornered, another one sobbing in the dirt, and my husband pirouetting on his toes like a ballet dancer. We agreed the tent wasn't much, but it was safe from a deer stampede.

The end of three weeks of camping found all of us "adjusting." Slapping the laundry against a flat rock, walking around with sand in our underwear, and taking a bath in a one-quart saucepan had become a way of life.

Sometimes at night when the campfire glowed and you sipped your coffee in the stillness of the night, you felt you might be present at the creation. The kids intent on listening to animals rustling in the bushes and watching the flickering patterns in the fire forgot to argue with one another. No telephones. No Avon ladies. No television. No lawn mowers. No committee meetings. No vacuum sweepers. Just peace.

Then one night, there was peace no more. A twenty-two-foot trailer slithered into the clearing next to us. We could hear their voices crack through the silence of the lazy morning.

"I swear, Clifford, I don't mind roughing it, but with no electricity to hook up to, this is ridiculous. What am I supposed to do about my electric coffee pot and my blanket and my heater?"

"Don't tell me your problems," he shouted. "What about my shaver and my electric martini stirrer."

"Well, I hope they have a laundromat and a shower house with hot water . . ."

"And a boat dock," he added, "and a swimming pool for the kids. They'll be sick if there's no swimming pool. You know how cold the lakes are."

"Did you check on whether or not they picked up the garbage every day? I don't want a lot of animals around the trailer. I didn't come out here in the wilderness to fight off animals. What in the world is that infernal noise?"

"I think we're near the beach. That water lapping and rolling in all night long is going to drive me crazy. Did you bring my pills, Arlene?"

"Of course, dear. Why don't you set up your screened cabana and listen to the radio? I'll try to rustle you up a drink. I don't suppose that little shopkeeper who looks like Gabby Hayes has ever heard of ice cubes before."

I turned to my husband. "Let's knock the other prop out from under our tent tomorrow and head up toward Blue Water Cove. I hear it's a 'hot lake' and 'the bass are running' like dishonest congressmen."

He grinned. "I think you've got 'the fever.'"

It's summertime and once again our daughter, the Midwest's answer to Tokyo Rose, has been circulating daily bulletins of our vacation plans.

I had one phone call from a woman two blocks over to look up her sister in San Juan, a request from a retired couple for a bushel of grapefruit from Orlando, and just yesterday a carry-out boy winked and said, "Are you really going to Berkeley to burn your library card?"

Actually I'm an advocate of separate vacations: the children's and ours. Or as comedienne Joan Rivers said, "They hated the children and would have separated years ago, but they're staying together for the sake of each other."

There is something about packing five people into a car with nothing to do but tolerate each other that leads to roughhousing, name-calling, eye-gouging, and eventually recoiling next to the spare tire in the trunk. Each individual pursues his or her own antagonistic topic.

The children, for example, will ramble on for miles about the last restroom they visited, describing in intricate details the messages written in lipstick on the walls. Then they will amuse themselves by the hour playing "auto roulette." This is a precarious game of trampling, jostling, and hurling of bodies to see which one gets a seat nearest the window.

Despite the enthusiastic reports from parents that their children broke out in hives from the excitement of viewing the Grand Canyon, we have noted ours couldn't care less. Their interests run toward amusement parks, souvenir shops, miniature golf ranges, zoos with souvenir shops, parks with swings and slides, restaurants with souvenir shops, pony rides, and national monuments with souvenir shops. I get the feeling if we drove the car to Lincoln's Memorial, climbed his leg and spread out a picnic lunch on his lap, one of the kids would observe, "Keep your eyes open for a motel with a heated swimming pool and a nearby souvenir shop."

The compulsive desire to buy a carful of souvenirs before we got to the city limits became so bad, we had to set down some explicit rules for souvenir buying:

Know your history. Don't be lured into buying a genuine replica of a ballpoint pen used by Stephen Foster when he wrote, "I Dream of Jeanie with the Light Brown Hair." (We paid a few dollars more and bought the typewriter used by Thomas Jefferson when he wrote the Declaration of Independence.)

Learn to be crafty. Beware of Indians selling electric blankets, authentic Japanese kimonas made in West Virginia, and President and First Lady T-shirts. (The barbecue sauce we bought, but T-shirts!)

Select a souvenir that will remind you of your visit. This is especially difficult with children who insist on buying a sweat shirt that proclaims, "I'M AN ALCOHOLIC. IN CASE OF EMERGENCY, BUY ME A BEER," from scenic Bar Harbor.

Don't pay exorbitant prices for souvenir items you can buy at home. Take that small Frankenstein toy we bought in Tennessee—the one where you pull a switch and his pants fall down and his face turns red—$3.95, batteries not included. With what I would have saved buying it out of a catalogue, I could have bought that beautiful satin pillow in the Smokies that read, "There's No Salt Like a Mother's Tears."

Lastly, consider how good a traveler your souvenir will be. Once when we bought a bushel of peaches from Georgia, we had to drive steadily with no stops for forty-eight hours to avoid being eaten alive by fruit flies.

On another occasion, all five of us had to ride together in the front seat to avoid conflict of interest with a small alligator in the back seat.

Next to children on a trip, there is nothing more trying than their father. He doesn't go on a trip to enjoy the scenery and relax. He's on a virtual test run to prove his car's performance in a grinding show of speed and endurance equaled only on the salt flats testing grounds.

First, there's the graphic charts he insists be kept listing the mileage, gasoline and oil consumption, and itemized expenses encountered during the trip. Three things usually happen to these charts: (a) They are used to wrap up a half-eaten Popcicle and discarded along the way, (b) They are grabbed in an emergency to squash bugs on the windshield, (c) They are committed to memory and used as a mild sedation on neighbors and friends upon your return.

Next, he will insist you read and interpret road maps. To do this you must consider that you are dealing primarily with a maniac, a driver who wants to arrive at his destination three hours before he leaves home. He abhors heavy traffic, detours, toll stations, construction, and large cities with a population of fifty or more. He is depending upon you to anticipate these discomforts and avoid them at all costs. In short, he is hostile. You will find your road map, folded incorrectly in the glove compartment. Usually it will be a little out of date (listing only the original thirteen colonies). Once when I told my husband we measured but a hairpin and a mint away from our destination, he beat his head on the steering wheel and openly accused me of moving the Mississippi River over two states.

Another challenge is getting the driver of the car to stop for food. Rationalizing that even at the "500," they have pit stops, our driver invariably feeds us on promises of what lies ahead at Futility City.

With bloated stomachs and sharp teeth from gnawing on our safety belts we hit Futility City only to discover one filling station, a hound dog in the middle of the road, and a brightly lighted stand where they sell shaved-ice cones. The hound dog looks interesting.

Since this is to be an honest account of the behavior patterns of the average vacationer, I can't leave out "Mother." Mother climbs into the car and, like an evangelist who just had the tent collapse on her flock, can't resist a captive audience. She goes the discipline route.

I have been known to go across an entire state, ignoring national monuments, freaks of nature, postcard countrysides, faces carved in mountains and herds of wild buffalo, while my long-playing mouth recites misdemeanors the kids made when they were on Pablum. My sermon on "All right now, which one of you clowns turned on the car heater?" extended over three states.

Sometimes mothers are permitted to drive, but only under the following conditions: (1) city traffic at 5 P.M. when the population is 250,000 or over, (2) unmarked dirt roads at midnight, (3) highways under construction with detour signs that have blown over, (4) in a tornado on an eight-lane highway where the minimum speed is 65 mph.

The irony of all this is that we don't know what a madcap time we're having until we see our vacation on our home movies. In the flickers, we hide our heads in our armpits, dance a jig, act like we're fighting Dempsey for the title, and pull down limbs of trees and point to them like we've just discovered a cure for arthritis.

We've got some wonderful footage on my husband where he is standing on his head removing a fishhook from his underside and mouthing obscenities into the camera. All the rest of us are holding our sides laughing fit to die. There's another classic where my Wallie the Whale waterwings spring a leak and I disappear beneath some lily pads and never surface again. Oh, and there's a thrilling shot of one of the kids being sick on a small fishing boat off the coast of Florida and we are hovering over him offering him salami and mayonnaise sandwiches. That one really breaks us up.

Another vacation this year? You bet. We're firm believers that at least once a year a family ought to get away from it all so they can appreciate good food, plush lodgings, convenient stores, and breathtaking scenery—upon their return home after two grim weeks of togetherness.

Must try to remember to send in the boys' camp applications early. You see, I *do* remember last year's disappointment:

Mr. Grim Gruber, Director
Camp Discouragement for Boys
City
Dear Mr. Gruber:

The afternoon mail brought me your fine brochure on Camp Discouragement for Boys. You may or may not remember me. My son attended your camp last summer for two weeks. (He was the blond boy whose soiled socks stuck to the light bulb in the mess hall.)

We were so pleased with the peace and tranquility we enjoyed in his absence, Mr. Bombeck suggested I rush down before Thanksgiving to make sure you have enrollment space. (He also wanted me to remind you he fought for your freedom in World War II, but I don't like to bring pressure.)

Your camp originally came to our attention as it was the only one we could spell. The previous summer we sent him to Camp Mini-something-or-other and discovered we were obviously misspelling the name of the camp. We kept getting letters from a chieftain in the Blackfoot reservation in North Dakota who thanked us profusely for the cookies and clean socks.

I do hope your fine counselor, Mr. Bley, is well enough to return this summer. I was surprised to hear of his "health problem" as he looked so well when I met him on the opening day of my son's camping period. Winning that flag for keeping the latrine clean seemed to mean so much to him. What a pity he had to relinquish it the following week. He will just have to get used to spirited boys, won't he?

I've been meaning to share with you some of my son's hilarious reports of your camp. He wrote us that when a boy talked after lights out, the boys got to slug him, and when he continued to talk, the counselor slugged him. I ask you, where would we be without a boy's imagination?

Incidentally, this is probably an oversight, but he has never received his camp award for throwing a frozen pancake thirty-two feet high. I understand from him this is some kind of a camp record. (Even if he was aiming it at a senior leader during evening meditation.) Although we are not "showy" people, we do have a spot for it in the trophy case in the hallway, alongside his birth certificate and a note saying he passed his eye test at school—his two accomplishments to date.

Did you ever solve the mystery of the missing bathing suits from camp? My son was terribly upset about the nude swimming as he is a sensitive boy.

Do write me your confirmation of my son's registration.

Sincerely

Dear Mrs. Bombeck:

We do remember your son.

Mr. Bley continues to improve and now is permitted a limited number of visitors on Sundays. We are enclosing your son's camp award and are sorry for the oversight.

The mystery of the missing bathing suits was solved soon after we searched your son's foot locker.

Registrations have been filled since just before Thanksgiving.

Sincerely,
Grim Gruber, Director
Camp Discouragement for Boys

## Nagging—American Style

AS THE BRIDE in the newspaper account told the police the other day after she shot her new husband at their wedding reception, "No marriage is perfect."

After I had read the story and had gone beyond the point of wondering why she was wearing a gun to her wedding, I got to wondering why she had shot him so soon. Surely they didn't have the time to approach the big problems that psychologists are always warning us about like: communications, consideration, honesty, thoughtfulness, in-laws, money, and children. It had to be then a perfect "case" for what I have always contended. The biggest problems in a marriage are all those little pesky differences that drive you behind a locked door in the bathroom, to the sofa to spend the night, to Mother's studio couch, to the lake with the boys, to the nearest bar, or straight into the arms of the Avon lady. Nagging one another about the most inane things you can think of then becomes one of the few ways you can give vent to these differences.

I have always said half of the arguments in this country are caused by a simple little thing like a mosquito in the

bedroom. It's true. The trouble festers when it becomes evident two opposites have married (a) those who don't mind mosquitoes in the bedroom and (b) those who find it impossible to exist with mosquitoes in their bedroom.

Usually this discovery is not made until the first summer after marriage. When it happens, it's enough to make World War II sound like a wet cap pistol.

Generally, but not always, it's the woman who can't stand the sharp, whining buzz about her head. Promptly she will throw back the covers, illuminate the bedroom with light, stand in the middle of the bed and announce, "Clyde, we can't sleep with that mosquito in this bedroom. Clyde! Clyde! I say, we can't sleep with that mosquito in this bedroom."

Now, Clyde comes out of his unconscious state mumbling, "Hold him, Tom, while I get the net. You don't want to lose him at the boat. He looks like a three-pounder."

"Wake up," he is ordered. "You're not fishing. We're chasing a mosquito. Here, take this paper and don't miss!"

"Look," he pleads sleepily, "why don't you just ignore him and go to sleep. What's a small mosquito?"

"They're noisy and they carry malaria," she states flatly.

He groans, "With malaria I can stay home from work and get paid. Exhaustion, they won't buy."

"Wait a minute," she says excitedly, "I think he's in the bathroom. Quick, shut the door."

"Now, can I go back to bed?" he asks.

"No, I think there's a pair of them. This dizzy wallpaper. You can't see anything on it at night. I hate this wallpaper. Be still. He was on my pillow a while back. There he is . . . get him! You missed! For a man who can hit a baseball, a golf ball, and can fly cast into a circle, you're lousy at hitting mosquitoes."

"It's *your* mosquito, Great White Hunter, you kill it!" he says.

"And how did we get mosquitoes?" she retaliates. "I'll tell you how. They slip through your homemade screens."

"Well, they had to go on a diet to do it," he yells back.

"And another thing," she shouts. "Your mother had no right to wear navy blue to our wedding."

"You always bring that up," he informs her. "It has nothing to do with mosquitoes."

"How would you like to sleep in this disease-ridden jungle all by yourself?"

"I'd sleep in a crocodile's stomach to get that bright light out of my eyes," he blusters.

"Okay, Clyde," she storms. "That tore it. I'm going to the sofa for a decent night's sleep. If you want to chase mosquitoes all night, that's your business!"

Second only to the mosquito is the problem of the electric blanket. When electric blankets came out, some simple-minded designer hung a single control box on it and hoped for a miracle.

I defy you to put any blissfully happy married couple under a blanket with a single control and have them speaking to one another in the cold light of morning. Quite frankly, I haven't seen such a home wrecker since they legalized the Watusi.

Why only last week, a pair of my dearest friends, Wanda and Lester Blissful, separated over a single-control electric blanket. Naturally the card club doesn't have the full details yet, but the way we understand it, Wanda was readying for bed one night when Lester said gruffly, "Are you wearing that little sleeveless gown to bed?"

"I don't usually wear a snowsuit," she smiled stiffly. (Wanda's a real corker.)

"If you're planning on hiking that blanket up to a seven again tonight, forget it," he said firmly. "Last night, I slept like the FBI was trying to wring a confession out of me."

She smiled. "You exaggerate. I had the control on five. The night before you had it on two and I nearly froze. You know, Lester, if I had known you were a No. two on the electric blanket, I would never have married you. There's something wrong with a man who would let his veins freeze over."

This is all hearsay, mind you, but we heard they sniped at each other all night long. Lester said, "I feel a Mau Mau is having me for lunch . . . literally!" Wanda said, "That's better than feeling like a prime beef in a food locker!" Lester retaliated with "Toasted marshmallows, anyone?" Wanda shot back, "Welcome to Ski Valley."

After a sleepless night for both of them, they decided things weren't working out between them and they made an appointment with their lawyer.

Their properties, holdings, and children were divided with cold efficiency. There was no problem here. Then Lester spoke, "Who gets custody of the electric blanket?"

"What do you need it for?" yelled Wanda. "You could get the same cold feet by hanging them out of the window."

"And you could get equally warm by wetting your finger and sticking it into an electrical outlet!" he charged.

At this point the lawyer interceded and suggested they buy an electric blanket with dual controls. He said he and his wife would assume custody of the blanket with the single control.

Their case comes up next month, so they say at card club.

Very frankly, two things have nearly wrecked our marriage: a home freezer and the checking account. Now, I know what you're going to say. Right away, you're going to jump to the conclusion that I bought an expensive home freezer without telling my husband and that I abuse the checking account by spending too much money. You are wrong. They are just small things to "nag" about.

For example, we've been arguing about that home freezer for three years now. It's been paid for since a year ago last August. (In fact, I heard there was a Conga line at the credit office that snaked out to the elevator and that the manager treated the staff to cranberry juice out of paper cups, but that could be a rumor.)

At any rate, I insisted we buy the freezer because I couldn't live through another "harvest" without it. I wanted to preserve some of that fresh corn on the cob, green beans, melon balls, peaches, and strawberries. So, my husband agreed to the freezer.

The first week, I snapped and broke thirty pounds of green beans. I blanched them, cooled them, put them into plastic bags, then into boxes where I duly marked the date: June 5. By June 28 we had consumed thirty pounds of green beans. I went the same route with corn and carrots. No matter what quantities I put into the freezer, we had it eaten clean by the end of the week.

In the fall I bought a bushel of apples. I peeled, cored,

blanched, cooled, bagged, boxed, and labeled. The yield was eight quarts which someone figured cost me $2.33 a quart, counting labor. (On a rice-paddy minimum wage scale.)

One day my husband decided to check out the freezer. I held my breath. "Well now, what do we have on this shelf?" he asked quizzically.

"Snowballs," I said softly. "The kids made them up when it snowed and then when it's summer, we've got this wonderful, rich supply of snowballs that we couldn't possibly begin to have if we just had the freezing compartment in the refrigerator."

"And what are all those brown paper bags filled with? Steaks? Rump roasts? Chops?"

"You're warm," I said, slamming the door shut.

"How warm?" he asked, opening it again.

"Chicken innards," I said.

"*Chicken innards!*"

"That's right," I explained. "You always said I wasn't to put them into the garbage can until the day of pick-up and I thought I could store them in the freezer until garbage day. I guess I forgot to put a few of them out."

"Is this what I think it is?" he asked tiredly.

"It is, I believe, a transistor battery. Someone said if you put them in a freezer, they'd recharge themselves."

"So, this is what I gave up cigarettes for," he whimpered. "This is why I painted my heels black so no one would know I was wearing socks with holes in them. This is why I didn't buy a library card . . . just to save money. All for a frozen patch of snowballs, batteries, and chicken necks!"

"Aren't you being a little dramatic?"

"You are some kind of a nut," he accused. "It's a good thing they don't try to match you up in some computer, or you'd be married to Bert Lahr and living on a Funny Farm."

I'd like to say I filled the freezer to capacity with a hind quarter of whatever it is you freeze and we lived happily ever after. I'd like to say it, but I can't. I figured if we didn't argue about all those chicken innards, we might argue about something serious.

As for the checking account, it's simply a little thing about being "neat." The first year we were married, we opened our first checking account. My first entries looked like the work of a monastery monk. They were bold and black, lettered evenly, and stood out in complete legibility.

As the months wore on I began to scribble, abbreviate, and write notes in the margin. Then I would rearrange deposits and dates with bent arrows. Finally, my husband said one day, "I am going to start you in a nice new bank tomorrow. Would you like that? Your checks will start with No. one again and your ledger will be spanking clean."

The next bank was the same story, only they had no sense of humor for my notes attached to the checks. ("Luvie, hang on to this one until Monday. Our new money isn't dry yet.") We pushed on to another bank and another account.

In time, I began to shop for banks like a new home owner. I can tell you in a flash which banks have dry inkwells, which ones sell bookends, and which ones flaunt lollipop trees and pastel checks. At one establishment I received a nasty note advising me to sign my name the way I signed it on the records. My husband was visibly annoyed with me. "How did you sign your name originally?" he queried.

"Alf Landon," I said.

He collapsed in a chair and it served him right for doubting me.

Another time they became quite oral about the omission of my account number. There followed another inquisition. "Well, what number *did* you use?" I tried to remember. "I think it was my social security number . . . or my oil company number . . . or my swimming club number . . . or was it my record club?"

Things did go a little better when my husband figured out

my checkbook abbreviations. For example, NS beside an entry meant "No Stamp" to mail the check. Thus that check would be re-entered as a deposit and added on to the total. An OOB meant "Out Of Balance" and was the amount the bank and I differed. Thus, a subtraction and we began even again.

FB was entered when the item was so frivolous and ridiculous I knew he'd raise the roof if he knew. It stood for "Fringe Benefits." Others took some explanation. "What's this entry for Nursery—seventy-one dollars? We haven't had a baby in eight years," he growled.

"Geraniums," I said.

"Seventy-one dollars worth of geraniums!"

"Oh, of course not, ninny, that bill was for seventeen dollars. I made a mistake and transposed the numbers and I had to record the check like I wrote it. I only subtracted seventeen dollars though because the nursery wouldn't cash a check for seventy-one dollars. No one buys that many geraniums." We were overdrawn and moved on to another bank.

To date, I have been in more banks than Jesse James. But I figure if my husband wanted a financial giant, he should have shopped a little longer and not snatched the first skirt to come down the pike.

I suppose I should condemn marital nagging, but I'm not going to.

The American Institute of Family Relations observed a while back there are three times during a day when wifely nagging is the most dangerous: at breakfast, before dinner, and again at bedtime.

So what's left? A spontaneous argument can be rather stimulating after a morning playing "Red Goose Run" with Captain Kangaroo. It picks up tired blood, clears the old sinuses, sharpens the reflexes, and gives you a chance to use words like: insidious, subversive, ostentatious, incarceration, ambiguous, partisan, incumbent, and other words which you don't know the meaning of either, but which you're reasonably sure are fit for children to hear.

Besides, it's a challenge. There's a sameness to nagging that occurs after you've been married awhile. The routines became as familiar as the dialogue of two vaudevillians. My husband has one called "Where's the table salt?" or as the kids call it, "The Great American Tragedy." I could serve eagle eyeballs under glass, wearing a topless bathing suit, and he'd shout, "What does a man have to do to get salt to his table!"

I have some old standards that I replay from time to time. There're "This house is a penal institution," "I didn't know you were allergic to grass when I married you," and "Why is it other men look like a page out of a Sears catalogue and you drag around in baggy pants like Hans Brinker?"

A little nagging is a healthy thing in a marriage. The way I figure it, you can either nag your way through fifty or sixty years or wear a gun to your wedding.

july 10 — september 5

# what's a mother for
# but to suffer?

OF ALL THE EMOTIONS enjoyed by a mother, none makes her feel as wonderfully ignoble as her "What's a Mother For But to Suffer?" period.

It doesn't happen in a day, of course. She has to build up to it through a series of self-inflicted tongue wounds. She observes, for example, "I could be St. Joan of Arc with the flames licking around my ankles, and Harlow would roast marshmallows." Or, "If I were on the *Titanic* and there was only one seat left in the lifeboat, Merrill would race me for it." Finally, at the peak of her distress, she will sum up her plight thusly, "I could be lying dead in the street and Evelyn would eat a peanut butter sandwich over me."

The image of her own sacrifice and thankless devotion to motherhood grows and grows until finally she is personified in every little old lady who scrubs floors at night to send a son through law school to every snaggle-toothed hag who sells violets in the snow.

Outwardly most women are ashamed of this emotion. They are loathe to admit that a small child, born of love, weaned on innocence, and nurtured with such gentleness could frustrate them to such cornball theatrics. They blame society, the educational system, the government, their mother, their obstetrician, their husband, and Ethel Kennedy for not telling them what motherhood was all about. They weren't prepared and they're probably bungling the whole process of child-rearing.

They just took a few of "what Mother always saids" and stirred in a generous portion of "what Daddy always dids" and said a fervent prayer that the kids didn't steal hubcaps while they were trying to figure out what they were going to do.

I've always blamed my shortcomings as a mother on the fact that I studied Child Psychology and Discipline under an unmarried professor whose only experience was in raising a dog. He obviously saw little difference.

At the age of two, my children could fetch and I'd reward them with a biscuit. At the age of four, they could sit, heel, or stay just by listening to the inflection in my voice. They were paper trained by the age of five. It was then that I noted a difference between their aims and goals and mine. So I put away my Child Psychology and Discipline volume and substituted a dog-eared copy of *Crime and Punishment*. I am now the only mother in our block who reaches out to kiss her children and has them flinch and threaten to call their attorneys if I so much as lay a finger on them.

Then a friend of mine told me she had a solution that worked pretty well. It was "Wait until your father gets home." This seemed to be working for me, too. It certainly took away the "acid stomach condition" that had been so bothersome. But one afternoon I heard the children making plans to either give Daddy up for Lent or lend him to a needy boy at Christmas and I felt a twinge of conscience.

We talked it over—their father and I—and finally conceded child-raising was a two-headed job, literally speaking. We would have to share the responsibilities. We have a list of blunders that span Diana Dors twice, not the least being our stab at sex education.

The sex education of a child is a delicate thing. None of us wants to "blow it." I always had a horror of ending up like the woman in the old joke who was asked by her child where he came from and after she explained the technical process in a well-chosen medical vocabulary, he looked at her intently and said, "I just wondered. Mike came from Hartford, Connecticut."

My husband and I talked about it and we figured what better way to explain the beautiful reproduction cycle of life than through the animal kingdom. We bought two pairs of guppies and a small aquarium. We should have bought two pairs of guppies and a small reservoir. Our breakfast conversation eventually assumed a pattern.

"What's new at Peyton Place by the Sea?" my husband would inquire.

"Mrs. Guppy is e-n-c-e-i-n-t-e again," I'd say.

"Put a little salt in the water. That'll cure anything," he mumbled.

"Daddy," said our son. "That means she's pregnant!"

"Again!" Daddy choked. "Can't we organize an intramural volleyball team in there or something?"

The first aquarium begat a second aquarium with no relief in sight.

"Are you getting anything out of your experience with guppies?" I asked my son delicately one afternoon. "Oh yeah," he said, "they're neat."

"I mean, have you watched the male and the female? Do you understand the processes that go into the offspring? The role of the mother in all this?"

"Oh sure," he said. "Listen, how did you know which one of your babies to eat when they were born?"

We added a third aquarium which was promptly filled with salt water and three pairs of sea horses.

"Now, I want you to pay special attention to the female," I instructed. "The chances are it won't take her long to be with child and perhaps you can see her actually give birth."

"The female doesn't give birth, Mom," said my son peeling a banana. (I felt myself smiling, anticipating a trend.) "Ridiculous," I said. "Females always give birth." The male began to take on weight. I thought I saw his ankles swell. He became a mother on the twenty-third of the month.

"That's pretty interesting," observed my son. "I hope when I become a mother, it's on land. I can't tread water that long."

We blew it. We figured we would.

If you want to know the truth, we haven't made out too well in the problem of sibling rivalry either. I think the rumor is that more parents have been driven out of their skulls by sibling rivalry than any other behavior phase. I started the rumor.

In infancy, it's a series of small things. Big sister will stuff a whole banana in the mouth of baby brother with the threat, "Shut your mouth, baby, or out you go." Or big brother will slap his toddler sister off her hobby horse with the reprimand, "Keep that squeak on your side of the room." It eventually reaches a point where they are measuring their cut of meat with a micrometer to see they are getting their fair share as set down by the Geneva Convention, and being represented by legal counsel to see who gets the fruit cocktail with the lone cherry on top.

The rivalry of each day, however, seems to culminate at the dinner table.

SON: She's doing it again.
FATHER: Doing what?
SON: Humming.

DAUGHTER: I am not humming.

SON: You are so. There, she did it again, Dad. Watch her neck. She's humming so no one can hear her but me. She does it all the time just to make fun of me.

FATHER: I can't hear anything. Eat your dinner.

SON: How come *he* got the bone?

FATHER: What difference does it make? There's no meat on the bone, anyway.

OTHER SON: Then how come *he* got the meat? I got stuck with the bone the last time.

DAUGHTER: I got dibs on the last black olive. *You* got the ice cube in your water after school and *you* got the bike for your birthday, so I get the black olive.

FATHER: What kind of logic is that! I swear it's like eating with the mafia. (*Turning to Mother*) How can you sit there and listen to all this drivel?

MOTHER: I'm under sedation.

This seemed to be the answer until recently, when some dear friends of ours confided in us that they had all but solved their sibling rivalry problems at the dinner table. We listened to them talk of peace, love, and tranquility throughout the meal by engaging in a new game called Category. It worked very simply. Each member of the family was allowed one night at the table where he alone named the Category and led that particular discussion. Hence, everyone had a chance to speak and sooner or later each child could talk about something that interested him.

I had to admit, Category sounded like a better game than we were playing at present called Trials at Nuremberg. This also worked rather simply. We would wait until we were all assembled at the table, then right after the prayer we'd confront the children with crimes they had committed in their playpens up to the present day. We'd touch upon bad manners, bicycles in the driveway, socks under the bed, goofing around with the garbage detail, throwing away their allow-

ances on paraffin teeth and anything else we could document. By the time we reached dessert, we usually had a couple of them sobbing uncontrollably into their mashed potatoes, begging to be sent to an orphanage. We decided to give Category a try.

"Tonight, I'm going to talk about 'Friends,'" said our older son.

"Don't talk with food in your mouth," amended his father.

He swallowed and continued, "My very best, first choice, A-1 top of the list, first class, Cadillac of a friend is Charlie."

"Charlie who?" someone interrupted.

"I don't know his last name," he shrugged. "Just Charlie."

"Well, good grief," I sighed. "You'd certainly think if you had a big, fat Damon and Pythias relationship with a real, live friend you'd get around to last names."

"Who's Damon and Pythias?" asked a small voice.

"Aw, come on," said the speaker. "It's not your turn until tomorrow night. Anyway, today my best friend, Charlie, threw up in school—"

"*Mother!*" screamed a voice. "Do I have to sit here and listen to stories about Charlie up-chucking?"

"Tell us about another friend, son," pleaded his father.

He continued. "Well, my second best B-2, second from the top of the list, Oldsmobile of a friend is Scott. Today, Scott went after the janitor to bring the bucket when Charlie threw up and—"

"Please!" the entire table groaned.

"Well, it's my category," he insisted, "and they're my friends. If I have to sit and listen to you talk about your junk, you can listen to me."

"I wish Charlie were here to eat these cold mashed potatoes."

"Yeah, well, when it's your turn to talk, I'm going to hum."

"All right, kids," interrupted their father. "While we're on the subject of cold mashed potatoes, who left the red bicycle right in the middle of the driveway tonight? And, as long as we're all together, which one of you lost the nozzle off the garden hose? (*Aside*) Hold up the dessert, Mother, I've got a few things to discuss. Now, about the telephone. I'm getting a little sick and tired of having to shinny up the pole every time I want to call out . . ."

Very frankly, I don't feel the problem of sibling rivalry will ever be worked out in our time. Especially after reading a recent survey taken among brothers and sisters as to what they liked or disliked about one another. These were some of the reasons for their contempt of one another. "He's my brother." "She says hello to me in front of my friends." "She's a girl." "He's always hanging around the house when I'm there." "She acts big and uppity." "She's a sloppy beast." "He knows everything." Only one brother said something nice about his sister. He wrote, "Sometimes when she takes a bath, she uses a neat deodorant." I ask you, how are you going to build a quiet meal around that!

The second-largest problem to parents is status. It changes

from year to year, beginning with "I'm five years old and *my* mama lets me stay up to watch the late, late show," to "I'm in the sixth grade too and I'm listed in the phone book under my own name."

It gets pretty ridiculous, of course, but it's just another hair-shirt in a mother's wardrobe. Another challenge for a mother who must make a decision not to measure her own children's happiness with another mother's yardstick. Just last month, I heard that the lastest status symbol around the bridge table is children's dental work. Wild? Not really. The more fillings, the more space maintainers, the more braces, the more status. If the orthodontist says your kid has a bite problem, lady, you're in.

Here's a conversation I overheard illustrating the point.

"You talk about dental work," said a small blonde. "Come here, George. Open your mouth, George." The lights danced on George's metal-filled mouth like Ali Baba's cave. "That," she said emphatically, "is my mink stole. A mother's sacrifice. And is he grateful? He is not."

"Think nothing of it," said her companion. "Come over here, Marcia. Let the lady look at your braces." Marcia mechanically threw back her head and opened wide. The inside of her mouth looked like it was set to go off. "That," she said, "is my trip to Europe. What do you think of that?"

"I think we worry too much about them," said the first one. "Always nagging. 'Brush your teeth, don't eat sweets.' I mean we can't run around after them like those hags on television, can we?"

"Wait till you see what I'm buying George for his mouth this month," the blonde confided. "You'll be dumbfounded. It's very new and expensive and I understand there aren't a half dozen people who have them in their mouths yet. George and I will be one of the first."

"What is it?" asked the first one breathlessly.

"Promise you won't tell anyone?" (*Hushed tone*) "It's a telltale tooth."

"A telltale tooth?"

"Right. They cram six miniature transmitters, twenty-eight other electrical components, and two rechargeable batteries into what looks like an ordinary 'bridge' of a first molar. Then, as they chew, the telltale tooth broadcasts a stream of information to the dentist that tells what the child has eaten and what is causing the breakdown of his teeth."

"A fink tooth! Well, I'll be. I think I'll get one of those for Marcia. Maybe we could hook up her transistor to it and do away with that wire coming out of her ear. Then the music could come from her teeth. Wouldn't that give the kids in her class a jolt!"

"Well, I thought I'd get an antenna for George's. Then maybe he could hook up to that Early Bird channel from Telestar and draw in something from overseas."

"There goes that patio cover you were saving for—but then, what's a mother for, but to sweat in the hot sun."

A mother's suffering—a privilege or a put-upon. Who knows. I only know that when you can no longer evoke any empathy from your children with it, then you must take a firm stance, throw back your head, look determined, and as my old Child Psychology professor advised, "Pull up hard on the leash!"

## Color Me Naïve

BOY, MAYBE I'M NAÏVE or something, but what's with these women who waddle into the hospital complaining of a bad case of indigestion and deliver twins two hours later? When presented with their case of indigestion swathed in pink blankets, they express shock and say, "I didn't even know I was pregnant!"

I'm the suspicious type. I think when they got to the stage

where they couldn't see their feet over their stomachs, couldn't
fit behind a car steering wheel, couldn't wear anything but a
tent with a drawstring neckline, they suspected, all right.

Granted, some women show less than others during pregnancy, but the only women I know who actually carry babies
"concave" are magazine models and television actresses. And
I never saw one of them I didn't hate! What they do is they
nail these fashion models in the second week of their
pregnancy, pour them into a Paris original and try to convince
Mrs. Housewife that even models have babies and they don't
look like Humpty Dumpty with a grouch.

Television is worse. On soap operas, for example, the
actress rarely gets out of her street clothes. Oh, she may
complain of a backache, tiredness, nausea, and swollen ankles,
but the straight skirts and severe sheaths continue. I have
also noted the length of pregnancies on a soap opera is no

more than eight or nine weeks, a decided improvement over the standard nine months. Finally, in the ninth week (when they have padded her with a cotton swab) she complains of labor. She is fresh from the beauty shop and is ready to deliver. The baby is never seen. She (a) loses it, (b) puts it up for adoption, or (c) never wants to see it again. This creates fewer problems for casting.

You can expect such an unrealistic approach from medias that deal in make-believe, but in real life it would sound like an old William Powell-Myrna Loy movie.

MYRNA: William, I should have told you before, but we're going to have a baby.

WILLIAM: (*The match he is holding burns his fingers.*) A baby, but when?

MYRNA: Tomorrow.

WILLIAM: But why didn't you tell me, my dear?

MYRNA: I was afraid you'd be cross with me. Are you surprised?

WILLIAM: I can't believe it. So that's why there's a baby crib in our bedroom . . . and I've been cooking all the meals . . . and your suitcase is packed . . . it's all beginning to make sense now. But how was I to know? Day after day I'd find you just sitting in that chair.

MYRNA: I can't get out of it.

WILLIAM: Could I get you something? A glass of water? An obstetrician?

MYRNA: Just a helping hand out of this chair. (*She stands up, forty-five pounds heavier than she was nine months ago, shoulders flung back, feet apart.*) There now, be honest, didn't you suspect something?

WILLIAM: Nonsense. You still look like the bride I married.

I recently became very interested in the story of a London housewife who was at odds with English automobile manúfacturers over the low position of steering wheels for expectant mothers who have to drive a car. The automobile manufacturers retaliated with "Why should pregnant women have to drive at all?" which is the type of answer you'd expect from a bachelor engineer whose mommy told him she got him with green stamps!

Actually, pregnant women don't have to drive cars. They could ride motorcycles sidesaddle, strap their feet to two skateboards, or raise their umbrellas and think Mary Poppins, but the fact remains automobiles are an intricate part of a woman's life and to give them up for six months or so is like going back to nesting in a rocking chair for nine months.

I know of what I speak. Before American cars were equipped with tilt-away steering wheels, I had a traumatic experience that I have not been able to relate to more than thirty or forty thousand of my most intimate friends.

I was going into my eleventh month of pregnancy (the doctor and I disagreed on this point) and had gone to the store to purchase a half gallon of ice cream and a loaf of bread. The car seat was back as far as it would go, which created a small problem. My feet no longer reached the brake pedal or the accelerator, so I had to crouch. When I crouched, my vision was impaired and I had to hang my head out of the no-draft. When I did this, I hit things.

No matter. I got to the store and parked the car, nose in, and made my exit without incident. However, on my return I noticed I had been hemmed in on both sides by parked cars.

I eased open the door a crack and proceeded to stuff myself into the car, stomach first. However, I became wedged between the arm rest of the door and the steering wheel. I could not go forward or backward. Now, try that on for laughs. My stomach was stuck and my ice cream was melting.

People began to stand around in curious mobs. Quickly I pulled backward, releasing me from the front seat. To save face, I nonchalantly opened the back door of the car and slid in like a guest. Now, to get to the front seat. Bent from the waist, I faced the rear of the car and tried rolling over the top of the front seat. The ashtray tore a hole in my bread wrapper.

Humiliated, I plopped down on the seat to think. What do you do when you go to the supermarket manager and ask him to announce over his microphone that the black station wagon bearing license plates ——— is blocking *a stomach?* I licked the sticky ice cream off my fingers and decided to give it one more try. I'd back into the front seat. I was doing fine until another fat part of me made contact with the horn. A small child pointed and said, "Mommy, is that woman sitting on her horn going to have a baby?"

Tears welled in my eyes. "Don't be ridiculous, kid! I'm carrying it for a dear friend."

Whenever I'd get really depressed over my plight, I'd think about a footnote I read once in a Population Study Patterns report. (I picked that up in a doctor's office. It beat reading *Gall Bladder Digest.*) It said an Austrian woman had set an "apparent world population record" by bearing sixty-nine offspring. What's more, she did it the government way: in carbons and triplicates. Here's her tally.

| BIRTHS | SETS | TOTALS |
|---|---|---|
| Quadruplets . . . . . . . . . . | 4 | 16 |
| Triplets . . . . . . . . . . . | 7 | 21 |
| Twins . . . . . . . . . . . . | 16 | 32 |
| | TOTAL: | 69 |

I used to think about her a lot. Without ever having set eyes on her, you can tell many things from these figures. Obviously this is a woman who hates the pesky details of packing a suitcase. You'll note she made only twenty-seven trips to the maternity ward. Likewise, she's a woman who doesn't waste time in repetition. If she had felt a single birth coming, she would probably haved phoned it in.

She's a person used to looking upward, not having seen her feet in twenty-seven years. Heartburn to her is a way of life, while a knit suit is as unreal as Santa Claus. In all probability, her sense of humor has been dulled. When she and her husband planned their marriage in the first full bloom of courtship, and he proposed, "We'll have thirty-one boys for me and thirty-eight girls for you," she probably blushed and said, "You're a regular card, Stanley."

As she tallied up the twenty-ninth, thirtieth, and thirty-first births, undoubtedly "Tell Mother we're expecting again" became a rather dreary chore. After arrivals forty-three, forty-four, and forty-five, she probably had reached the yellow pages of the phone book for names and was reduced to calling number forty-six the Aufderheiden Bottling Company. Upon the birth of fifty-one and fifty-two, the problem of how to get to thirty-seven PTA Open Houses likely threw them. When the children reached the sixties, it was undoubtedly a strain to remember not whose birthday was Saturday, but how many.

I can visualize many problems with sixty-nine children in the house. Taking numbers to get into the bathroom, getting your clothes issued from a quartermaster, substituting the word "invasion" for "visit" and tactfully suggesting to two redheads they've been sleeping with the wrong family for three years.

The story goes on to reveal that the average woman has a potential capability of producing something like twenty off-spring, discounting the possibility of multiple births. (If that doesn't make your day, it's beyond help.) So, if you stand now at the national average, which is 2.7 children per family, you and your husband are going to have to go some to make a footnote out of yourself!

No story on motherhood these days is complete without mention of two static words, "The Pill." I'm inclined to go along with the sign on a diaper service truck I saw last week. As it whizzed through town at a law-breaking speed, I caught the sign painted on its rear doors, "What Pill?"

Actually, there are two things in this country directly opposing The Pill, both birds.

First, Europeans are staging an all-out effort to increase the population of the storks. To keep them from becoming extinct, sympathetic French citizens are keeping them in their kitchens to protect them from cold snaps, an emergency stork committee has been named to make sure the birds survive the hazards of high-tension wires and television antennae, and at one point an airlift was staged to transport young birds from Algeria to France. And how do you think these grateful birds will repay the French citizens for their hospitality? By moving on to Chicago, Los Angeles, New York, Denver, and Philadelphia, what else?

Frankly I'm pretty jittery about the whole deal. I get panicky when I see a dove fly in Clara's window.

The other bird who is blocking the breakthrough of The Pill to American women is the pigeon. With the projected people population running into the billions, overcrowded schools, limited housing, lack of food and threat of unemployment, the birth control pill was awarded by the government to the pigeons so that they could control their numbers.

I suppose if you're a pedestrian who walks under high window ledges, this might have some meaning for you, but I don't think the pigeons were even seeking assistance from the government.

Crawling out on a rather narrow ledge of the courthouse, I talked recently with a spokesman—the only bird who knew pigeon English—about the talked-about Pill.

"Well, if people don't want us around, why don't they say so?" he cooed. "I'm sick of this shilly-shallying. When we first moved from the suburbs into the cities, the natives took potshots at us. Of course, they were severely criticized by the ASPCA—not the barbershop harmony group, dear, the Society for the Prevention of Cruelty to Animals.

"Next, they tried a variety of insecticides to make us leave our perches. Finally, they put electrical charges on the buildings where we walk. And if you think that doesn't give you a jolt when you set down for a landing, you haven't changed radio stations while you were in the bathtub lately.

"No, I think they've gone too far. Oh, I suppose we do produce at a rather astounding rate. But there's nothing else to do up here all day long but fly over parked cars and mess around the statues in the parks."

I asked him how the women of this country should go about getting The Pill.

"All I can offer is some advice on how we got to be a menace. We just made our numbers felt in the downtown area."

"I'll tell them," I said.

The more I think of it, however, the more I'm convinced that fertility, or the lack of it, doesn't depend on a pill, a chart, or a clinic. It rests solely with the predisposition of women.

For example, go buy a new bathing suit, go on a diet, invest twenty dollars in a pair of stretch pants so tight you can trace your lunch and *voilà!* Pregnancy! Or more drastic measures: Let your Blue Cross lapse, buy a small sports car with two bucket seats, or adopt a baby. You asked for it. Instant parenthood.

If you're really serious about limiting your family, you should follow the following advice:

1. Young mothers are urged to hang on to maternity clothes, sterilizers, bottle warmers, beds, baby tenders, sheet blankets, pads, and reusable pacifiers. If storage space is needed, dig a hole under the house if necessary.

2. Don't make vacation plans in September for the next summer at Lake Erie or in New York. Clinical records have indicated women who planned to scale the inside of the Statue of Liberty were so pregnant by vacation time they were lucky the ferryboat didn't capsize.

3. Resist the impulse to sign up for self-improvement courses in the daytime or academic study at the university in the evening. This is a sure way to get back to testing strained liver with the tip of your tongue.

4. Do not be tempted by the job markets until you are beyond sixty. Remember. Roads to fertility begin at the employment office—especially for those who make a big deal inquiring about vacations and retirement benefits.

5. Keep a keen eye on budget spending. Deferred accounts, long-term credit buying is like waving a red flag before the odds.

6. Don't become too enamored with water sports such as expensive boats, water skiing, and scuba diving. This could be awkward and limiting later on.

7. Don't make any public speeches over bridge tables on topics such as, "I named my last one Caboose. And that's it!" or "Did you hear about Fanny and she's forty-two!"

I may be naïve, but I'm no fool!

## The Disenchanted

SOME WOMAN once nailed me in a restroom in Detroit and said, "I can hardly wait until your children are a little older. You will have such fun writing about them during that stage." The woman, an obvious sadist who hangs around restrooms and stirs up trouble, never mentioned the precise age at which child-rearing got to be a fun thing. I am still waiting.

When the children were quite young, I used to envision a time when they would gather at my feet and say, "Now don't you lift an arthritic finger, Mother. I know exactly where your pinking shears are. Let me run and get them for you." Frankly I cannot remember a time when our popularity as parents has been at such an all-time low.

Our children barricade themselves behind locked bedroom doors, emerging only when the telephone rings. The "phono-mania" is probably our doing. We noted long ago that some of our friends had a real phone problem with their children. (One couple had the run of the phone from 4 to 6:30 A.M. weekdays only, during the months with R in them.) So we decided that when our children were old enough to point to the telephone and say, "Mommy, what is that?" we'd answer, "It's a cavity machine to check the cavities in your teeth." (We also told them steak made little children sick, but that is another story.) Our yarn about the cavity machine began to leak holes when our daughter discovered by lifting the handle of the cavity machine and dialing a few numbers she could be in touch with thousands of cavity machines throughout the world. She has had a Princess phone stuck in her ear ever since.

The key word with growing children—are there any other kind?—seems to be communication. If you're a lip-reader of any repute whatsoever, you have no problem. However, if you must compete with local disc jockeys which feed hourly through their earplugs this could get pretty sticky. We have solved this problem by buying time on the local station and reporting personal messages: "We moved last week." "Daddy's birthday is in September." "Do you still lisp?"

Naturally you can't live among all those decibels and not be affected by it. I didn't know how noise could become a way of life until the other day when I answered the door and a young man said, "Pardon me, madam, I'm doing a survey among mothers to see whether or not they agree with an acoustical engineer from Arizona that rock 'n' roll may cause teenagers to go deaf."

"No, I don't need any rolls or bread today. If you've got any of those little buns with the jelly inside, though—"

"No, madam," he said, raising his voice, "you don't under-stand. I'm not a bakery man. I'd like to get your opinion on what hearing experts are saying about rock 'n' roll music and whether or not you think excessive—"

"*Oh, Excedrin!* You want me to do a commercial? My yes, I have headaches all the time. It's this loud music. You see, we've got four radios in the house. Along about four o'clock it sounds like the U. N. General Assembly singing a serenade in four languages to Red China. I simply crawl under the sink with a shaker full of Excedrin and—"

"Madam," he said facing me squarely, "we're not doing a commercial. We're doing a survey. Do you have a teenager in your home?"

"You're going to have to keep your lips in full view of my eyes at all times," I explained. "And talk a little slower."

"I'm sorry," he said. "Do you have a teenager in your home?"

"I think that's what it is," I said hesitantly. "The bangs are two inches above the hemline and there's a lump on the hip shaped like a small transistor, two button eyes, and a long cord that connects the hip to the ear."

"That's a teenager," he added impersonally. "Now, have you noticed any impairment in her hearing since she started listening to rock 'n' roll music?"

I pondered. "Nothing unusual. She still doesn't respond to simple commands like 'Clean your room,' 'Change your clothes,' 'Get the door.' On the other hand she picks up phrases like 'Have you heard the story about . . .' 'The bank balance is down to . . .' and 'Let's feed the kids early and slip out to dinner . . .' like she was standing in the middle of the Capitol rotunda in Washington."

"Then you have noticed that increased decibels have made a change in your teenager?"

"Pardon me while I get the phone."

"I didn't hear anything," he said.

"It's always like that after I've listened to three hours of Maurice and His Electric Fuse Boxes. Did you know that group once recorded the guitar player's hiccups and sold two million records? Are you saying something, young man? I told you you'd have to keep your lips in full view of my eyes at all times. *And speak a little slower!*"

Other than noise, possibly nothing is more perplexing to parents than the current hair styles. In our family it all began when our daughter said she was going to let her hair grow. Like a fool I thought she meant down her back! Little did I dream it would cascade over her face and that only a slight part in the middle would stand between her and asphyxiation.

Quite frankly the whole thing got on my nerves. "Are you awake under there?" I'd ask, my eyes squinting for a peek of flesh. "If you are, just rap twice on the table." Sometimes when the hair wouldn't move for a while, I'd get panicky and take her pulse. Then a voice would come out of the hair, "Mother! Please! I'm on the phone." For all I knew she could have had a ouija board and another friend in there with her. Occasionally she would style her hair in such a way that a single eye would be exposed. The eye would follow me about the room, not moving and rarely blinking. I often found myself addressing remarks to it.

One day when I came to the conclusion that she looked more like a troll than a human, I ventured a wild suggestion, "Why don't you cut your hair?"

I saw the hair part and a pair of lips emerge and say, "You've got to be kidding! I'd be the laughingstock of the school. No one cuts their hair anymore."

I saw my chance and took it. "That's it. Be a pace setter. Dare to be different. There is absolutely nothing more fresh and feminine in this world than short-cropped, clean hair with a little curl in the end and a little side bang. I tell you, you'd stand out like a pom pom girl in St. Petersburg, Florida. For the first time in your life, dare to look like a girl."

She pondered it for three weeks. Then her eyes glistening

with sentiment, she was sheared and was once again able to distinguish light from darkness. I admit I was pretty proud of myself. "You really look the way a young lady should look. I wouldn't be surprised if all the girls in your school followed your lead. It's so girlish . . . so ladylike . . . so feminine."

We were both standing in line at the local hamburger emporium when we heard it. An elderly couple quite frankly stared at my daughter's tapered slacks, boots, short jacket, and cropped hair for a full three minutes. Then they clucked, "Look at that boy! It's disgusting! What kind of a mother would let him dress like that!"

I will be glad when the hair grows back in again. Then I will only have one sad eye to follow me about.

Truly I wish I could collar that woman in Detroit and ask her when I get to laugh. Maybe it was the other night when the kids were talking with one another at the dinner table and they began to spell in front of us. Maybe it was when I overheard one of them asking their father if he wasn't a little old for a button-down collar. Or maybe it was when one of them shot me down for saying hello to them on the playground in front of their friends.

A parent gets a lot of theories these days on how they should raise their children. Treat them as children. Treat them as adults. Treat them as equals. Treat them as pals. Okay, when my children stop telling me Doris Day is three years older than I am and looks ten years younger, I'll consider them as associates. Until then, when do I get to laugh?


## Reflections at Summer's End

THE END OF SUMMER is to me like New Year's Eve. I sense an end to something carefree and uninhibited, sandy and warm, cold and melting, barefoot and tanned. And yet I look forward with great expectation to a beginning of schedules and appointments, bookbinders with little tabs, freshly sharpened pencils, crisp winds, efficiency, and routine.

I am sadly aware of a great rushing of time as I lengthen skirts and discard sweaters that hit above the wristbones. Time is moving and I want to stop it for just a while so that I may snatch a quiet moment and tell my children what it is I want for them and what all the shouting has been about.

The moment never comes, of course. I must compete with Captain Kangaroo, a baseball game, a Monkee record, a playmate, a cartoon or a new bike in the next block. So, I must keep these thoughts inside . . .

Too fast . . . you're moving too fast. Don't be in such a hurry to trade formulas for formals. You're going to own your own sports car before you've tried to build one out of orange crates and four baby buggy wheels. You're going to explore the world before you've explored the wonders of your own back yard. You're going to pad with cotton what the Good Lord will provide if you are just patient.

Don't shed your childhood like a good coat that's gotten a little small for you. A full-term childhood is necessary as is all phases of your growth. Childhood is a time for pretending and trying on maturity to see if it fits or hangs baggy, tastes good or bitter, smells nice or fills your lungs with smoke that makes you cough. It's sharing licks on the same sucker with your best friend before you discover germs. It's not knowing how much a house cost, and caring less. It's going to bed in the summer with dirty feet on clean sheets. It's thinking anyone over fifteen is "ancient." It's absorbing ideas, knowledge, and people like a giant sponge. Childhood is where "competition" is a baseball game and "responsibility" is a paper route.

I want to teach you so much that you must know to find happiness within yourself. Yet, I don't know where to begin or how.

I want you to be a square. That's right, a square! I want

you to kiss your grandmother when you walk into a room even if you're with friends. I want you to be able to talk openly of God and your love for Him. I want you to lend dignity to the things you believe in and respect for the things you don't believe in. I want you to be a human being who needs friends, and in turn deserves them. I want you to be a square who polishes his shoes, buttons the top button of his shirt occasionally, and stands straight and looks people in the eye when they are talking to you. There is a time to laugh and a time to cry. I want you to know the difference.

I want you to be a cornball, a real, honest-to-God, flag-waving cornball, who, if you must march, will tell people what you are for, not what you are against. I'm so afraid in your ultimate sophistication of growing up, you'll look upon Betsy Ross as a chairman who needed a service project, upon Barbara Frietchie as a senile who should have been committed to an institution by her son, upon the little old man who doffed his hat as the flag went by as the town drunk who never missed a parade.

Please cry when school children sing "The Battle Hymn of the Republic," when you see a picture of the Berlin Wall, when you see the American flag on the silver suit of an astronaut. Maybe I'm in a panic for nothing. It just seems that during the last few years the flag has become less symbolic to people. I think all of last year I only read two stories concerning a flag: one was about a flag being burned in front of a foreign embassy, the other involved an undergarment manufacturer who was under fire from the DAR for daring to make panties out of the Stars and Stripes. Have some feeling for it and for what it stands for. Wear it on you as big as a conventioneer's badge.

Please remember to have compassion. It's funny, a mother rarely forgets the first time her child leaves his small, self-centered world and thinks of someone other than himself. I remember when our youngest was six years old he came home from school one afternoon and demanded, "I need an old toothbrush and a toy truck."

"Don't tell me," I said laughing, "you're making a Thanksgiving centerpiece for the dining room table."

"Nope," he said proudly. "We're winning the war in Vietnam."

"With a toothbrush and a toy truck?"

"Mom," he said patiently, "you don't understand. Let me explain it to you. You see, we're fighting a war in a place called Vietnam and there are people over there who have nothing to brush their teeth with or anything. They don't need money. They just need toothbrushes. Can I have yours?"

"Well, don't you think we ought to send them a new one?"

"That's okay," he reasoned. "Now I have to pick out a truck . . . not one that's all beat up, but something a soldier would want to play with."

My eyes fairly popped out of my head. "A *soldier wants to play with!* You mean the Vietnamese children, don't you?"

Now his eyes widened. "You mean there are children in Vietnam? In the war?"

"Right in the middle of it," I explained. "Now go back and pick out a truck."

I found him sitting in the middle of the floor with a truck on his lap, preoccupied with his own thoughts. "I never thought there would be children in a war," he said.

"Few people do," I answered.

"Well, what do the children do all day while the soldiers fight?"

"Try to act like the war's not there."

"Do they play in another language?"

"No, it's a universal one."

"Will I be a soldier when I grow up?" he asked solemnly.

"I hope not. Why?"

"Because it's a crumby trick sending a neat package to a kid and having him open it and finding a silly toothbrush and someone's secondhand birthday truck. It's a rotten trick on a kid."

If I could only be sure all the lessons are sinking in and are being understood. How can I tell you about disappointments? You'll have them, you know. And they'll be painful, they'll hurt, they'll shatter your ego, lay your confidence in yourself bare, and sometimes cripple your initiative. But people don't die from them. They just emerge stronger. I want you to hear the thunder, so you can appreciate the calm. I want you to fall on your face in the dirt once in a while, so you will know the pride of being able to stand tall. Learn to live with the words "No! You can't! You're out! You blew it! I don't know." And "I made a mistake."

Adults are always telling young people, "These are the best years of your life." Are they? I don't know. Sometimes when adults say this to children I look into their faces. They look like someone on the top seat of the Ferris wheel who has had too much cotton candy and barbecue. They'd like to get off and be sick but everyone keeps telling them what a good time they're having.

Do not imagine for a moment that I don't feel your fears and anxieties. Youth does not have an immunity from disappointments and heartbreaks. No one does.

Fears begin the day you were born: fear of baths, bed wetting, the dark, falling off the sink where you are being bathed, strangers throwing you into the air and not catching you, going hungry, noises, open pins.

Later, it's monsters, parents leaving and not coming back, death, hurts, and bad dreams. School only adds to anxieties. Fear of not having friends, being called upon and not knowing the answers, telling the truth when you're going to be punished, not getting to the bathroom in time, not being liked by a baby sitter, not loved by your parents when a new baby arrives in the house. As you mature, they continue to multiply. Fear of not achieving, not having friends, or not being accepted, not getting the car, worrying about war, marriage, career, making money, being attractive to the opposite sex and making the grades to graduate

Fears are normal. We all have them. Parents have the greatest fears of all. For we are responsible for this life which we have brought to this world. There is so much to teach and the time goes so fast . . .

Was that brisk draft of air a prelude to another fall, or did someone just rush by me in a hurry to turn on Captain Kangaroo?

## Out of the Nest

WE CALL HIM "the baby."
He weighs forty pounds, stands stove-high and can kick a football higher than the house. Somehow, I have the feeling we will call him "the baby" when he is forty, has children of his own, and a hairline like the coast of Florida.

This day, in particular, is special. It's the day when "the baby" goes to school for the first time. I don't know why I feel so irritable. One minute I'm yelling at him, "You slam that door once more, fella, and I'll mail you to a school in Nebraska with no return address."

The next I'm scooping him to my bosom and saying, "Let's run away to Never-Never land, you and I, where little boys never grow up and I could get the job of Mother that Mary Martin gave up."

This should be a happy morning. I remember all those promises I made to myself while sloshing over diaper pails and shaking boiling hot milk over my wrists at 2 A.M. just six short years ago.

"Just wait," I told myself. "When this whole mess is behind me I'll go back to bed in the mornings, have lunch with someone who doesn't eat his meat with a spoon, shed fifteen pounds, do my nails, learn how to play bridge, and blow this firetrap called home that has held me a virtual prisoner."

I nurtured this dream through measles, fractures, tensions, traumas, Dr. Spock, and nursery school. And now that I am so close to realization, I feel guilty. What am I doing? Sending this "baby" off to learn calculus before the cord is healed. How can I possibly think of my own comforts when he is harboring all those insecurities? Indeed, how does the State of Ohio know my son is ready for the first grade? They look at him and what do they see? A birth certificate and a record of immunizations.

I look at him and I see a smile . . . like Halloween. I see two short legs that won't get him a drink of water without a stool under them. I see two pudgy hands that can't work together to hold a slippery bar of soap. I see a shock of red hair that doesn't come up to his father's belt buckle. I see a little boy who never went to the restroom all during nursery school because he didn't want to admit he couldn't spell the difference between B-O-Y-S from G-I-R-L-S on the door.

I should have prepared him more. I piffed away all that time on Santa Claus, Easter Bunny, Tooth Fairy, and Mary Poppins. I should've dealt with the basic realities like tolerance, forgiveness, compassion, and honesty. For from this day forward his world can only widen. An existence that began in a crib, grew to a house, and extends over a two-block bicycle ride will now go even beyond that. I will share him with another woman, other adults, other children, other opinions, other points of view. I am no longer leading. I am standing behind him ready to guide from a new position.

Who is this woman who will spend more daylight hours with him than I? Please, Miss Chalkdust or whatever, give him the patience and gentleness he needs. Please have a soft lap and a warm smile. Please don't be too pretty or too smart, lest I suffer from the comparison.

A note. Maybe I should pin a note on his sweater to make sure she understands you. I could say, "Dear Miss Chalkdust or whatever: I submit to your tender, loving care my son who is a little shy and a lot stubborn. Who can't cope yet with zippers that stick or buttons on sweaters that don't come out even. One who makes his 5's sideways but works seriously and in earnest. I may sue you for alienation of affection, but for the moment, God Bless You!"

Note. There is no time for a note. The bus is here. It's such a big bus. Why would they send their largest bus for someone so small? He is gone. He didn't even look back to wave.

Why was I so rotten to him all summer? I had five summers to be rotten to him and I had to concentrate all my rottenness into this one. It's funny when you think about it. You give six years of your life readying a child for school and all of a sudden you find you're being replaced by a stranger and a thirty-five-cent plate lunch.

The house is so quiet. It's what I've always wanted, isn't it? A quiet house. I wonder who my tears are really for. I hate to admit it, but I think they're for myself.

I think I'm afraid. What kind of a woman am I? Am I going to be the woman who wanders through the house, unfulfilled and bored, who occasionally plucks a pair of sticky socks off the ceiling and sobs into them, "My baby, my baby!"? Will I dust and vacuum the house every day and be tidied up by ten-thirty only to sit and drink coffee and watch for the big, yellow bus to deposit my brood at the curb that I may once again run and fetch like a robot that has been programmed for service?

Will my children go on being my crutch? My excuse for not stirring from this house? Will I dedicate my entire life to their comforts?

Or could I be like that robin in our spouting last spring? What a time to be thinking about robins in the spouting. I watched that little feathered mother-to-be all spring as she and her mate built the nest and she perched on her eggs to wait. Then, day of days, the babies were born and both she and the father scratched and carried to fill the demands of those ever-open mouths in the nest.

Finally the day came when they lined them up and one by one the babies flew. At first they hesitated and hung back until they were nudged out of the nest. Then, they swooped up and down like an early prop plane gone out of control. They exhausted themselves flapping their wings. Some set down in makeshift landings that were unbelievable. Others perched precariously near the danger of cats and barking dogs, but the mother never budged. She just watched and observed, her snappy, black eyes never missing a move. Day by day the birds flew more, flew better, and flew farther until the day came when they were all ready to take their place in the sky with the parents.

I thought of my friends and I remembered the ones who were as wise as the robin. They too nudged their youngsters out of the nest, and then the youngsters sprouted their own wings and led the way. They emerged from a cocoon existence of peanut butter and naps into great beautiful butterflies. The sound of the school bell was like V-E Day to them. They assumed leadership, developed, and grew into active citizens in the community, unearthed talents that surprised everyone (including themselves), and set about restoring order to their lives and rejuvenating their own appearance.

The bus? It's here so soon. Before I've scarcely had time to get my bearings. There he comes hopping off the step and yelling excitedly, "I passed!" It's such a small bus. Why would they send such a small bus for such a group of big, boisterous boys? Or could it be . . . the same bus they sent this morning and my son just grew a lot?

Maybe we've all done some growing today.

**grandma** (grand'ma), *n.* The mother of one's father or mother.

THE ROLE of a grandmother has never been really defined. Some sit in rockers, some sky dive, some have careers. Others clean ovens. Some have white hair. Others wear wigs.

Some see their grandchildren once a day (and it's not enough). Others, once a year (and that's too much).

Once I conducted an interesting survey among a group of eight-year-olds on grandmas. I asked them three questions. One, what is a grandmother? Two, what does she do? And three, what is the difference between a grandmother and a mother?

To the first question, the answers were rather predictable. "She's old (about eighty), helps around the house, is nice and kind, and is Mother's mother or Father's mother, depending on the one who is around the most."

To the second question, the answers again were rather obvious. Most of them noted grandmothers knit, do dishes, clean the bathroom, make good pies; and a goodly number reveled in the fact that Grandma polished their shoes for them.

It was the third question that stimulated the most reaction from them. Here is their composite of the differences between a mother and a grandmother. "Grandma has gray hair, lives alone, takes me places and lets me go into her attic. She can't swim. Grandma doesn't spank you and stops Mother when she does. Mothers scold better and more. Mothers are married. Grandmas aren't.

"Grandma goes to work and my mother doesn't do anything. Mom gives me shots, but Grandma gives me frogs. Grandma lives faraway. A mother you're born from. A grandmother gets married to a grandfather first, a mother to a father last.

"Grandma always says, 'Stay in, it's cold outside,' and my mother says, 'Go out, it's good for you.'"

And here's the clincher. Out of thirty-nine children queried, a total of thirty-three associated the word "love" with Grandma. One summed up the total very well with, "Grandma loves me all the time."

Actually this doesn't surprise me one small bit. On rare

occasions when I have had my mother baby-sit for me, it often takes a snake whip and a chair to restore discipline when I get them home.

"Grandma sure is a neat sitter," they yawn openly at the breakfast table. "We had pizza and cola and caramel popcorn. Then we watched Lola Brooklynbridgida on the late show. After that we played Monopoly till you came home. She said when you were a kid you never went to bed. One night you even heard them play 'The Star-Spangled Banner' before the station went off."

"Did Grandma tell you I was twenty-eight at the time?" I snapped.

"Grandma said twenty-five cents a week isn't very much money for an allowance. She said we could make more by running away and joining the Peace Corps. She said you used to blow that much a week on jawbreakers."

"Well, actually," I said grimacing, "Grandma's memory isn't as good as it used to be. She was quite strict and as I recall my income was more like ten cents a week and I bought all my own school clothes with it."

"Grandma sure is neat all right. She told us you hid our skateboard behind the hats in your closet. She said that was dirty pool. What's dirty pool, Mama?"

"It's Grandma telling her grandchildren where their mother hid the skateboard."

"Mama, did you really give a live chicken to one of your teachers on class day? And did you really play barbershop once and cut off Aunt Thelma's hair for real? Boy, you're neat!" They looked at me in a way I had never seen before.

Naturally I brought Mother to task for her indiscretion. "Grandma," I said, "you have a forked tongue and a rotten memory. You've got my kids believing I'm 'neat.' Now I ask you, what kind of an image is that for a mother?"

"The same image your grandmother gave me," she said.

Then I remembered Grandma. What a character.

In fact, I never see a Japanese war picture depicting Kami-kaze pilots standing erect in their helmets and goggles, their white scarfs flying behind them, toasting their last hour on earth with a glass of sake, that I don't think of riding to town with my grandma on Saturdays.

We would climb into her red and yellow Chevy coupe and jerk in first gear over to the streetcar loop where Grandma would take her place in line between the trolley cars. Due to the rigorous concentration it took to stay on the tracks and the innumerable stops we had to make, conversation was kept to a minimum. A few times a rattled shopper would tap on the window for entrance, to which Grandma would shout angrily, "If I wanted passengers, I'd dingle a bell!"

Once, when I dared to ask why we didn't travel in the same flow of traffic as the other cars, Grandma shot back, "Laws, child, you could get killed out there." Our first stop in town was always a tire center. I could never figure this out. We'd park in the "For Customers Only" lot and Grandma would walk through the cool building. She'd kick a few tires, but she never purchased one. One day she explained, "The day I gain a new tire is the day I lose the best free parking spot a woman ever had."

I don't have Grandma's guts in the traffic or her cunning. But I thought about her the other day as I sat bumper to bumper in the hot downtown traffic. "Hey, lady," yelled a voice from the next car, "wanta get in our pool? Only cost a quarter. We're putting odds on the exact minute your radiator is going to blow. You can have your choice of two minutes or fifteen seconds." Boy, Grandma would have shut his sassy mouth in a hurry.

We had an understanding, Grandma and I. She didn't treat me like a child and I didn't treat her like a mother. We played the game by rules. If I didn't slam her doors and sass, then she didn't spank and lecture me. Grandma treated me like a person already grown up.

She let me bake cookies with dirty hands . . . pound on the piano just because I wanted to . . . pick the tomatoes when they were green . . . use her clothespins to dig in the yard . . . pick her flowers to make a necklace chain. Grandma lived in a "fun" house. The rooms were so big you could skate in them. There were a hundred thousand steps to play upon, a big eave that invited cool summer breezes and where you could remain "lost" for hours. And around it all was a black, iron fence.

I liked Grandma the best, though, when she told me about my mama, because it was a part of Mama I had never seen or been close to. I didn't know that when Mama was a little girl a photographer came one day to take a picture of her and her sister in a pony cart. I couldn't imagine they had to bribe them into good behavior by giving them each a coin. In the picture Mama is crying and biting her coin in half. It was a dime and she wanted the bigger coin—the nickel— given to her sister. Somehow, I thought Mama was born knowing the difference between a nickel and a dime.

Grandma told me Mama was once caught by the principal for writing in the front of her book, "In Case of Fire, Throw This in First." I had never had so much respect for Mama as the day I heard this.

From Grandma I learned that Mama had been a child and had traveled the same route I was traveling now. I thought Mom was "neat." (And what kind of an image is that for a mother?)

If I had it to do all over again, I would never return to Grandma's house after she had left it. No one should. For that grand, spacious house tended to shrink with the years. Those wonderful steps that I played upon for hours were broken down and rather pathetic. There was a sadness to the tangled vines, the peeling paint, and the iron fence that listed under the burden of time. The big eave was an architectural "elephant" and would mercifully crumble under the ax of urban renewal.

Grandmas defy description. They really do. They occupy such a unique place in the life a child. They can shed the yoke of responsibility, relax, and enjoy their grandchildren in a way that was not possible when they were raising their own children. And they can glow in the realization that here is their seed of life that will harvest generations to come.

september 6 — november 2

# don't sweat the small stuff

SEVERAL YEARS AGO I adopted an expression to live by. I don't know where I picked it up, probably from some immortal bard on a restroom wall, but it has worked like therapy for me.

To begin with, I used to be a worrier. I worried about whether or not our patio doors were covered by insurance if they were hit by a polo ball. I worried about that poor devil on television who flunked his nasalgraph test. I worried about Carol Channing going bald. I worried about who would return our library books if my husband and I both "went to that great split-level in the sky" together.

When the children were babies, it was worse. I used to get up at night and hold mirrors under their nostrils to make sure they were still breathing. I worried about their spitting out more food than went into their stomachs. I developed a "thing" about germs. When I changed diapers, I washed *their* hands. When we went bye-bye in the car, it was like moving the circus. I had a fetish about the kids drinking their moo-moo from any cup that didn't have their name on it.

Then, along came the thought-provoking slogan, "Don't Sweat the Small Stuff," and my entire life changed.

The things I couldn't do anything about I ignored. The things I could I numbered and filed them in their respective places. I stopped worrying and started relaxing. I quit scaring the kids half to death at night with the mirror routine. I discovered I could pack baby's entire needs for the weekend in a handbag and they could drink out of animal skins if they had to. As for germs, I conducted an experiment one night and found to my delight that a pacifier recovered from a package of coffee grounds in the garbage can rinsed well under hot water and jammed quickly into baby's mouth, actually enjoyed improved flavor.

I quit worrying about Mao Tse-tung, the population of India, litterbugs filling up Grand Canyon, and our wading pool becoming polluted. I quit worrying about what would happen to me if I wore white shoes after Labor Day. Before, I rather imagined Saks would fly their flag at half mast. Maybe *Life* magazine would send a reporter-photographer team to follow me about and record the shock of the man-on-the-street. Or maybe Brinkley would use me in one of those amusing little sign-off stories that Huntley pretends he doesn't hear.

It used to be that getting the jump on fashions each season was like running through your lifetime after a train and never catching it, or waking up each morning and discovering it is always yesterday.

It's true. If you want to buy a spring suit, the choice selection occurs in February: a bathing suit, March: back-to-school clothes, July: a fur coat, August. Did I tell you about the week I gave in to a mad-Mitty desire to buy a bathing suit in August?

The clerk, swathed in a long-sleeved woolen dress which made her look for the world like Teddy Snowcrop, was aghast. "Surely, you are putting me on," she said. "A bathing suit! In August!"

"That's right," I said firmly, "and I am not leaving this store until you show me one."

She shrugged helplessly. "But surely you are aware of the fact that we haven't had a bathing suit in stock since the first of June. Our—no offense—White Elephant sale was June third and we unload—rather, disposed of all of our suits at that time."

"Are you going to show me a bathing suit," I demanded, "or do I tell everyone that you buy your fitting-room mirrors from an amusement park fun house?"

"Please, madam, keep your voice down. I'll call our manager, Mr. Wheelock, on the phone. (*Lowers voice*) Mr. Wheelock, we've got this crazy woman on the floor who insists upon buying a bathing suit. You heard me right. A bathing suit. I told her that. What does she look like? W-E-I-R-D. She's wearing a pink, sleeveless dress, carrying a white handbag and has (ugh) white shoes. I agree, Mr. Wheelock, but what should I tell her? Very well. (*Louder*) Madam, Mr. Wheelock says since you are obviously a woman of fine taste, we will call you in February when we unpack our first shipment of swim suits. Would you like that?"

Now, normally, I would have jumped up and down pounding my head with my handbag and become quite physical about it. Instead, I simply smiled and said, "Of course I'll return in February when I will personally release a pregnant moth in Mr. Wheelock's fur vault!" I didn't, of course, but with a crazy woman who wears white shoes in August, the salesperson couldn't really be sure, could she?

I quit worrying about removing upholstery labels that said, DO NOT REMOVE LABEL UNDER PENALTY. I quit worrying about

the goonie birds becoming extinct and the communists infil-
trating Cub Pack 947.

I stopped taking seriously all this nonsense about hand-me-
down clothes having a traumatic effect on your children.

I mean, any mother with half a brain knows that children's
apparel comes in three sizes: "A little large, but you'll grow,"
"Just right—so enjoy," and "A little small, so stoop a little."

I think it was last year when we had a rare phenomenon
at our house. All the coats were "Just right—so enjoy." By
my rough calculations, this event will not occur again in my
life span. Now, did the children appreciate the aesthetic
beauty of a sleeve that hit smack between the wristbone and
the hand, and hems that neither hit midthigh nor dragged
behind them like a train? They did not.

"I'll be the only boy in the sixth grade wearing white go-go
boots with tassels." "What are you complaining about? I'll
be the only patrol boy wearing Cinderella mittens." "You're
kidding with this hat. I know I'll grow, but how big can a
head get?"

I just rationalized that I was supplying them with a lifetime
of laughs. It's a curious tradition, this passing down of
clothes within a family. It's the American way, you know.
If you're the oldest in the family, you wear new, but you
learn early, "Don't tear it, stain it, sweat in it, or drag it
across the floor. It's got a long way to go." If you are somewhere in the middle, the attire is a little lighter from constant
washings, a little frayed around the buttonholes, and a little
smoother in the seat. If you're "the baby," heaven help you.
When style was passed out, you weren't born yet. You're in
line for the dingy diapers, the sweaters that were washed by
mistake in hot water, the pajama bottoms that don't match
the tops and the snowsuit that "cost a pretty penny in its
day." (No one seems to remember the day *or* the year.)

Traumas! Hogwash! I have never seen people enjoy such

unrestrained belly laughs as when they're reminiscing about the hand-me-downs of their childhood. The long underwear tucked inside the shoes so people would think you were wearing your Sunday-best white hose to school. Wearing your mother's boots—the skinny pointed heels—and stuffing the heels with paper. The first snow when kids emerged like patchwork refugees who had just climbed out of a ship's hold.

No, I rather think kids will have to look back kindly on their days of hand-me-downs, for they'll just have to remember with warm, wonderful nostalgia, the year the coats were, "Just right—so enjoy."

I don't worry anymore about whether or not my light bulb goes off in the refrigerator when I shut the door . . . or what my dog thinks about when he sees me coming out of the shower . . . or whether or not de Gaulle wants the Statue of Liberty back.

I even adjusted to the family's nonconformer, the child who is a rebel, a loner, a renegade—the one I'm convinced the hospital gave me by mistake.

Every family has at least one. He's the preschooler with the active thyroid who gets locked in restrooms because he stayed behind to find out where the water went after you pushed down the handle. He's the one who wanders away from home and gets his arm stuck in a piece of construction pipe. He's the one who rejects store-bought toys in favor of taking the registers out and making tunnels out of old oatmeal boxes. He gets more lickings than all the other kids in the family put together.

In school he gets checkmarks for daydreaming, for not being neat, for not working to capacity. It doesn't seem to bother him. In his preoccupation for other things he is unaware that he drives his family crazy, arriving late for dinner every night, wearing his socks and underwear to bed to save time in the mornings, cutting the grass only when he needs money.

I used to worry about him a lot. Had he been a genius I'd have been properly awed by it. Had he been a slow learner, I'd have shown due compassion. But to be neither of these things only confused, puzzled, and tried my patience.

I feared for this unpredictable child who was not only out-of-step with the world but whose feet rarely touched the ground. With his insatiable curiosity and hardheaded drive would he beat paths of greatness and discovery, the likes of Winston Churchill or Michelangelo? I wanted to believe that. Or would he find his measure of happiness drifting in and out of this world, living solely off his enthusiasm, imagination, and penchant for living life to its fullest?

Then one day I saw him clearly in the lines of Henry David Thoreau. He wrote, "If a man does not keep pace with his companions, perhaps it is because he hears a different drummer. Let him step to the music which he hears."

I quit beating my drum for conformity and listened to his beat for a while. His pace was a bit more relaxed, the order of his schedule a bit different. For example, watching a caterpillar cross the driveway took precedent over taking a bath. Finishing a pair of homemade stilts preceded dinner. The awe of discovering newborn robins in the spouting beat reading about Columbus discovering America.

I was not aware of how "far out" I had traveled with his drums until the other day. I was in the process of interviewing a woman to spend a few days with the children while my husband and I went out of town.

As we talked, my nonconformer entered the room. Now, had he been a usual child he would have been holding a conventional water tumbler filled with water. As it was he had seen fit to fill an old-fashioned glass with two ice cubes and float a cherry and a slice of orange on top of it. Did I panic? I did not. I took a deep breath, smiled at my horrified visitor, and said, "I don't sweat the small stuff anymore."

To which she gasped, "You mean with a kid drinking in the afternoon the stuff gets bigger?" and bolted for her car. Oh well, she wouldn't have lasted around here two days.

## A Man and His Car

I SHOOK MY HUSBAND AWAKE out of a sound sleep. "I've had that bad dream again," I said.

He yawned, "What bad dream?"

"The one where Lady Bird Johnson comes knocking at our door and asks us to get rid of those junk cars in our driveway."

"Didn't you tell her we're still driving them?" he asks sleepily.

"Yes. Then she looked very concerned and said we should apply for federal funds. She said those rusty heaps in front of our house have set her beautification program back ten years and that no matter what our politics we should care about our country. Then, she just faded away."

"That sounds like a nice idea."

"Wake up. We've got to talk about those cars. They're eyesores. We should replace one and I think it ought to be yours."

"Nonsense," he grumbled, "I just spent an entire Saturday touching up the rust spots with black paint."

"On a mouse-gray body, that's hardly a secret," I snarled. "It looks so garish with all those stickers on the rear window, SEE ROCK CITY, BUY LIBERTY BONDS, NRA. Why don't you scrape some of them off?"

"Because they're holding in the rear window." He yawned again.

"I'll bet it was that rusty tailpipe that caught her attention. We could wire it up off the ground."

"Okay, tomorrow take a little wire off the door handles and wire up the tailpipe. You can reinforce the running boards if you want to."

"Yeah, and I might shine up the chrome around the headlights and get a new set of wicks for them. That'll spruce things up a bit."

"While you're at it, why don't you spend a little time on *your* car? It's not exactly a Grand Prix entry, you know."

"Well, I haul twenty or thirty kids a week around in it. What do you expect?"

"All I know is, the insurance company wouldn't insure it. They just sent us a survival kit. Those springs in the seats are exposed so badly if you weren't buckled in with seat belts, you'd be driving from the roof. There's no door on the glove compartment, the rear window won't go up or down, and you have to turn on the radio with a pair of pliers. And who in heaven's name scratched 'Official 500 Pace Car' on the door? You know the best thing we could do for Lady Bird would be to erect a billboard in front of both of them."

"She suggested that," I said quietly.

"Then it's settled," he sighed, pulling up the covers. "Now will you turn off the light and let me go to sleep?"

I ignored him and reached in the headboard bookcase for something to put me to sleep. I thought I had made a wise choice. It was one of those books that lists surveys and studies conducted by industries and researchers to find out what motivates people to buy as they do. For example, I discovered that people buy home freezers because they are emotionally insecure and need more food than they can eat. Then I bolted upright. There in front of me was a chapter on what motivates men to buy the cars they do. It said researchers found when dealers put a convertible in their show windows men flocked to look at it. But they invariably bought a sedan. Why?

Psychologists who studied the problem came up with the fact that convertibles were symbolic mistresses. They were flashy. They brought out the eyeballs. They attracted attention. Men looked at them longingly, dreamed a little, lusted a lot. But, in the end, man's common sense, his practical side, his down-to-earth rationalization, told him it was not for him and he bought the sedan. The sedan represented the symbolic wife, the plain, safe girl who would be a substantial mother to his children.

As one "practical sedan" to another, I don't mind telling you this bothered me. Especially, when I began thinking back to the women—er, cars my husband had picked out in the past.

Our first car—which he obviously identified with me—was a secondhand, plain, drab-looking, black you-know-what with a broken window—on my side—and a glove compartment door that sprung out in your lap every time the motor turned over, plus a small printed note on the fender that read, "Please, Don't Kick the Tires."

It was good, clean transportation despite the fact it was an obvious alcoholic and couldn't pass a service station without stopping for a slug of gas with an oil chaser. It was hot in the summer and cold in the winter and asthmatic all year round.

Our first new car, in 1951, indicated I still had not changed. It was as proper as a hearse—no chrome, no extras, and no nonsense. I don't think any self-respecting tiger would have been caught dead climbing into its tank!

We bought another new car in 1955. Only the color and the mortgage balance changed.

I slipped out of bed and peered through the window. Suppose men really picked cars like they picked wives. Was this a car to have an affair with? Was this the jaunty sports cap, silk scarf flying crazily in the wind type of car? Was this a mistress, or a mother in sturdy, sensible sneakers?

In the driveway was our small cheapie foreign car that boasted it never changed body styles year after year. The pitiful bit of chrome on the bumper was rusted from the salt on the streets in winter, and a paper towel was stuffed around the windshield because the thermostat was broken and the heat was intense. The color was mouse gray.

I shook my husband awake. "Let's go out and buy a new

car tomorrow. Something impractical. Something wild. It's important to me."

"Are you crazy?" he groaned sleepily. "Why, I've got too much money tied up in that old heap to let her go. She's good till the fuel pump goes. Besides, she's comfortable."

"That's a rotten thing to say to anyone," I sobbed and went to sleep.

I suppose I'd still have that mouse-gray image in the driveway today if it hadn't been for the garbage truck that plowed into me. As I told my husband when I returned his car minus two fenders, two headlights, and a trunk lid, "That tears it. This car is Hitler's Revenge and it must be replaced. I can't drive a car I can't communicate with."

"If I've told you once I've told you a hundred times," he said, "the car doesn't understand a word of English. It responds only to German commands."

"I tried that," I said. "I saw this garbage truck begin to back up and I said, 'Das ist ein garbage truck, lunkhead, let's get out of here.'"

"What happened?"

"Nothing happened. It just sat there like a stick until the truck hit us. I tried blasting the horn and it peep-peeped like it was apologizing. Incidentally, the horn broke off in my hand. It's in the glove compartment."

"Then what happened?"

"I ran out of German, that's what happened. The truck still didn't know I was back there and started at me again. I tried every German word I knew: glockenspiel, pumpernickel, Marlene Dietrich. I even sang two choruses of 'O Tannenbaum.' That's when the second impact hit. That did it. I whacked it on the instrument panel and said, 'Du bist ein cheapie, that's what you are. One more hit and we're going to look like a crock of sauerkraut.' Just about that time the driver got out of his truck and said, very surprised, 'I thought I hit a bump in the road.' How's that for humiliation!"

"Don't worry. I think we can fix her up," said my husband.

"Fix her!" I shouted. "You wouldn't dare. Not after what she's put me through. Just think of the merits of a big car. No more shinnying into the seat like a snake into a sleeping bag. No more mud goggles on rainy days. No more massaging your cold feet and shifting gears at the same time.

"Think what it would be to pass cars on a hill. And to ride with your legs outstretched, instead of in a foetal position. Just imagine. We could talk to a car in English. No more having to say, 'By the way, what is it you say when you want the car to go in reverse?' "

"Mutter, bitte," he said.

"Which means?" I sighed wearily.

"Mother, may I?"

"It figures. Tomorrow, we buy a new car."

I never realized it before, but there's an umbilical cord connecting a man to his car. It is perhaps the most possessive, protective, paternal relationship you'll ever encounter. Bound together by a thirty-month loan contract, their hearts beat as one until the car goes back on the lot and is exchanged for a new model to which he transfers his love and affection.

The book was right, of course. He eased onto the seat of the sports car in the show window, his arm slipping ever so slyly over the back of the seat. He caressed the steering wheel and the visor with a gentleness I had never seen before. (I thought I saw him pinch the directional lights.) Then he took a deep breath of resignation, walked over to the conventional model and sighed, "We've got the children to consider."

I was pleased to note my image had improved considerably. It had a radio that didn't take ten minutes to heat up. It had power steering and power brakes. And the color was a deep purple. (Which my husband noted matched the veins in my nose.)

Then I went too far. One night I asked to borrow his car.

You'd have thought I wanted to borrow his dental plates to eat caramels.

"Isn't there any other way you can get to card club?" he asked.

"Yes," I replied. "I could tape peanuts to my arms and maybe attract enough pigeons to fly me there, but I'd rather drive the car."

Reluctantly he walked me to the door. "You have your license? Your key ring? Extra money? Witnesses?"

I grinned. "I don't want to marry it, just drive it to card club."

"You have to understand about this model," he explained patiently. "She starts cold. Now some cars need pumping. Don't pump her. *She hates to be pumped!* Get that? All you do is ease the choke out about a quarter of an inch. Then push the accelerator all the way to the floor and just ease up on it a bit. Okay? Not too fast. At the same time, turn the key and gently now, slide the choke back in."

Given the least kind of encouragement—like keeping awake—he also delves into "baby's sluggish crankcase, her puny pistons, her fouled plugs, and her dulling points."

As I slid into the seat, he let fly his last arrow. "Don't gun it and you'll make it."

I turned off the motor. "Don't gun what and I'll make it where?"

"Don't gun the motor and you'll make it to the gas station. The tank says empty, but I know there's enough to coast you in, especially if you make the light on the corner and roll the last fifty feet. Oh, and if it keeps dying on you there are emergency flares in the trunk."

A man and his car—he loves and cherishes it from the first day forward, for richer for poorer, for better or for worse, in sickness and in health, and if Detroit ever turns out a model that sews on buttons and laughs at his jokes, ladies, we're in trouble!

*The Watercress and Girdle Group*

THE NAME OF THE GAME is clubwork.

It's played from September through May by thousands of women who spend billions of volunteer hours every year deciding whether to put kidney beans or whole tomatoes in the Circle Meeting chili, or whether to spray-paint the pipe cleaners for the PTA Easter luncheon pink or purple.

Some women readily recognize the overorganization, the tedious details, the long drawn-out devotion to three-hour meetings. But they rationalize that the real cause is worth it. Other women become impatient with sloppy leadership, dull monologues, and that "why-do-today-what-you-can-talk-about-for-three-more-hours-next-Wednesday" syndrome.

Clubwork is therapy for a lot of women. It gets them into their girdles and out among people. It gives them something else to think about besides how to disguise leftovers and how to get crayon stains out of a shirt pocket that has gone through the dryer. Let's face it. The government couldn't afford to buy the services that come out of women's groups if it cashed in the President and all his holdings.

I like clubwomen. Some of my best friends are clubwomen. I even took one to lunch last week. Some I like better than others. Program chairmen, for example. I have always had a soft spot in my head for them. Those of us in the business of giving speeches have concurred unanimously that program chairmen rate a special place in heaven, where the sun always shines, birthdays cease to show after the age of thirty-three, and John Mason Brown sits at their right hand.

Of all the offices on the duty roster, possibly none is more underrated than the woman who must entertain the membership during an entire club year. For audience variety, she has the elder pillars of the club who attend once a year on Founder's Day and who are too proud to wear their hearing devices. ("The speaker was a sweet little thing, but she mouthed her words.") She has the strait-laced group who objected vigorously when a speaker reviewed *The Scarlet Letter.* ("That hussy! She treated it like a piece of costume jewelry!") She has the new bloods who are pressuring her into arranging a "wine tasting" program. ("Preferably *before* the business meeting, honey.")

While the rest of the membership and the officers spend a quiet summer, the program chairman never sleeps. Oh, the president spends a few anxious evenings rolling and tossing and making plans to have her appendix taken out early in September so she can relinquish the gavel to the vice president.

There's the vice president looking suspiciously at the president whom she suspects is not above having her appendix out to get out of the job of president.

There's the recording secretary in a state of numbness, as she has only attended one meeting as a guest before they elected her to the office. There's the corresponding secretary, who is three years behind in a letter to her mother, wondering how all this is going to work out. And there's the bewildered treasurer, who is setting her husband up as a pigeon for the club's books in the fall.

Not the program chairman. She is haggling with a department store to stage a free fashion show for women with large thighs. She is buzzing the "hot line" to her president every two days with cries of "I can't get Arlene Francis for twenty dollars . . . shall I try for Betsy Palmer?" She is fighting the battle of personages on vacations, unlisted phone numbers, and speakers who won't commit themselves beyond next weekend.

And she is probably anticipating a scene typical of the one I was involved in recently when the program chairman said brightly, "Marcia, you haven't been to one of our meetings in a long time. I'm sure it's due to the popularity of our speaker, Mrs. Bombeck." To which Marcia looked annoyed and snarled, "*Bombeck!* Good Lord, I thought someone said *Steinbeck* was coming!"

Another clubwoman for whom I have great empathy is the perennial Chairman of the Bazaar. Here is a small lump of helplessness who couldn't say no. Molded by flattery and strengthened by self-confidence, she is put adrift in a sea of home-baked bread and knitted toilet tissue covers.

I know of what I speak. Several years ago I was a bazaar chairman. The doctor tells me in time I may be able to hear a telephone ring without becoming incoherent. I wish I could be sure.

One of the first things a bazaar chairman must adjust to is what happened to all the well-wishers who, only a week ago, hoisted you to their shoulders, marched you around the gym, and sang, "For She's a Jolly Good Pigeon." Their generous offers of "I'll donate thirty quarts of my famous calf's-foot jelly" and "Leave the raffle tickets to me" now sounds like, "Are you kidding? This has been a nothing year for calves' feet" and "Honey, I couldn't sell an inner tube to a drowning man."

In desperation, a bazaar chairman will eventually take on the guise of a Mafia moll, stopping at nothing to "firm up" her committees. I've heard ruthless threats behind the coffee urn that would make your hair stand on end. "All right, Eloise, you take that White Elephant chairmanship or the entire world will know you've got a thing going with your son's orthodontist. I'm not bluffing either. And you just never mind why Jeannie Crabitz took the fish pond. That's between the two of us."

The families of bazaar chairman are also affected by this new-found diversion. Plaintive pleas of "Daddy, when is Mommy coming home for a visit?" are often answered with a sour, "She has to come home on Wednesday—it's the night she defrosts our dinners for the week."

As the bazaar draws near, the fever increases while the house takes on all the physical properties of urban renewal. "I can't sleep," complains her husband, staggering into the living room. "My bed is full of plastic cigarette holders and Hawaiian leis."

"Well, stack them in the closet," she says tiredly.

"What!" he snaps, "and disturb the goldfish that are stacked on top of the stuffed poodles and the Japanese fans?"

The last two days before the bazaar are the wildest. With a lot of luck, the raffle prizes will have been delivered to another state . . . the kitchen committee resigns en masse, resolving only to speak to one another in church on Sundays . . . and there's a strong possibility Santa Claus may not "dry out" in time to make the scene for the kiddies.

Each phone call brings a new trauma: "She insists on donating a size forty-eight angora pullover and I refuse to have it in my booth" . . . "My pickles were solicited for the Country Store booth and if the kitchen wants some, let them do their own telephoning" . . . "I will not have my pitch and throw game in the schoolroom. Last year we broke the blackboard and I had a migraine for a week."

When the last bit of popcorn is swept from the gym and the blackboard repaired and the angora pullover en route to the "missions," some poor, unsuspecting newcomer is bound to remark, "It was a lovely bazaar."

She doesn't know it yet, but that lump of innocence is next year's bazaar chairman.

One of the most overzealous groups of clubwomen I know are the Garden Clubbers. They cannot comprehend that some of us are born into this world to plant glad bulbs upside down. Some of us are resigned to a life without manure and mulch. And that when some of us have a green thumb, it's a skin condition.

Don't misunderstand me. I have nothing but respect for Garden Club women. Especially after the episode my mother and I endured with the dried weeds project. We just couldn't imagine there being much skill to throwing clumps of fall foliage into a pot!

"Why, they must think we're a couple of rubes who just blew into town with the egg money," Mother said. "Imagine! Paying $7.95 for a pot of dried milk pods, a few pine cones, and a couple of sticks with berries on them. We could fill a bathtub with this stuff for forty-nine cents of spray paint."

Maybe it was the vision of a floral-filled bathtub that prompted us to do it. Looking back, we like to think one of the kids left the cap off the glue and we inhaled enough to make us fly. At any rate, the next weekend found Mother and me hacking our way through the woods like Jon Hall and Sabu.

Cattails, we discovered, flourished only in swamps where the bog was knee-high. The prettiest leafy specimens were always at the top of the trees. The most unique pods were always situated in the middle of a livestock relief station.

And the most graceful Queen Anne's lace was always over the next hill.

I have no intention of humiliating my mother by relating that grim scene of her up to her knees in jungle rot, clutching a bundle of poison sumac to her chest and shouting hysterically at a snake slithering over her gym shoes. (Only to report that she shouted to the heavens, "Oh please! I'm Evangelical and I tithe!")

I think our little excursion can best be told by a tabulation we compiled of the expenses incurred in the pursuit of dried stock for floral arrangements.

### Expenses

| | | |
|---|---|---:|
| 1 can gold spray paint | $ | .69 |
| 1 can silver spray paint | | .69 |
| 1 gallon paint thinner | | 1.25 |
| (Used to remove spray paint from patio floor) | | |
| 1 ironing board cover | | 2.00 |
| (Note to amateurs: put the leaves *between* wax paper before pressing) | | |
| 1 pair gym shoes | | 4.00 |
| 1 sweater (Abandoned at snake pit) | | 5.95 |
| 1 car wash and vacuuming | | 2.00 |
| 1 doctor (for sumac) | | 5.00 |
| 1 prescription (for sumac) | | 3.57 |
| 1 overdue book on *Dried Flowers for Fun and Profit* | | .62 |
| Personal Aggravation | | 500.00 |
| | TOTAL | $525.77 |

It's not that I don't appreciate Garden Clubbers' talents, it's just that they are always trying to convert you to Gardenism. One enthusiast, in particular, bugs me all the time. She's always pinching my brown leaves off my indoor plants and feeling the soil around my pots to see if they've been watered lately. She makes me nervous.

"What did you do with that slip of creeping phlox I gave you?" she asked the other day.

"It crept into the soil and died," I said.

"If I've told you once," she sighed, "I've told you a thousand times plants are like little people. You simply have to give them a little water, a little love, and a lot of understanding. Now, this is lovely and green. What do you call this?"

"I call that a rotten onion that has been around for nine weeks and is pithy and mushy on the inside, but has bright green sprouts on the outside."

"You're terrible. You really are," she chided. "You should belong to a Garden Club. Then you could exchange ideas and learn from the other members."

"I belong to the 'Wilt and Kill,'" I offered.

"The 'Wilt and Kill'?" she asked her eyes widening. "I don't think I know it."

"We're a group of Garden Club rejects . . . meet the first rainy Monday of the month . . . answer roll call with our current houseplant failure."

"You're putting me on."

"No, I'm not. It's not too easy to qualify. One girl used a nine-foot sunflower plant as a border. She got in. Another padded her beds with plastic flowers from the dime store . . . in the winter. She qualified. I call every flower Semper Fidelis. It's the only Latin I know. I'm an officer."

"Incredible. I've never heard of it."

"We have a wonderful time. At the last meeting Maybelle Mahonia set up the projector and showed home movies of her garden. It was as barren as a missile site. We got a prize for every weed we could identify. Would you like to hear our slogan?"

"I don't think so," she said, feigning dizziness.

"It's 'From Futility to Fertility We Stand Together.'"

"Oh dear. I must be going. Incidentally, how is your sweet potato vine?"

I smiled. "It was delicious."

Ah clubwork . . . the escape hatch from the land of peanut butter and the babblings of children. If it bothers you that so much leadership ability is dormant somewhere, not because of apathy, but because these women don't want to pay the price of boredom to do the job, you could lure them back into the meeting halls easier than you think.

1. Pick a leader because she's a leader, not because she owns the punchbowl and the folding chairs.

2. Frisk all grandmothers and new mothers at the door for snapshots of children. (Check knitting bags, bras, garters, and umbrellas.)

3. Forget the democracy bit. Run the meeting like a railroad or you'll never get home in time to thaw the hamburger.

4. When ankles swell and handbag handles cause red marks to streak up the arm, adjourn the meeting.

5. Plan brief, meaningful meetings and get something done. I wouldn't be surprised if capable women beat a path to your mousetrap!


*While You're Down in the Dumps . . .*

WHEN MY HUSBAND AND I appear at an antique show there is a scurrying of feet while one dealer whispers to another, "Stick a geranium in that slop jar, Irving, here comes a couple of live ones."

This is partly our fault. We stand there openmouthed and bug-eyed, clutching green cash like we just hit town long enough to buy the fertilizer. On at least one occasion I have rushed over to a large hulk of metal and shrieked, "Is this a 1900 milk separator?" "No," someone replies patiently, "that's a 1962 drinking fountain."

We have maintained a rule of thumb. If you can sleep on it, plant flowers in it, frame it, play it, eat it, stuff it with magazines, records or blankets, ring it or open a conversation with it, we'll buy it.

Then we have an open category of things we're going to do something with some day. This takes in a cast-iron angel with a broken foot, a hand-driven child's washing machine, a Civil War grave marker, and a collection of "Go with Willkie" campaign buttons.

In Maine one summer we picked up a faded, musty chessboard for two dollars. It hung in our garage like a conscience for two years before my husband painted it bright red, mounted it on a turntable, and called it a "lazy susan for gracious eating." "This is going to revolutionize our eating habits," he said. "No more bloated stomachs from waiting for the kids to pass the food. No more flesh wounds from knife cuts and fork pricks. No more unnecessary conversation at the dinner table." He put the lazy susan on the table, placed our food on it, and whirled it. It looked like a fattening roulette wheel. "The success of this device," he went on, "can be summed up in two words: *keep alert.* When the turntable stops at your plate, take whatever is in front of you. You will have eight seconds to spear or spoon the food to your plate. We cannot make exceptions. I'll blow a whistle and the turntable will move again. This way in thirty-two to forty seconds we will all have our plates loaded with hot food and ready to eat. Get it?"

We got it. The first night the food was not placed in its proper order and we had whipped potatoes *over* gravy and strawberries *under* shortcake. The "whistler" promised us this would be remedied at the next meal. Then, we had the problem of overhang. That is, a coffee pot handle, a large plate or an onion ring strategically placed could conceivably clip the glasses or cups and throw the entire timetable off schedule by as much as four or five seconds.

It was time for another lecture. "All right, group, I've noticed this time your performance was a little ragged. You spoon drippers and bowl clangers all know who you are. No need to mention names. Now, let's put our shoulders to the wheel and shape up!"

Within two weeks, I noticed some drastic changes. I was five pounds lighter and—due to the centrifugal force whirling around before my eyes at mealtime—I was hopelessly hooked on Dramamine.

I did what any mother would do—I stole his lousy whistle!

Other antiques we bought were equally popular. A dear little 1809 collapsible rocker attacked the baby when he tried to sit in it and he's avoided it like a penicillin shot ever since.

The pump organ that was to bring togetherness to our brood also brought disharmony to the family circle. But how do you tell this to a man who has just displaced a disc and two old friends lugging it into the hallway?

Add to that a bill for $140 to replace the reeds and keep its bellows from becoming asthmatic and you've got a pretty good argument for sentiment.

"Where are we going to put it?" I asked.

"Think of it," he said, "a bowl of popcorn, a basket of juicy apples, and all of us locked arm in arm singing, 'Kentucky Babe.' Doesn't that just make your flesh crawl?"

"I'll say. Where are we going to put it?"

"I still remember a chorus or two of 'There's a Fairy in the Bottom of My Teacup.' If you promise not to drown me out, I might let you read poetry in the background on Sundays."

"We can't leave it here in the hallway. It's on my foot."

"And home weddings," he rambled. "Think of it, with a vase of . . . what are those flowers at weddings?"

"Orange blossoms, and get this thing off my foot!"

The organ, with all its scrolls, ornate panels, carpeted pedals, and elevated candle holders, was christened "The Heap" and was placed in the living room. Its stay here was a short one. Guests complained the organ, the candles, and the flowers were a little much and gave them a creepy feeling. (The fact that the only song my husband knew with two hands was "The Old Rugged Cross" didn't help things either.) "The Heap" was reassigned to our bedroom. Here, it became a living tabernacle for unpaid bills, unanswered letters, ties that needed cleaning, old road maps, car keys, and odd bits of change. Occasionally we'd crack our shinbones on it, which prompted us to move it to the family room. It lasted there two days. A cry of dissension went up among the young television viewers who were forced to read lips over the roar of the foot pedals and the gasps of the bellows. The next stop was the porch solarium where "The Heap" developed a decided wheeze in her bellows from the moisture. She came to rest in the kitchen.

Our problem is twofold. Serving five people seated around a pump organ and living in constant fear of a spontaneous chorus of "There's a Fairy in the Bottom of My Teacup."

Very frankly, it is next to impossible to instill respect in small children for antique furniture. Cries of "Get your feet off that distressed table!" or "Don't sit on that woodbox, it could go any minute," leaves them confused and mumbling, "She's got to be kidding."

At roadside shops on Sundays, they make snide remarks about "all this junk" and end up buying a bag of hoarhound candy which they immediately discover they hate and spit out in my hand.

Those of us who don't have Early Grandmothers with attics, or an "in" with a dealer who reads the obituaries daily, must come by antiques the hard way, via the dump.

My affinity for dumps dates back further than my affinity for antiques. As a child, I lived three blocks from a Discount Dump. It was outside the high-rent district and it was every man for himself. I could canvass that dump in fifteen minutes in my bare feet, taking in every seatless wicker chair, canning jar carton, and soiled lampshade.

When we were married, the dump seemed a logical place to accessorize our home. Of course, I'm not attracted to all dumps. Certainly not the status dumps. They have their own curator. They're no fun at all. The curator lives in a small shack and spends his days cleaning and stacking old bricks, boxing sundry tools for easy inspecting, putting cast-offs in some kind of order and reading *House Beautiful*.

He usually greets you at the car with a brisk "May I help you?" When you say, "No, I'm just browsing," he follows along closely at your elbow, pointing out how that rusty auto crankcase would make an adorable planter for a solarium or how that little bamboo birdcage was owned by one bird in East Brunswick who slept a lot.

Other dumps are literally for the birds. Last summer in New England, for example, our garbage was becoming a conversation piece. Also, a health hazard. It was packaged and laid wall to wall throughout the kitchen, dining room, and half of the living room. When I asked a neighbor about it, she said, "You mean you haven't seen the dump? You have to go there yourself to believe it. Also to get rid of your garbage."

"*To the dump!*" I shouted wild with excitement.

"What are we going to buy?" asked one of the kids.

I ignored him. Why hadn't I thought of going to a dump in New England. It was probably lousy with Americana— Revolutionary troops marching over the wasteland dropping sabers by the dozens, pewter cups, personal letters to General Washington, signet rings—I could hardly contain myself.

We drove around a long, dusty road until finally we saw more seagulls than we had seen in the travel folders. So this was where they hung out! No sabers, no pewter cups, no antique goodies at all, just garbage. We backed up the car and started to unload. "What are we going to buy?" a small voice persisted. "I saw a rat," said another. "Of all the parents in the world, we had to get the funny ones," snarled the other one.

No matter. I will go on sewing my heirloom quilts on hot summer days and collecting old hatpins. They're lethal-looking, but they're marvelous for releasing the lock on the bathroom door when someone gets locked in. How the kids will divide all those Willkie buttons when they grow up is their problem.

## "Mums the Word for Dad"

THE NEWS that the television networks are telecasting a record number of football games again this season is being met with some violent reactions from housewives across the country.

A few women in the Peaceful Acres development in Connecticut smashed television screens with broom handles. A group of California housewives focused national attention on the problem with their "Psychiatric Drive-Ins" open twenty-four hours a day during the football season. The most notable effort was a group from Virginia who heaved a football through Lady Bird Johnson's window with a terse message, "Would you want your daughter to spend a weekend with one?"

I talked briefly with a group of Ohio women. "It isn't the several hundred games we object to," said the spokesman. "This is only the beginning. Add to that the state and the local games and you've got ten or twelve football games being aired each day of the weekend. Roughly this amounts to one husband propped up in a chair like a dead sponge surrounded by bottle caps."

Heaven knows, men aren't the more talkative of the species. In fact, I have just come by some statistics that claim men average no more than six words a day in their own homes. Furthermore, their only hope of increasing this total is through conscientious massage of the throat muscles.

Even out of football season, men approach their homes in the evening with all the detachment of a census taker. He garages the car, feels the stove to see if there's anything going for him, changes his clothes, eats, and retires to the living room where he reads the newspaper and engages in his nightly practice of finer isometrics—turning the television dial. He remains in a state of inertia until the sound of his deep, labored breathing puts the cork on another confetti-filled evening.

The frustration of wives who want to talk with someone who isn't teething is pitiful. While some accept the silent evenings as a way of life, others try desperately to change it. When one woman attempted to apologize at the dinner table for the children—who were performing a native tribal dance through the mashed potatoes—her husband looked up sharply from his plate, glanced at the children, and shrieked, "You mean they're all ours?" (five words)

One of the most disappointing attempts at starting a conversation is, "What kind of a day did you have, dear?" One husband reportedly answered by kicking the dog, another went pale and couldn't form words, another bit his necktie in half. Some just stared blankly as if they hadn't heard the question. Only one man formed a verbal reply. It was "Shut up, Clara."

Other women work constantly to raise the odds.

WIFE: Know what we're having for dinner? Braised cue tips with sumac topping, onion balls in sour cream, and a bird of paradise nesting in a floating sea of chicken fat.

HUSBAND: I had it for lunch. (5 words)

WIFE: There's another man, Lester. We're civilized people. Let's talk about it.

HUSBAND: Wait till the commercial. (4 words)

WIFE: I broke my leg last week, Wesley. I was waiting for you to notice. See how well I'm doing on crutches?

HUSBAND: Get me a cold one while you're up. (8 words, but he was stoned)

"With the football season it's worse," said a small blonde. "My husband sits down at eight o'clock on a Friday night and never takes his eyes off the screen. I say to him, 'You wanta eat now, Ed?' and he just sits there. I say to him, 'You comin' to bed now, Ed?' and he just sits there. I said to him the other night, 'The woman is here to buy the kids, Ed,' and he didn't move a muscle. I finally took his pulse. It was weird."

"I know what you mean, honey," said a small brunette. "My Fred says to me, 'We need a color TV set. The networks have eighty-three games in color this year.' I said to him, 'If you like to see all that red plasma and those blue bruises, it's okay with me. Frankly, I like to see a man with his front teeth.' He gets real sore. Plugs the high school game into his ear, puts one eyeball on the state game and the other on the National Football League and yells, 'Keep those kids quiet.' We don't have kids."

"If you're thinking of joining them, forget it!" said another voice. "I used to watch football games at college and loved 'em. But on TV. First, I sat through shots of last week's game, then a preview of this week's line-up. When the game finally started, we saw it in live action, then slow motion, then stop action and instant replay. After that we switched to another camera to see if he got a better 'side' of the ball carrier. At the half we had highlights of the first half, followed by interviews of people who chewed over the way they played the first half and predicted what they were going to do the second half. Finally, the game over, we had a recap of the game by the announcer topped off by fifteen minutes of Scoreboard."

"Then what's the answer?" someone asked.

"We fight back with *Peyton Place*," said a newly-wed snapping her fingers with inspiration.

"Here's the deal. We get the network to bring on *Peyton Place* thirty minutes early and watch exciting shots from last week's show, followed by previews of this week's action. Then we have Betty Furness interview Old Man Peyton and his grandson just for a little flavor.

"When the action starts, the camera will replay in slow motion all the scenes, then stop-action all the dirty parts and have an instant replay of all the violent parts. After that, we'd switch to another camera for another view of Betty Cord in her negligee. At the 'break' they'd show action from the first half followed by an interview by Ann Landers, who would chew over the first half and offer advice on how it should be played the second half.

"When the show is over, Dr. Joyce Brothers would tally up

the marriages for each, the divorces, the surgery, and their standing in the league."

"It's just got to work," said a quiet brunette. "I'm so desperate, I'm beginning to talk to my kids."

NOVEMBER 3 — JANUARY 1

# EAT YOUR HEART OUT, HELOISE!

IT HAPPENS every November. I don't know why. I suffer an attack of domesticity. I want to bustle about in a starched apron, bake bread, iron sheets, and make my own soap. I want to beat mattresses, mend cleaning rags, wax the driveway, and can green beans. I want to dust the coffee table and arrange it with a vase of flowers and a copy of Norman Vincent Peale. In short, I am nauseating.

I call it my "Eat Your Heart Out, Heloise" syndrome. It's like a strange power that overcomes me and lasts no longer than two days. During that span I can hardly remember what I have done or why I have done it. All I know is when I return to my old self, I usually have a pot of ox tail soup brewing and am sitting in my rocker reading, "How to Remove Kite String Marks from the Spouting," and wondering what I am doing here.

Last November's seizure was a doozie. When I returned to

my slovenly ways I discovered I had rearranged the furniture, giving it all the personality of a bus station restroom. Ignoring the advice of experts, I washed the draperies, causing the lining to sag like a toddler's underwear.

I discovered I had gone to town and returned home with twenty yards of red corduroy for bedspreads. Heaven knows what I would have purchased if I owned a sewing machine. They tell me I alerted the entire household, lined them up on the front lawn and insisted we begin fertilizing early for spring, putting in the screens and beating the rugs. I have never viewed such sickening efficiency in my life. The woodwork glistened. The windows sparkled. I had even taken the paper clips out of the tea canister and replaced them with tea.

I have talked with other women about this strange phenomenon and they assure me it is normal. This return to order is sparkled by cool weather, an anticipation of the holidays and a large guilt complex that I shouldn't be enjoying myself so much with the children in school.

I have found that a cold shower shocks me back to my slovenly ways. I know I am slovenly because I gave myself one of those magazine quizzes once to find out if I was "children-geared," "husband-geared," or "house-geared."

The "child-geared" mother often referred to her husband as what's-his-name and took a tape recorder to the labor room to record her suffering so she could play it at her children's weddings. I wasn't that. A "husband-geared" woman fed her husband steak and the kids hamburger. I wasn't that. A "home-geared" woman fixed up the basement for the family to live in and cried whenever someone splashed water on her kitchen tiles. I wasn't that.

According to my score, I wasn't crazy about any one of the three. In fact, in homemaking I only scored five out of a possible hundred points. (I changed the paper in my birdcage with some kind of regularity.)

What makes this confession so incongruous is that fifteen years ago, I did a three-times-a-week newspaper column on housecleaning. As I remember it, one day I slipped out of my office for just a moment to go to the coffee machine. When I returned I had been elected by the department as its next homemaking editor. (Incidentally, newspapering is the only profession in the world so full of finks you have to have your own food taster.) In short, I had been had.

I called it "Operation Dustrag" and set about advising the housewives of the city how to develop a positive attitude toward cleaning so they wouldn't become cranky and irritable with their family. I assured them if they stuck with me and my thrice-weekly household cleaning schedule, we could restore order to their houses and literally tap-dance our way to House Beautiful. (I think I promised them prosperity, an end to World War II, and a cure for the common dustball, but no one got legal about it.)

What really amazed me was how seriously women took their housekeeping chores. To some, it was a way of life. Their plaintive pleas rolled in daily: "How do I clean my alabaster?" (Madam, I didn't know birds got dirty.) "How can I prevent scrub water from running down my arms to my elbows?" (Hang by your feet when you wash the walls.) "Is there a formula for removing chocolate from overstuffed furniture?" (No, but there's one for beating the stuffings out of the little boy who ate the chocolate on the overstuffed furniture.)

After several irate calls from women who had tried my little balls of paraffin in their rinse water to make the chintz look chintzier—one woman said if her curtains had wicks they'd burn right through Advent—I promised my editor I would try these things at home first. My home began to take on all the excitement of a missile at count-down.

I concocted a mixture of wall cleaner that nearly blew our

house off the foundation. I tried samples from manufacturers that took the coin dots right out of the kitchen tile. I had so many sample-type gloves, I wore them for everything from cleaning out the dryer lint trap to shaking hands with my husband.

My succinct advice went on day after day.

To make a towel for the children's bath, simply take two towels and monogram each with an F. One F will represent face, the other, feet. Then, simply toss both towels into a corner on the floor. This sounds primitive, but after three days they won't even want to know which F they're using, and at least the towels will always be where they belong, on the floor.

For mildew or musty odor on the shower curtain, simply take a sharp pair of scissors and whack it off. Actually, the more mildew, the more interesting the shower curtains become.

To clean piano keys, try having your children wear chamois gloves moistened with clear water. I daresay their practice sessions won't sound any different and you'll have a clean keyboard.

To remove gum stains, pick off as much gum as possible, then soften by applying egg whites. An egg white stain is better to live with than chewing gum.

A sterilizer that has boiled dry will make an interesting conversation piece on the ceiling over your stove. Small rolls of dust under the bed will entertain small children for hours. (Likewise in-laws, malicious neighbors, and the Board of Health.)

The end of "Operation Dustrag" came as a shock to no one. It was entered in statewide competition under the category "columns." As I sat at the banquet table listening to the names of winners, I was numb. If I won something it was another year of "Help Stamp Out Dirt." If I didn't, I couldn't trust myself to go to the watercooler without drawing some other dreary chore.

Needless to say, the column went unnoticed. By Wednesday of the following week, I had been assigned to Society where "the bride walks to the altar on the arm of her father" and other funny things happen.

Several years later when I retired to actually keep house, I discovered the real keyword to housecleaning was incentive. I was a fool not to have realized it before. There had to be a reason for cleaning house. At our place, the motivation seems to center about one word: *party.*

When we can no longer "dig out," we simply announce to twenty or thirty of our most intimate friends, we are going to entertain. Then we swing into action. My husband knocks out a wall or two, gives the baseboards that long-promised second coat, changes the furnace filter, replaces light bulbs where there has been no light for five years, squirts glazing compound into holes and wall cracks, and hot-mops the driveway.

The children are in charge of scouting the sandbox and toy chests for good silverware, hauling away the debris under their beds, disposing of a garbage full of bottles and returning the library books.

I have my own busy work. I discard all the jelly glasses and replace them with "matched" crystal, exchange all the dead houseplants for new ones from the nursery, and of course plan the menu and the guest list.

Our parties have always been memorable. We always have the wet picture frames that someone invariably leans against and has to be cut out of with sharp scissors. We always have the freshly laid fire in the sparkling clean grate and the closed draft that sends our guests coughing into the dark streets. We always have one guest who is rude enough to inquire why our living room wall is sagging and suggests perhaps our attic is a little overloaded.

The "day after party day" then is always designated "Clean

the attic day." Now let me offer this bit of advice. If your marriage is already a little unstable to begin with, forget the attic. We never do, but then we've been written up several times in the *Ladies' Home Journal* feature, "Can This Marriage Be Saved?"

Usually we let down the attic stairs—which the Good Lord knows is enough of a physical strain the day after a party—and we scale the heights together. After considerable effort, my husband speaks, "Let me begin by saying that you can't be illogical or sentimental about this stuff."

"Well, that's pretty pompous coming from a man who still has his Jack Armstrong signet ring, a book of shoe stamps from World War II, and his first bow wow!"

"Those are collector's items," he explains. "That's different. I'm talking about junk. Right now, we are going to establish a rule of thumb for saving things."

We sit down on a carton marked RAIN-SOAKED HAL-LOWEEN MASKS. "Now," he continues, "if we can't wear it, frame it, sell it, or hang it on the Christmas tree, out it goes! Understand?"

At the end of two hours we haul four pitiful items to the curb: a broken hula hoop, an airline calendar showing Wiley Post spinning a propeller, an empty varnish can, and one tire chain.

"This is ridiculous," he growls, crawling back into the attic. "Let's take this stuff one by one. What's this?"

"That's our summer cabin inventory."

"What summer cabin?"

"The one we're going to buy someday. So far, we have a studio couch, a lamp with a bowling pin base, six Shirley Temple cereal bowls, two venetian blinds, and a chair with a rope seat."

"And this?" he sighs.

"That's my motherhood insurance. They're all my old maternity clothes, bottle sterilizer, potty chair, layettes, baby bed, and car seat. You lay a hand on this stuff and we'll both live to regret it."

"And all this trash?"

"That belongs to you. Consecutive license plates from 1937, old fertilizer bags, a rusted sickle, a picture of the Cincinnati Reds, autographed by Bucky Walters, the medical dictionary wrapped in a plain, brown wrapper, cartons of English quizzes from the class of 1953, eighteen empty anti-freeze cans, a box marked 'Old Furnace Filters' and a bait box that is trying to tell us something."

"Okay," he sighs, "I won't raise a finger. Put it out at the curb and call the junk man."

I grinned. *"The junk man.* You've got to be kidding. Gone is the simple, little peddler who used to beat a path to your curb in search of a bushel basket of cast-offs. Gone are the agency trucks who used to be in your driveway before you

got the receiver back on the hook. Hustling junk is a real art nowadays."

And I meant it. It had been my experience that if you're stuck with an old swing and gym set, it is easier to start a second family than to try to unload it. If you're saddled with an extension ladder with a couple of rungs missing, hire an adventurous painter with no dependents. As for having a car in the driveway that won't run, fella, that's about as thrilling to move as a dead horse!

On the day the agency trucks go by, I find myself running around the garage like a frustrated auctioneer, spreading my wares out attractively in the driveway and adjusting spots to highlight the plastics. "Boy, have I got goodies for you to-day," I yell. "I've got a set of corn holders, a size-twelve wedding gown worn only once, a box of Mason jars that will drive antique collectors mad, and a carton of coat hangers that are still in their productive years. That is, if you'll take this bed.

"You don't want the bed? Tell you what I'm gonna do. I'll throw in two pairs of ice skates, a garden hose, and a pressure cooker. No deal? All right, sir, you seem like a man of some discernment. As a special offer this week, I am offering your truck first choice on a nearly new beer cooler, thirty-five back issues of *Boy's Life*, and a hand-painted Nativity scene. If you'll take the bed off my hands.

"Really, sir, you do drive a hard bargain. To show faith, I'll tempt fate by giving away my layettes. That is positively my final offer. After all, this bed is a real find. It was only used by a little old lady from Pasadena who had insomnia. What do you mean, who told me that ridiculous story? You did when I bought the bed at your outlet store for ten dollars."

"Your story is touching," said my husband, "but what are we going to do with all this trash?"

I shrugged. "Bring it downstairs and we'll plan our next party."

### "One More 'Ho Ho Ho' and I'll Paste You in the Mouth"

"WHO CARES if it fits? She takes everything back anyway. Billie Joe, if you get hit by a truck, the next time I'll leave you at home! Why did I wear these boots? It never fails. I wear boots and the sun comes out! Will you please stop pulling at me. I did buy my Christmas cards last January. I just can't find them. Cheap stuff. They always put out cheap stuff at Christmas. Did you see that man shove me? Same to you, fella!

"Don't dilly-dally to look at store windows. I've got all my baking to do, the house to decorate, presents to wrap, the cards to mail . . . mailman! I forgot to get something for the mailman. Boy, everyone's got their hand out at Christmas, haven't they. Well, did you see that? I was here first and she hopped in right in front of me. We oughta get numbers like they do at the butcher counter. That would take care of those pushy ones. Same to you, fella!

"I don't care if the box fits, just any box will do. So don't send it. Let me occupy a whole bus with it. You tell the policeman when I occupy a whole seat that your truck driver couldn't deliver it. Lines . . . lines . . . I'll have to get in line to die . . . Billie Joe, you're too old for the Santa Claus bit. Don't think I don't know why you want in line . . . for a lousy candy cane. You'd stand in line if they were handing out free headaches.

"What music? I don't hear any music. I think I'll just give Uncle Walter the money. He's always liked money. In fact, he's never happy with anything else you give him. And that gift exchange. Wish we could get out of that. I always get something cheap back. My feet hurt. You'd think some man would get off his duff and give a woman a seat. No one cares about anyone anymore. I don't hear any music.

"My headache's back. Wish I could take off these boots. I think we're ready to . . . wait a minute, Billie Joe. I forgot Linda's birthday. Doesn't that beat all. It's what she gets for being born on Christmas Day. Now, I've got to run up to fourth floor and fight those crowds all over again. You wait here with the shopping bags and don't wander do you hear? No sense running you all over the place. Boy, some people have a fat nerve having a birthday on Christmas Day. I don't know of anyone who has the gall to be born on Christmas Day. What did you say, Billie Joe?"

"I said, 'I know SomeOne.'"

*"Deck the Halls with Boughs of Holly . . ."*

MY IDEA OF DECORATING the house for Christmas is to light up the rooftop with bright strings of bulbs, drape garlands of greenery from pillar to post, flash spots of bauble-studded trees, garnish the garage door with a life-sized Santa Claus, and perch a small elf on the mailbox that says "Y-U-L-E" where his teeth should be.

My husband's idea of decorating for Christmas is to replace the forty-watt bulb in the porch light with a sixty-watter.

"You act like I'm against Christmas or something," he said defensively. "Why, no one gets any more excited about the holidays than I do."

"Yeah, we've noticed how emotional you get when all those cars line up and breathless little children point to our house and say, 'Wowie, that's some sixty-watt porch light bulb!'"

"The trouble with you," he continued, "is that you overdo. If you'd just keep it simple. But no! You can't rest until you have me shinnying over the rooftops in a snowstorm with a shorted string of light bulbs in my teeth."

"I don't want to talk about it. You've been crabby ever

since you dropped your GI insurance. Heaven knows, it isn't the children's fault."

"What do you want to say dumb things like that for? And where are you going with those bulbs?"

"I am going to hang them on the bare branches of the tree in the front yard."

"I hope they're weatherproof. Remember the year you hung those little silver birds from the branches? I don't think I shall ever forget looking up from my breakfast and seeing those little feathered devils disintegrating before my eyes. It was like watching their intestines unravel."

"You've told that story a thousand times. These bulbs are waterproof."

"Junk . . . nothing but junk!" he said, pawing through the boxes. "I wouldn't be caught dead standing out there in the snow draping this wretched stuff over the trees."

"I know. You're the type who would buy roller skates for Tiny Tim!"

"Do you have a ladder?"

"I don't need one. I'm going to balance a bar stool on the milk box."

"I knew it," he said, "you just couldn't stand to see me sit in here where it's warm. You've got to involve me in your Disneyland extravaganza. All right, we might just as well do the job right. First, I'll make a sketch of the tree and we'll figure out mathematically how many blue, gold, and red bulbs it will take to make it look right."

"You ruin everything," I grumbled. "You and your planning. Did anyone ever tell you you're about as much fun as a fever blister under the mistletoe?"

"I tell you what," he shouted, jumping out of his chair. "Let's keep it simple this year. I'll put a sixty-watt light bulb in the porch light and we'll all stand around and sing, 'Good King Wenceslaus.' You know, I bet I'm the only one here who knows the second stanza by heart . . ."

*"Up On the Housetop Reindeers Pause . . . Out Jumps Good Old Santa Claus . . ."*

IF THERE IS one man singularly responsible for the children of this country, it's Doctor Spock. (That reads strange, but I don't know how to fix it.)

What I'm getting at is, this man is the great white father of every parent who has bungled his way through a vaporizer tent or a two-year-old's tantrum. Why, there was a time when, if Doctor Spock had told me to use one-legged diapers, I would have done so without question.

Now he has shaken me up. He has said there is no Santa Claus and urges us to tell our children the truth.

"Kids, brace yourselves," I said. "Doctor Spock says there is no Santa Claus and that I should never have taken you to see a live one in the first place because his behavior is noisy and his clothes are strange. Also, he inspires greed."

They looked at each other, obviously stunned.

"That's just not true," one said. "You know there's a Santa Claus, just as you believe there are fairies dancing on our lawn."

"Knock it off with the 'Yes, Virginia' bit. I told you that. Now I'm telling you Santa Claus is an upsetting experience. There can't be a Santa Claus."

"There can if you want him to be," they said cautiously.

"I don't know," I hesitated. "He does have a certain magic that makes people happy and kind toward one another. He does keep the work economy steady for elves and gives seasonal employment to reindeer. Heaven knows, he has your father spending more money than he earns and all of us crawling around on the rooftops with strings of lights in our teeth. I don't know what to believe anymore. I've always had such faith in Dr. Spock!"

"Have you ever seen Dr. Spock?" asked one.

"No, but . . . now *cut that out!* I know he exists. The point is how can I go on believing in a Santa Claus who parachutes from a helicopter over a shopping center parking lot, breaks his leg and ends up in a hospital?"

"Well, where else would you go with a broken leg?" asked another.

"The point is, kids, he's merely a mortal man, and mortal men don't go around pushing their fat stomachs down skinny chimneys."

"Of course he's mortal," they explained. "Otherwise, how could he have eaten all those cookies you put out for him last year?"

"That's right," I said excitedly, "he really did come, didn't he, and left me that dreamy black jacket that I *know* your father wouldn't have bought. You know something? I believe in Yogi Bear, and his behavior is noisy. I believe in Phyllis Diller and her clothes are strange. I believe in the Bureau of Internal Revenue and they're not exactly philanthropic. Kids, there is a Santa Claus!"

As the curtain closed on this domestic scene, the seven-year-old leaned over to whisper in his father's ear, "Boy, Dad, she gets harder to convince every year!"

Memo to: Mr. Kravitz, principal
From: Katherine Courageous
Re: Christmas Pageant

The Christmas Pageant will be a little late this year. Possibly January 23 if that date is agreeable with you.

Although an enthusiastic Pageant Committee has been at work since October, we have had some problems. To begin with, there were several on the committee who insisted on making a musical out of the Nativity story. At one point, we had the precision drill team making a "B" for Bethlehem in the background while a trio of baton twirlers marched around the stable. This idea was scratched when someone remembered batons hadn't been invented yet.

Remember how excited we were about the donation of a "live" donkey? Our custodian, Mr. Webber, does not share our excitement. Although his phrasing was a little less delicate, he intimated that if the animal was not "gym-floor trained" by January 23, we could jolly well go back to papier-mâché. He also said (this is quoted out of context) that the smell of the beast wouldn't be out of the auditorium in time for the Lions' annual Chili Supper next May.

We have had a few casting problems to plague us. I had to award the Mary, Mother of Jesus, role to Michael Pushy. (His parents donated the donkey.) Michael refused to wear a wig, which might be a little confusing to the audience, but I'll make a special note on the program. I've had great pressure from Mrs. Reumschusser. It seems her son, Kevin, is a Ted Mack loser who plays "Rudolph the Red-Nosed Reindeer" on the spoons. I am using him at intermission.

The costumes didn't arrive until three days ago from the Beelzebub Costume Company of New Jersey. There was obviously an error. Instead of thirty Roman soldier uniforms, there were thirty pink suede bunny leotards with matching ears. It was quite apparent to me that after I had tried a few on our "little people," this was not our order. Miss Heinzie and myself couldn't help but speculate that somewhere there is a tired businessman with a Roman soldier sitting on his lap.

The shop department is not yet finished with the special scaffold for parents wishing to take pictures and tape-record the program. We felt this necessary after Mr. Happenstance's accident last year when he panned in too closely and fell into the manger.

I hate to ask, but could you please do something diplomatic with Mrs. Ringading? She has threatened the refreshments committee with her traditional whiskey balls and rum cookies. You know what a fire hazard they created last year.

In view of the fact that two of our shepherds have diarrhea, we respectfully request the Pageant be postponed until January 23 or after.

## "God Rest Ye Merry Gentlemen . . ."

THAT CLICKING SOUND you hear about this time is the result of fourteen million husbands pushing the panic button. They are pushing it because they are hours away from Christmas and still have no gift for what's-her-name, mother of his four children.

One of the more conscientious husbands can always be counted upon to come up with the item mentioned last July when his wife snarled, "What I need around this house is a decent plunger!" Inspired by his power of retention he will sprint out and have a plunger wrapped as a gift. No one will be more surprised than he when his wife cups it over his mouth!

Others will seek out the advice of young secretaries who have read all the magazines and know that happiness is an immoral nightgown. Depending upon the type of wife she will (a) return the nightgown and buy a sandwich grill, or (b) smile gratefully and wear it to bed under a coat, or (c) check out the secretary.

For the most part husbands are cast adrift in a sea of confusion and bewilderment, sniffing perfumes, fingering sequins, and being ever on the lookout for a woman who looks like his wife's size.

Don't ask me why my heart goes out to these desperate men. Maybe it's that time of year. Maybe it's the den mother in me. Maybe I have really forgotten the rotten gift I found in my stocking last year: a gift certificate for a flu shot! At any rate, some of my women friends have asked me to pass along to men some guideposts to shopping.

First, women are never what they seem to be. There is the woman you see and there is the woman who is hidden. Buy the gift for the woman who is hidden.

Outwardly, women are a lot of things. They're frugal souls who save old bread wrappers and store antifreeze during the summer in the utility room. They're practical souls who buy all black accessories and cut their own hair. They're conservative souls who catch rainwater in a saucepan, and take their own popcorn to the drive-in. They're modest souls who clutch at sofa pillows to cover their exposed knees. Some still won't smoke in front of their mothers. So, they're dependable, brave, trusting, loyal, and true? Gentlemen, take another look.

Hidden is the woman who sings duets with Barbra Streisand and pretends Robert Goulet is singing to her. Who hides out in the bathroom and experiments with her eyes. Who would wear a pair of hostess pajamas if everyone wouldn't fall down laughing. Who reads burlesque ads when she thinks no one is watching. Who would like to feed the kids early without feeling guilty. Who thinks about making ceramics, writing a play and earning a paycheck.

That's all the help I'm going to give you birds. You've got just a few hours to get to know your wife. If you still think she rates a monogrammed chain saw, that's up to you!

There is a wonderful story of Christmas, about a great cathedral whose chimes would not ring until, as the legend goes, the real gift of love had been placed on its altar.

Year after year, great kings would offer up the riches of their land, but the chimes would not ring.

One year, a small waif in a shabby coat entered the great cathedral and proceeded down the long aisle. He was stopped and asked what he could possibly give that kings had not already offered. The small boy looked down and hopelessly examined his possessions. Finally, he took off his coat and laid it gently at the foot of the altar.

The chimes rang.

To receive a gift, molded from love and sacrifice, selected with care and tied up with all the excitement the giver has to offer, is indeed rare. They don't come along often, but when they do, cherish them.

I remember the year I received my first "Crumb Scraper." It was fashioned from half a paper plate and a lace doily. I have never seen such shining pride from the little four-year-old girl who asked, "You don't have one already, do you?"

The crumb scraper defied description. When you used one part of the cardboard to guide the crumbs into the plate, they bounced and scattered through the air like dancing snow-flakes. But it didn't matter.

I remember a bookmark created from a piece of cardboard with a picture of Jesus crayoned on the front. It was one of those one-of-a-kind collector's items that depicted Jesus as a blond with a crew cut. Crayoned underneath the picture were words to live by, OH COME HOLY SPURT.

My favorite, though, was a small picture framed with construction paper, and reinforced with colored toothpicks. Staring out at me was a picture of Robbie Wagner. "Do you like it?" asked the small giver excitedly. "I used a hundred gallons of paste on it. Don't put it near heat or the toothpicks will fall off."

I could only admit it was beautiful, but why Robbie instead of his own picture. "The scissors slipped and I goofed my picture up," he explained. "Robbie had an extra one."

There were other gifts—the year of the bent coat hanger adorned with twisted nose tissues and the year of the matchbox covered with sewing scraps and fake pearls—and then the small homemade gifts were no more.

I still receive gifts at Christmas. They are thoughtful. They are wrapped with care. They are what I need.

But oh, how I wish I could bend low and receive a gift of cardboard and library paste so that I could hear the chimes ring at Christmas just once more.

*Let Faith Be Your Guide*

I WAITED until the end of the book to tell you why I wrote it.

I figured if you got this far, you might need an answer. If you didn't get this far, it wouldn't make any difference.

It goes back to the first time I saw authoress Faith Baldwin in a full-page magazine ad admonishing, "It's a shame more women don't take up writing." I said aloud, "Ain't it the truth, Faith."

She looked directly at me and said, "If you're a woman who wants to get more out of life, don't bury your talents under a mountain of dishes. Writing will provide a wonderful means of emotional release and self-expression, to say nothing of the extra income. You don't have to go to an office with half your mind on your household, wondering if it rains, did you close the windows. (I liked that.) Even though you are tied down to your home, you can still experience fulfillment."

Faith, you had me pegged, all right. I had been a little bored at home. (A *little* bored. Who am I kidding? I was picking lint off the refrigerator.) So, I began to write about what I knew best: the American Housewife. Very frankly, I couldn't think of anyone in the world who rated a better press.

On television she is depicted as a woman consumed with her own bad breath, rotten coffee, underarm perspiration, and irregularity problems. In slick magazines, she is forever being brought to task for not trying to "look chi chi on her way to the labor room," for not nibbling on her husband's ear by candlelight, and for not giving enough of those marvy little intimate dinner parties for thirty or so.

In cartoons, she is a joke. In erudite groups, an exception.

In the movies, the housewife is always the one with the dark hair and the no-bust. Songwriters virtually ignore her. She's the perennial bad driver, the traditional joiner, the target of men who visualize her in a pushbutton world. (All of which are contingent on service repairmen whose promises are as good as the word of Judas.)

If she complains, she's neurotic. If she doesn't, she's stupid. If she stays home with the children, she is a boring clod who is overprotective and will cling to her children till they are forty-eight years old. If she leaves her home to work, she is selfish, ambitious, and her children will write dirty words in nice places.

Faith didn't tell me about the secondhand typewriter that tightened up when it rained or had a "7", an "s", and an "o" that stuck. She didn't tell me how I'd have to set up a table at the end of my bed and how my files would spill over into the bathroom. (The Internal Revenue Service didn't buy it either. They're still questioning my expenditure for a new shower curtain for my office.) She didn't tell me about the kids reading over my shoulder and saying, "What's so funny about that?" or interrupting one of my rare literary spasms to tell me that if you filled a washcloth full of water and squeezed it, it would take fourteen drops to fill your navel.

She didn't tell me about the constancy of a column that makes no allowances for holidays, vacations, literary droughts, or kidney infections.

She just said, "Write about home situations, kids—things that only a woman who stayed at home could write about."

At first, I began writing for one woman. I visualized her as a moderately young woman, overkidsed and underpatienced with four years of college and chapped hands all year around. None of the popular images seemed to fit her. She never had a moment alone, yet she was lonely most of the time. She worried more about toilet training her fourteen-month-old than Premier Chou En-lai. And the BOW (Big Outside World) was almost a fable to her.

After a while I began to visualize other women as I wrote. The woman with no children who made a career out of going to baby showers, the teenagers with wires coming out of their ears, hair cascading over their eyes and looking for the world like hairy toasters, the older woman who gagged every time someone called her a senior citizen, and the career girl who panicked when she saw the return of the dress with waistlines and belts. ("God only knows what I've grown under these shifts for four years.")

Through the columns and through the mails, we shared some common ground together. It was—in essence—group therapy. They'd write, "Honey, do something about your picture. You look like a fifty-year-old woman who has just been told by her obstetrician that she's pregnant!" Or they'd say, "You had to tell the world about my urban renewal living room, didn't you? Are you sure you don't live next door to me?" Sometimes their loyalty knew no bounds. "Erma, you're the only woman I let my husband take to bed with him. (Via the Sunday Section) He says you're like an old friend."

Other readers were not so enamored. "Who do you fancy career girls think you are, sitting in a plush office telling us housewives what it's like?" Or the note from an obvious health fadist, "Lady, you make me sick!"

These women and many more make up this book. They represent a myriad of moods, situations, frustrations, and humor that make up a housewife.

When my son learned that I was writing a book his first reaction was, "It isn't going to be dirty, is it?" I turned to him and said, "Kid, I couldn't get this thing banned in a Christian Science reading room." Then, that began to worry me a bit. Other than a small portion dealing with the sex education of our son in the fourth chapter, I have acted like

Sex and the Married Housewife do not live in co-existence with one another.

To be perfectly honest, I didn't know how to handle it. I grew up in an era when sex education was a dirty word. I didn't read *Little Orphan Annie* until I was twelve because Mother thought Daddy Warbucks was a dirty old man. I didn't even know *National Geographic* ran pictures until after I was married. Daddy always cut them out.

I can remember, of course, slipping a book by Kathleen Norris off the shelf and putting it between the pages of *Girl's Life*. The heroine, usually named Hiliary, was "pouty, wild, untamed, spoiled, breathless and rich." She always had sensuous lips. (I thought that meant a fever blister until I was fourteen.) The hero was usually Brad who was stubborn, tough, square-jawed, and who spoke huskily when he made love. My eyeballs fairly popped as I got to the meaty parts where Brad and Hiliary met to embrace. Then, it was always the same. "The fire in the fireplace flickered and died." I don't know how many books I plowed through where "The fire in the fireplace flickered and died," leaving me in a world of ignorance and speculation. I hadn't the foggiest notion what was going on while the fire was going out. So you can blame my omission on Kathleen Norris!

I have purposely not let my husband read the manuscript. With a book without sex in it, I can use all the lawsuits I can get to publicize it.

I could be terribly heroic and say I wrote the book because the American Housewife deserved a new, honest image.

I could be terribly sentimental and say I wrote the book because four men have always told me I could do it when I knew I couldn't. There is James W. Harris, my high school journalism teacher, who first had the kindness to "laugh when I sat down at the typewriter." There is Glenn Thompson, editor of the Dayton *Journal Herald*, who took me out of a utility room and is responsible for any measure of success I enjoy. There is Tom Dorsey, director of Newsday Specials, who took a "flyer" on an unknown writer whose credits consisted of bad checks and grocery lists. And not the least my husband, Bill, who when I cling to his knees and beg for criticism of my work, has the wisdom not to give it to me.

To be honest, however, I will have to admit that I wrote the book for the original model—the one who was overkidsed, underpatienced, with four years of college and chapped hands all year around. I knew if I didn't follow Faith's advice and laugh a little at myself, then I would surely cry.

# "JUST WAIT TILL YOU HAVE CHILDREN OF YOUR OWN!"

*With Illustrations by Bil Keane*

To Thel Keane and Bill Bombeck,
without whose cooperation with the authors
the teen-agers and consequently the book about them
could not have been produced

*Dear Bil:*

*I hope you will understand why I cannot start the book today as promised. It was our original idea to write and to illustrate a volume on teen-agers that was not a put-down, but would be filled with love, humor and poignancy.*

*How does aggravation, hostility and pain grab you?*

*Some women are lucky, you know. They gave birth to babies. I gave birth to teen-agers. Our daughter was born with a Princess phone growing out of her ear. Our son was born with his foot extended in an accelerator position and a set of car keys in his little fist. The third was born hostile. (Even in the nursery he staged a protest to lower the age of birth to a five-month fetus.)*

*This morning was unbelievable.*

*"Mother, is that all the breakfast you're going to eat?"*

*"I'm not hungry."*

*"You say that now but later on you'll eat a lot of junk that will only give you acne. Here, at least eat a piece of toast."*

*"If I keep eating, I'll outgrow my new suit. And I want to look spiffy for Maxine Schmidlap's Tupperware party."*

*"You use that word a thousand times a day. Is that the only word you know?"*

*"I can't help it. It says what I want to say. By the way, I need the car today."*

*"You should get more exercise, but if you really need it, pick me up at school exactly at three. Oh, and do something*

about those white socks, Mom. They're absolutely orthopedic looking."

"All the other mothers wear them."

"But you're not everybody. You're my mother."

"You kids better hustle or you'll be late for school," I said.

"Have a good day," they chirped, "and remember you can't do housework and watch 'As the World Turns' at the same time. Get your dishes and laundry over with. Then you can watch TV."

When will they understand that I am grown up, Bil? When can I have a life of my own? When will they stop smothering me? Criticizing me? Spelling in front of me? I'm forty-three years old. I want to be treated as an adult.

Truly, I am sorry I cannot start a humorous book on teen-agers today, Bil. Maybe tomorrow . . . when I am not so g-r-o-s-s and my acne clears up.

Erma

*Dear Erma,*
*Tomorrow might be*
*a better day here, too.*

# 1

## How I discovered I was living with a teen-ager

# Acute withdrawal

"I'll be in my room."

*"Gosh, Mom, nobody's PERFECT!"*

In my mind, I always dreamed of the day I would have teen-agers.

Young boys would pinch me in the swimming pool and exclaim, "Gee, ma'am, I'm sorry. I thought you were your sensuous daughter, Dale."

The entire family would gather around the piano and sing songs from the King Family album. And on Friday nights, we'd have a family council meeting to decide what flavor of ice cream their father, Ozzie, would bring home from the ice-cream parlor.

It never worked out that way. Our teen-agers withdrew to their bedrooms on their thirteenth birthday and didn't show themselves to us again until it was time to get married. If we spoke to them in public, they threatened to self-destruct within three minutes. And only once a young boy grinned at me, then apologized quickly with "Gee, sir, I'm sorry. I thought you were Eric Sevareid."

Heaven knows, we tried to make contact. One day when I knew our son Hal was in his bedroom, I pounded on the door and demanded, "Open up! I know you are in there staring at your navel."

The door opened a crack and I charged into my son's bedroom shouting, "Look Hal, I'm your mother. I love you. So does your father. We care about you. We haven't seen you in months. All we get is a glimpse of the back of your head as you slam the door, and a blurred profile as the car whizzes by. We're supposed to be communicating.

How do you think I feel when the TV set flashes on the message 'IT'S ELEVEN O'CLOCK. DO YOU KNOW WHERE YOUR CHILDREN ARE?' I can't even remember who they are."

"I'm not Hal," said the kid, peeling a banana. "I'm Henny. Hal isn't home from school yet."

Another time I thought I saw Hal race for the bathroom and bolt the door.

"I know this isn't the place to talk," I shouted through the keyhole, "but I thought you should know we're moving next week. I'm sliding the new address under the door and certainly hope you can join us. I wouldn't have brought it up, but I thought you'd become anxious if you came home and the refrigerator and the hot water were gone."

A note came slowly under the door. It read, "I'll surely miss you. Yours very truly, Hartley."

Finally, my husband and I figured out the only way to see Hal was to watch him play football. As we shivered in the stands, our eyes eagerly searched the satin-covered backsides on the bench. Then, a pair of familiar shoulders turned and headed toward the showers.

"Hey, Hal," said his father, grabbing his arm. "Son of a gun. Remember me? I'm Father."

"Father who?" asked the boy.

"You're looking great, Hal. I remember the last time I saw you. You were wearing that little suit with the duck on the pocket. Your mother tells me you're going to be joining us when we move."

"You have me confused, sir," said the boy. "I'm not Hal, I'm Harry."

"Aren't you the guy I saw poking around our refrigerator the other night? And didn't you go with us on our vacation last year?"

"No sir, that was Harold. Incidentally, could you give me a lift to your house? I'm spending the night with Hal."

We thought we saw Hal a few times after that. Once when we were attending a movie and they announced a car bearing our license number that had left its parking lights on, a rather thin boy raced up the aisle, but we were never sure.

Another time at a Father-Son banquet, someone noticed a resemblance between my husband and a boy who hung on the phone all night mumbling, "Aw c'mon, Wilma," but that was also indefinite.

One day in the mail I received a package of graduation pictures and a bill for $76. It was worth it. "Look, dear," I said to my husband, "it's Hal." Our eyes misted as we looked at the clear-skinned boy with the angular jaw and the sideburns that grew down to his jugular vein. It made spotting him at graduation a snap.

"Son of a gun," said his father, punching him on the arm, "if you aren't a chip off the old block, Henny."

"Hartley," I corrected.

"Harry," said a mother at my elbow.

"Harold," interjected another voice.

"I'm Hal," said the boy graduate, straightening his shoulders and grimacing.

"Hal who?" we all asked in unison.

# Sibling bill of rights

*"Mom! It's lookin' at me again!"*

"Notice anything different about my face?"
"Yeah. Your acne stands out more."

I know it is too late now, but I have long felt that I was foolish not to limit my family . . . to a parakeet with his tongue clipped.

That way, I would have escaped a confrontation with the Sibling Bill of Rights.

For years, I have deluded myself into believing I was raising children. Wrongo. I am not raising children at all, but cold, austere computers who are equipped with memory banks. When one child is fed a gift or a favor, the eyeballs of the other one roll around wildly. His entire body shakes, a buzzer sounds, two bells ring and a voice says mechanically, "They never bought me a watch until I could tell time."

What the memory bank lacks in logic, it makes up for in sheer volume.

One will say, "You got the biggest piece of pie for supper. That means I get to sit by the window the next time we go on vacation."

Or, "Richey's broken arm cost $55. Since I wasn't stupid enough to break my arm, can I have the $55 for a car?"

Or, "I made the last tray of ice cubes. That means you have to pass ball with me the next time I ask you."

It is not important that they cannot remember where they left their Sunday shoes. What is important is that they have retained in their memory banks how much allowance they received in the third grade, what they got for their second birthday from Grandma Tibals, the exact hour they were put to bed when they were five and the precise moment they stopped getting those lousy home haircuts.

The memory banks go into full gear at bedtime.

*Teen-ager:* You little creep. You used half a can of deodorant. I wasn't even allowed to use deodorant until last year.

*Little Brother:* Can I help it if you're a late smeller?

*Teen-ager:* Keep it up. I'm going to tell Mom why she has ants in her registers. You think I don't see you kicking your crusts down there. When I was little I had to eat everything on my plate.

*Little Brother:* And I'll tell her how you stare at me at the table and say "eeeeeee" under your breath.

*Teen-ager:* You get away with murder. Just because Mom and Dad had you late in life. (twenty-six!) Do you know how old I was before I got my first bicycle? I was five. You got one before your diaper dried out. And the bike I got didn't have five gears and a hand brake. I got one with the skinny tires and dumb-looking bell and we wore fat pants that always got caught in the chain. (Editor's Note: The more this story is told, the more primitive the vehicle becomes until he will eventually be driving a chariot in a loincloth.)

*Little Brother:* Big deal. I gotta do my homework.

*Teen-ager:* Wow. If that doesn't beat all. I didn't have homework until I was a freshman.

Finally, I could stand it no longer. "Boys!" I yelled, "I want you to run down to the shopping center and get some bird seed. Petie acts hungry."

I saw their eyeballs start to roll. Bodies began to shake as a buzzer and two bells began to sound. Finally, a voice said mechanically, "We never get to eat before we go to bed."

"It's simple," said the other voice, "Mom always liked the bird best."

# Telephone fever

"Something wants to mutter to you."

"Kathy?"

The other night I nearly fell off my chair when a voice said, "MOM! TELEPHONE!"

I wandered through the house shouting, "Where! Where!"

"IN HERE!" shouted my daughter. "IN THE HALL CLOSET!"

I crawled in under a topcoat and felt my way along the cord to the phone.

"Are you going to talk long?" she asked.

"I don't even know who it is," I answered.

"I didn't ask who it was," she said, "I asked if you were going to talk a long time."

"I won't know until I know who it is," I said firmly. I grabbed the receiver and said, "Hello."

"Who is it?" she asked impatiently.

"An obscene phone caller," I whispered.

"Are you going to be long?" she persisted.

"I don't know," I said, listening intently.

In the small bit of light that was available, I saw my daughter dance up and down in front of me, grabbing her throat while her eyes bugged and her tongue began to swell.

"Pardon me, sir," I said to the caller. "Could you hang on just a minute? My daughter, Karen, is in front of me and is trying to tell me one of three things: (a) Her pantyhose are too tight and have cut off the blood supply to her kidneys, (b) she is thirsty and is asking permission to split a soft drink with her brother, or (c) she will die if she does not get the phone within the next minute and a half."

Covering the phone I said, "Karen, what do you want?"

"I have to call Celeste," she said. "It is a matter of life and death."

"In a minute," I said and returned to my caller.

The closet door opened and my son poked his head in and pantomimed, "Who is it?"

"It's an obscene phone call," I mouthed back. "What do you want?"

"Do you have a no. 2 tomato can? Fifteen jelly beans? Four buggy wheels? And a box of cocktail toothpicks?"

"Not on me," I said.

Another figure crawled into the closet. It was getting crowded. "Mom, who are you talking to?"

"An obscene phone caller."

"The dog wants out," he said. "What's obscene mean?"

"Get a dictionary."

"You want the dog to go on the dictionary?"

"I want you to look up obscene." Into the phone I said, "Really, I am too paying attention. It's just that . . ."

My daughter crawled in the closet with a poster that read, "FIVE MINUTES WILL BE TOO LATE."

My son persisted, "It can be a no. 2 can of orange juice if you don't have the tomatoes."

"PLEASE!" I said aloud.

Finally, my husband poked his nose in the closet.

"Is that Grandma from Florida? Why wasn't I called?"

"It's not Grandma," I said. "It's an obscene phone caller."

"Oh. We really oughta call Grandma now that we know where the phone is. We haven't talked with her since Christmas."

Finally, I said to my caller, "Look, the timer on the stove is going off because I have been on the phone ten minutes now, my daughter is demonstrating right here in the closet, my son is forcing me to drink down a no. 2 can of orange juice and my husband wants me to call Florida. If it isn't too much trouble, could you call back?"

There was a silence on the other end, then a curt, "Forget it, lady," before the click.

# The but-everybody's-got-a-pony syndrome

This phase is sometimes diagnosed as measles. The teenager will become hot and feverish (often breaking out in a rash on his or her stomach), will stand on the threshold of hysteria and shout, "But you don't understand. Every kid in school has a three-armed sweater and if I don't have one I might just as well drop out."

This is his need to conform and become acceptable. As a mother, I often wonder what would happen if one day word got around that the class president wore raggy underwear. I can just visualize a morning at our house.

"Mother, where are my raggy underwear?"

"I just polished the piano with them. They're in the dirty clothes hamper."

"You *didn't!* Why do you always have to take my things?"

"I'm sorry. I also threw away three apple cores under your bed, a used nose tissue and a stack of toenail clippings in your bathroom. If you rush, you can save them from the trash can."

"Really, Mother, just because you and Dad don't know anyone personally who wears raggy underwear, you jump to the conclusion there is something wrong with it."

"Who's jumping? Did I say anything when you chopped the legs off those slacks and fringed the bottoms? I did not. Did I say anything when you decided to go without socks? I did not. Did I even complain when you took Daddy's old Army coat, rolled up the sleeves and wore it with a three-foot wool scarf tied around your head? I did not."

"Sure, but now I'll be the only one in school without raggy underwear and I'll feel ridiculous."

"Okay," I said, "I wouldn't want you to grow up to be weird. Why don't we take a good pair of underwear and grub them?"

"You know what you are, Mother, you're g-r-o-o-v-y."

Spurred on by instant popularity, I proceeded to distress all of my daughter's underwear. When she arrived home from school I proudly displayed them.

"See what I've done? You're going to be so 'in' with raggy underwear, we may be under surveillance by the welfare department."

"You didn't," she screamed.

"But I thought it was in," I stammered.

"That was this morning," she sobbed. "Tomorrow, everyone is wearing credit card earrings and skirts with broken zippers. I'll be a c-l-o-d."

"And I'll have the shiniest piano in town."

"A SCARF? Nobody wears a SCARF!"

"Mom, have you seen my scarf?"

# 2

# How to build a teen-ager—if you want to

Sometimes I wake my son up in the middle of the night and ask him to smile. Those braces that twinkle in the darkness represent my fur coat, my trip to Monaco, my second car, my college education, my insurance policy (for my old age next week), the operation on my sinus passages.

It seems like only $2000 ago that we sat in the dentist's office and discussed my son's teeth.

"Have you looked in your son's mouth lately?" he asked.

"Actually, no."

"He has a bite problem," he said.

"I find that hard to believe."

"Do you base this on something scientific?"

"I base it on the fact that I go to the grocery store every three hours to keep him fed."

"He has one tooth erupting in the roof of his mouth and if you will note, his molars do not meet."

"You're trying to tell me my son is a werewolf?"

"I am simply trying to tell you if the teeth are not corrected he may suffer some permanent damage to the formation of his teeth."

"What would happen if we ignored it?"

"He could try to develop his personality and buy his way to the prom but . . ."

"I understand. What do you want me to do?"

"I want you to schedule the boy with an orthodontist. He'll take X rays, give him fluoride treatments and set up a long-range plan for his teeth."

My husband reacted with his usual parental concern. "How much is all this going to cost?" he asked.

"A couple of thousand dollars."

"Why couldn't he have had something cheap like bad breath?" he snapped.

"Ask your side of the family," I retorted. "They're the ones with all the crooked teeth. If your grandfather hadn't been so tight with a buck he could have improved on the genes and your son might have straight teeth today."

"It's no use blaming people," he said. "What's done is done. We'll go the orthodontist route."

The orthodontist route, if not a rocky one, was a steady one. At least once every three weeks found me sitting in the waiting room reading the *Bleeding Gums Journal.* After every visit I would have the same conversation with my son.

"When are you going to open your mouth?"

"Never."

"You can't go on day after day clenching your lips together. How are we going to know if your tonsils are bad? And if they are, how are we ever going to get them out? Through your nostrils? You're being ridiculous, you know. Thousands of teen-agers wear braces."

"Name me two."

"Personally, I think they're rather sexy."

"I look like a computer."

"You do not look like a computer. Did I ever tell you what my grandmother told me when I had to wear a bag of garlic around my neck during freshman orientation?"

"Yes."

"Oh, well, anyway one day you'll forget yourself and open your mouth and laugh right out loud and some beautiful girl will say, 'Oh, are those $2000 worth of braces in your mouth? I hardly noticed them at all.' Are you sure I told you the story my grandmother told me when I had to wear a bag of garlic around my neck during freshman orientation?"

"Yes."

This went on nearly two years. Then one afternoon my son and I were standing at the bus stop when I noticed a pert, little brunette ogling him. She smiled shyly at first, showing a dimple in the corner of her mouth. Then she smiled broadly.

Suddenly, all the resentment in me began to build. I thought of all the sacrifices for those lousy braces. The new slipcovers . . . the permanents . . . the colored TV set . . . the support stockings and something in me snapped. I went over to the girl and whispered, "Believe me, darling, my boy is not for you. I know you think that now, seeing that row of straight, white teeth that become straighter by the hour. But just believe me when I say that someday you'll meet some nice boy with a bite problem who will make you a wonderful husband."

Later, my son said to me, "Mom, what did you say to that girl at the bus stop? She didn't even wait for the bus."

"I didn't bring you this far to have you run off with two front teeth that overlap!"

We rode home in silence.

*"But, Mom! I can't get glasses!*
*They make a person look GROSS!"*

Call it a mother's intuition. I can always tell when my son loses his glasses. On arriving home from school, he will nod to the dog and rub me playfully on my stomach. Then he will open the dryer and yell, "What's for snack?"

Actually, my son has been wearing glasses for nearly three years. I saw him in them just once. It was in the doctor's office when he was being fitted. For nearly twenty minutes the doctor adjusted the frames with meticulous accuracy, bending the stems to give just the right amount of pressure to the head and nose.

"How does that feel, son?" he asked.

"Swell," was the answer.

"I can adjust them to set a little farther down . . . just a fraction."

"No," said my son, "it's perfect."

They both faced the mirror and with agonizing preciseness the doctor angled the glasses at $\frac{1}{32}$nd of a degree to attain just the proper balance. The doctor seemed pleased with himself. "Perfect," he said. "Here is a genuine cowhide case for carrying them."

My son whipped off the glasses, jammed them into his rear pocket and left the glass case (genuine cowhide) lying on the counter.

You would not believe the places we have found my son's glasses. Try.

Inside a boot with a hockey puck and a lost mitten.

In a leftover dish in the refrigerator.

On page 73 of *Catcher in the Rye.*

Tied to the handlebars of his bicycle with a gym shoe string.

In the spin cycle of the washer.

In the glove compartment of the car belonging to his best friend whom he only knows as "Moose."

On top of a soft-drink machine in a service station in northern Michigan.

In the U.S. mail box with a stack of Christmas cards.

Held captive under a fat woman on a bleacher at the city league basketball game.

In a soap dish in the shower of the YMCA.

Looking for what's-his-face's glasses has become as organized as the Ohio State marching band. As the call to alarm sounds, each member of the family goes to his or her appointed area to begin the search with cold, impersonal, detached thoroughness.

The one who needs the glasses (the glassee) sits on a stool in the middle of the kitchen and serves as a central message center in case the glasses are found. (He falls a lot.)

The youngest marches to the bathroom area where he checks under the lid, sifts through the wet towels and personally goes through all the pants pockets in the laundry hamper. "The bathroom is secure," he reports. "Only item found were your car keys in the medicine chest."

The oldest has the living-room detail. She leafs through books, magazines, under sofa cushions and the loose dirt around the planters. "Living room negative," she reports. "Only a few popcorn hulls in the large chair. When was the last time we had popcorn?"

My husband has the outside grounds which include the interiors of the car, garage, flower beds and garbage cans.

"Nothing out here that a brush fire couldn't cure," he yells.

I get the kitchen area which is a bit more detailed. "Call everybody in," I shout, "the glasses have been found in the breadbox."

Sometimes I am tempted to let the kid grope his way through life, but then I say to myself, "What kind of grandchildren will I get from a boy who squints at a pay phone and says, 'She's tall, but she's pretty groovy, isn't she, Mom?'"

"*I was just ironing out some things for Debbie.*"

I didn't mind when my daughter's hair covered her eyes.

I didn't mind when it cascaded over her shoulders like a cape.

I didn't even complain when it hung longer than her hemline.

But when I discovered it wasn't my daughter at all, but my son, I became alarmed.

The unisexual approach to hair is frightening to most parents. It takes some getting used to. Like, did you ever try to carry on a conversation with an eyeball? For a period of months, it's all I ever saw of my daughter. I'd hear a swish, swish of hair and I'd whisper to my husband, "How would you like to see that emerge from a dark lagoon some night? I bet that would cure your drinking problem!"

"Good morning, dear," I'd say to the mass of hair. "How's every little thing on Eye Island this morning?"

The eye flinched.

"Have some juice?"

The eyeball closed to show annoyance and somehow I felt relief that it indicated life.

"Want your father to drop you off this morning?"

The eyeball went up and we both translated this as acceptance.

"I worry, dear, that all that hair is taking the strength away from your body. You haven't been eating well lately."

In reply, she jerked her head in an affliction that stirred up the long tresses for a second but only until they came to rest again in a straight line that exposed only one eyeball.

"The eye is angry at me and I am sorry," I said. "Incidentally, did you hear the amusing story of the mother who painted her garbage cans orange so the children would think they were eating at Howard Johnson's?"

I should have known better. The eye hardly ever laughs.

The saga of the hair should stop right here, but it doesn't. Very frankly, I got bored with the game. So I said to my daughter one afternoon, "Do you dare to be different? I mean, are you gutsy enough to be a pace setter?"

The eye started to leave the room, then hesitated and finally blinked, showing a flash of interest.

"Have you ever wondered what would happen if you were to cut your hair in a short, feminine style? Imagine, you could sit down without pulling your hair. You could turn your head at the table and not have it fall into the gravy. You could dry your hair in less than three days. Look at it this way. You wouldn't be losing your conformity; you'd be gaining an extra eye."

"I don't know," she hesitated. "That's pretty weird."

"You're a girl," I pressed. "Look like one!"

I never question the forces that move teen-agers. I only know that three days later she had her hair cut to her shoulders. As I looked into both her eyes, I felt like I was seeing Halley's comet for the first time.

"You look wonderfully feminine," I squealed. "Believe me, you are going to be so pleased at the reaction of people. They'll look at you and say, 'Now there's my idea of a wholesome American girl!'"

The first outing with the short hair took us to a hamburger emporium. We were standing in line waiting for eight 21-cent hamburgers to go when across from us an elderly couple was taking her in. Their eyes traveled from her short, clean-clipped hair to her bulky sweater, her hip huggers and right on down to her safety shoes with the silver buckles. I nudged her. "You see, already you're causing quite a stir. You know something? You might just bring girls back into style."

The woman spoke first. "If that were my son, I'd cut his hair with a razor strop!"

The man nodded, then looked straight into my daughter's eyes and said, "Why aren't you in the Army?"

All the way home I tried to get the eyeball's attention. One just stared straight ahead and glistened with tears. One remained closed. "Maybe if you enlisted for a few months the hair could grow out," I suggested.

The other eyeball snapped open and looked at me. I wish it hadn't.

# 3

# The hands that hold the car keys rule the world

"If you're teaching Glen to drive, shouldn't the car have training wheels?"

*Dialogue between a mother who was told having a daughter drive would be a blessing and a daughter who up until now believed everything a mother did she did out of love*

*Mother:* I'm not a well woman, Debbie. You know that. After the last baby, fifteen years ago, the doctor said I would experience periods of tension and depression. I am tense and depressed now. What are you doing?

*Debbie:* Putting the key in the switch.

*Mother:* DON'T TOUCH A THING IN THIS CAR UNTIL I TELL YOU TO First, I want you to relax. You cannot drive a car when your hands are gripped around the door handle and the whites of the knuckles are showing.

*Debbie:* You're the one clutching the door handle.

*Mother:* That's what I said. Just relax and put all the anxieties about driving out of your mind. Forget that behind the wheel of this car you are a potential killer. That you are maneuvering a ton of hard, cold steel which you can wrap around a telephone pole just by closing your eyes to sneeze. Are you relaxed?

*Debbie:* I think so.

*Mother:* All right now. Let's go over the check list. Do you have flares in your trunk for when you get a flat tire?

*Debbie:* Yes.

*Mother:* Do you have a dime so you can call AAA when the motor stops dead on you?

*Debbie:* Yes.

*Mother:* Do you have your license so you can show it to the nice officer when he stops you for violating something?

*Debbie:* Yes, Mother.

*Mother:* All right then. Just turn the key and at the same time step on the accelerator.

*Debbie:* Aren't you going to fasten your seat belt?

*Mother:* Are you crazy? I may want to leave in a hurry. Let's get on with it. Just gently touch the accelerator.

*Debbie:* Like this?

*Mother:* HOLD IT! STOP THE CAR! Let us get one thing straight. The radio has to be off. There is not room in this car for Dionne Warwick, you and me. One of us has to go. You're driving. It can't be be you. I'm supervising. It can't be me. Dionne is singing. She is expendable. Now, just relax and push on the accelerator. Any idiot can drive. I do it every day. Just ease along, unwind, hang loose and don't think about the drunk over the hill waiting to slam into you. What are you doing?

*Debbie:* Stopping the car.

*Mother:* What for?

*Debbie:* There's a stop sign.

*Mother:* Why are you stopping back here? That stop sign is forty feet away, for crying out loud. Pull up. Pull up. Give it a little gas. Go ahead. NO, WAIT! Do you realize you almost sent me sailing through the windshield?

*Debbie:* I guess I'm not used to the brakes yet. I'm sorry.

*Mother:* I know. So was Sylvia's daughter. Remember I told you about her? Her MOTHER was teaching her how to drive. She took off so fast she gave her mother a whiplash. I think she's out of traction now. Her daughter is wonderful, though. Never complains when she has to drive her mother to the doctor or adjust her braces. Now then, where were we? It looks all right. Just sneak out and . . . YOU'RE

TOO CLOSE TO MY SIDE OF THE ROAD. We're all tensed up. Maybe if we pulled over to the curb here and relaxed a bit. You're doing fine. It's just that you lack experience. Like, when you meet a car you have to remember that anything on his side of the line belongs to him. We can't be greedy, can we? Are you relaxed? Good. Just put your hand out and enter the stream of traffic. Not too fast now.

*Debbie:* But . . .

*Mother:* If they want to go over twenty-five miles an hour, let 'em pass. The cemeteries are full of drivers who passed.

*Debbie:* Do you suppose you could show me how to park?

*Mother:* To what?

*Debbie:* To park.

*Mother:* There's nothing to it. You just go to the shopping center and make a small right angle and there you are. When your tires bump the concrete island, stop.

*Debbie:* No, I mean parallel park between two other cars. One in front and one in back.

*Mother:* Where did you hear talk like that? You're driving ten minutes and already you want to get cute with it. It sounds like a wonderful way to get your fenders dented, missy.

*Debbie:* Our Driver's Ed teacher says that's part of the test.

*Mother:* So the Driver's Ed teacher is smarter than your mother. Then why isn't he sitting here getting stomach cramps? That's the trouble with teachers today. No guts. I think we're getting tired, Debbie. I have a headache and an acid stomach. Let's head for home. There's a pamphlet I want you to read on "Highway Statistics Compiled on a Labor Day Weekend by the New Jersey Highway Patrol."

*Dialogue between a daddy who was instructed to check out the driving ability of his wife's reckless daughter and daddy's little girl*

*Debbie:* You don't mind if I play the radio, do you, Daddy?
*Daddy:* Ummmmmmmmm.
*Debbie:* Want me to go over the check list?
*Daddy:* Neh.
*Debbie:* Could I also dispense with "Mother, may I?" every time I shift gears?
*Daddy:* Sure.
*Debbie:* Want to test me on the "Highway Statistics Compiled on a Labor Day Weekend by the New Jersey Highway Patrol?"
*Daddy:* No. You're doing fine, dear. Wake me when we get home. Szzzzzzzzzzzzz.

*Dialogue between a father who regards his car as a mistress and a son who is moving in on his territory*

*Father:* Do you know how long it took me to get a car of my own?

*Ralph:* You were twenty-eight years old.

*Father:* I was twenty-eight years old, boy, before I sat behind the wheel of my first car. Got my first pair of long trousers that same year. And I apprecia . . . I wish to heavens you'd stop making those noises.

*Ralph:* What noises?

*Father:* You sound like the sound track from the Indianapolis 500. Sitting around shifting imaginary gears and making those racing sounds. It makes your mother nervous. Now, first off, before we even start the motor I want to familiarize you with the mechanics of the car. (Lifting hood.)

*Ralph:* Okay.

*Father:* Here's the motor . . . this big thing over here. This gizmo is the cooling system and the big square box over there is the battery. Understand so far?

*Ralph:* You got a real doggie here, Dad. Boy, if it were my car I'd put a spoiler in the front and back to hold the car down, and a four-barreled carburetor . . . maybe even a super charger. Then I'd put slicks on the back wheels for a faster getaway and this old buggy would be out of sight. Incidentally, Dad, you could use some work on your points.

*Father:* Get in the car, Ralph. And pick that chewing gum wrapper off the floor. Any questions before we get on with the driving?

*Ralph:* I hope you're not going to get sore or anything. It's not that I'm too proud to drive a heap around but could you take out the dog in the rear window whose eyeballs light up red and green every time you touch the brakes?

*Father:* Now see here, boy, your mother bought me that for my birthday and I have no intention of taking it out of the car. It would break her heart. And what do you mean with that "heap" crack?

*Ralph:* My buddy, Steve, has a vet four-speed, tri-power with mag wheels, Fiberglas body and four-wheel disc brakes.

*Father:* Well, there's a lot of it going around these days. You'll notice over here is the glove compartment. Know your glove compartment. You'll find everything you need here for emergencies. Here's a map of the state, a cloth for wiping moisture off the inside of the windows, a box of nose tissue, a pencil, a pad and . . . YOUR GLASSES. That's the third time this month. You know it's immaturity like this that makes me doubt whether or not you are old enough to drive a car. And while I'm about it: What are you going to do about your rusty bicycle?

*Ralph:* Dad, could we get on with the driving lesson?

' *Father:* Don't use that tone with me, boy. You probably think you got a pigeon sitting next to you. You're not fooling around with the typically square parent. What would you say if I told you I knew what "laying a patch" meant? Huh? I know what I'm dealing with. The insurance companies know what they're doing when they set the highest rates for young boy drivers.

*Ralph:* In a few months I'll have a car of my own. I've been saving for three years.

*Father:* How much do you have saved?

*Ralph:* $27.12.

*Father:* That dog with the traffic light eyeballs in the rear window cost more than that.

*Ralph:* All the guys get heaps and fix them up.

*Father:* We'll see how well you drive this one.

*Ralph:* Okay, Dad, hang on.

*Father:* Look, son, this isn't a test run for Platformate. Slow down. You're bruising the tires. And watch out for that car. Defensive driving, boy. That's the name of the game. It's the only way anyone can survive on the highways these days. And don't race the motor. Wait until she shifts into drive by herself.

*Ralph:* Well, Dad, what do you think?

*Father:* (Looking ashen) Take me home. I have never seen such an abuse to a car in my life. And slow down. You're driving a lady, boy, and don't you forget it.

*Dialogue between a mother and her misunderstood driver son*

*Mother:* You remembered to open the door for your mother.

*Ralph:* It's nothing.

*Mother:* Remember, young man, nothing fancy.

*Ralph:* Don't worry. You're not nervous and high strung like Dad. Hey, look at the Daytona 500 and behind it the Duster 340.

*Mother:* Where? Where?

*Ralph:* Over there. Waiting for the light to change.

*Mother:* Oh.

*Ralph:* A fella at school has a new TT 500 and another one a GTX. Dad wouldn't understand any of this. He thinks a goat is an animal with whiskers.

*Mother:* Isn't he a scream?

*Ralph:* Mom, do you suppose you could get Dad to take that miserable dog that lights up out of the rear window?

*Mother:* Of course. I can't imagine where he got such a corny thing in the first place. Probably something he got with a lube job.

*Ralph:* You're groovy, Mom.

*Mother:* It's nothing. Drive.

# OUR BOY, THE DRIVER

# 4
# Theories I have blown

"Mo-THER!"

"With emotions ranging from despair to rage, parents look at their sons with matted hair curling over their shoulders and their daughters with ropy skeins over their faces, and wonder why they MUST wear dirty blue jeans, flapping sandals, and assorted bits of clothing usually found in very unthriving thrift shops.

"I have developed a theory about this which may be offensive to mothers and housewives but contains, I believe, a germ of truth. The young like to look dirty because their homes are too neat."

MARYA MANNES, journalist, author, lecturer and political commentator (The Cleveland *Plain Dealer Sunday Magazine,* October 12, 1969)

"Know what's nice about bein' around home? Everybody can
do their own thing."

We have an unmarried friend who visits our house about once every three years. Preparation for her visit makes the coronation look like an impulse.

"This place looks like a bus station rest room after a protest march," I announce to the group. "We've got to restore order."

"Why?"

"Because my friend Lydia Spotless is not married and does not understand why we have poker chips in the planter in the hallway. Come to think of it, why do we have poker chips in the planter in the hallway?"

"Because you made us get them out of the knife-and-fork drawer to make room for the keys that don't fit anywhere else and the fourth-class mail."

"Oh. Well I'm going to assign you areas to work. YOU defrost the refrigerator."

"What's defrost, Mom?"

"That's where you turn off the electricity and melt all the ice in the freezer and then turn it on and start all over again."

"Won't the leftovers get ugly if we turn off the electricity?"

"Throw them out."

"You can't throw them out," harped my son. "I was just on the verge of discovering a cure for penicillin."

"Don't be cute. You can clean the stove. I'd do it but I'm a high school graduate."

"How long will it take?"

"Counting superficial burns and skin grafts, you should be finished in two or three days. Oh, and I want one of you to put a pencil beside the phone. I've been in Lydia's house and she has one."

"You're sure doing a lot of fussing for her."

"I know. It's just that her house is decorated in Early Antiseptic. When I visited there last spring, I went into her bathroom and there wasn't one basketball in sight."

"Where does she keep her basketballs?"

"I have no idea."

"She certainly sounds weird."

"Whatever she sounds, we are going all out for her. You all get busy. I am going to take the ironing board down."

"A kitchen without an ironing board? Are you kidding, Mom. It's un-American. It's like Simon without Garfunkel."

"I never told you this before, children, but there are some homes in America where mothers put up the ironing board once a week, do their ironing in a day and take it down again."

"That's easy for you to say," said my daughter. "But where do their kids put their schoolbooks when they come home from school? Or throw their coats? Or put the dog after a bath? Or stack the groceries when they bring them in from the car? Or do their homework? Or eat breakfast? Or shine shoes? Or iron their hair? Or press dirty gym shorts?"

"That ironing board is family," said my son dramatically. "I don't care what Lydia Spotless thinks."

"Okay," I said tiredly, "I'll give in on the ironing board, but get the Punch and Grow tomato plants out of the dining room, the dog collar and the trading stamps out of the bowl of fruit, the Christmas tinsel out of the carpet and the ping-pong paddles off the washer. Oh, and get the tropical fish food out of the spice rack. Lydia would never understand that."

"Older children, particularly, should be allowed to have clothes that are not too different from the standards acceptable to their friends. A boy with brown shoes in a class where blue suede is the standard for that year is being exposed (perhaps unnecessarily) to attack and ridicule. Parents should be aware of what is considered 'cool' and square among children.

"The realm of responsibility in relation to clothes can be stated as follows. We do the selecting; they do the choosing."

DR. HAIM G. GINOTT
(*Between Parent and Child*,
The Macmillan Company, 1965)

"Aw, for pete's sake! Let's switch to SEWN-ONS!"

Teen-agers generally rate their clothes much the same as movies are rated.

"G" clothes appeal to a general audience. This is any apparel that is fake and furry, short and tight and looks like a donation the missions in Bwantanga sent back.

"R" usually applies to items like raincoats and clean tennis shoes. It means they're restricted to boys under sixteen who are accompanied by their parents.

"M" is a rating for boots and clip-on ties. You wear these only after you are married.

"X"s are no-nos and include pastel socks, red lipstick, tie shoes, warm hats with bills, and zip-in linings.

The other day in the fitting room, my son slipped into a pair of trousers and asked for my opinion.

"Personally," I said, "I would rate those trousers 'T.'"

"What's a 'T' rating?" he asked, puzzled.

"Terminal. If you ever cough, the entire seat will go."

"They're not tight," he challenged.

"Then how come your face is beginning to bloat?"

"You don't like them because I picked them out," he said.

"That's not true," I said defensively. "I just think there is something wrong when a boy has to unscrew his feet to get his trousers on. Look," I continued, "I am going to give you a choice. Here is what I've selected. You pick out what you want."

"You're kidding."

"Don't judge them just by looking. Try them on."

Later, he emerged from the fitting room.

"Control yourself," I snapped. "You are really too old to cry. What's wrong with them?"

"What's wrong," he blubbered, "I feel like a wind socket."

"Then it is the fullness that bothers you?"

"FULL!" he shouted, "I haven't seen trousers like this since Hans Brinker and his Silver Skates."

"It beats wearing a tourniquet, doesn't it?"

"Mom, can you imagine what would happen if I wore them to school?"

"Let me guess. The band would form on the front lawn and play Lawrence Welk polkas. The cheerleaders would chant, 'He can sing and he can dance, but he is wearing baggy pants.' Seniors would put 'PANTS IS POWER' stickers on your locker. Under your picture in the yearbook, they would list, Weird Trousers 1, 2, 3, 4. The Varsity Club would give a dance to raise funds to have your pants altered. *Life* magazine would follow you around with a cameraman who snickered a lot."

"You said I had a choice," he said biting his lip. "What's the alternative?"

"Wear your old trousers."

"Boy," he said shaking his head. "It's government like this that brought Adolf Hitler to power."

"Take it or leave it," I said.

"I tell you what," he said, "let's compromise. How about this pair of bell bottoms?"

"If the good Lord had meant for you to wear bell bottoms, he'd have flared your ankles."

"Look," he said, "I can sit down in them, bend, stretch, kneel and carry on a conversation in them."

"But you can't zip them all the way up," I said.

"Nothing's perfect," he sighed.

"Oh well, I look at it this way. If you get cut anywhere on your body, you can't bleed. There's some comfort in that."

"Honest, Dad, it's NOT a masquerade costume!
It's my BEST SUIT!"

"Thou shalt not use threats. Threats weaken a child's self-concept. The psychological effect of threats on a child is bad. But this does not mean that firm limits are bad. Therefore, threats are useless in improving the future behavior of a child."

DR. FITZHUGH DODSON,
(*How To Parent*, Nash Publishing Co.,
Los Angeles, 1970)

*"You're grounded!"*

I was raised on threats. I was thirty-five years old before I realized that if I imitated Aunt Hazel one more time my face would not freeze into a mass of warts.

It was also around that time I discovered I could hang my arm out of the car window and the wind wouldn't blow the fingers off. I could cross my eyes and they wouldn't "set permanently." I could kiss a boy and not break out in red heart-shaped blotches to announce what I had been doing to the world.

By the age of ten it became apparent that my mother had an inexhaustible supply of all-occasion intimidations. And I believed every one of them.

"If you don't go to sleep," she threatened, "the tooth fairy Mafia will pull all your teeth and sell them in the black market." Or, "You wet the bed one more time and a rainbow will follow you around for the rest of your life."

The other day I called Mother in desperation. "I need help," I said. "I've used every threat on the kids you ever used on me and I've run out. Do you have anything stronger that you held out on me?"

"Come over," said Mother. "We'll talk about it."

She met me at the door with a small, black notebook. "I never had to use these on you," she said. "You were such a ding-a-ling I could tell you anything and you believed it."

"I guess I was gullible then, wasn't I, Mother?" I giggled.

"I wouldn't have phrased it in quite that way," she said.

"This book is a collection of 'I WISH YOU MARRIED' threats. Are you sure you're ready for them?"

"Oh yes," I said. "I feel like a door mat. The kids don't care about me at all. All they need me for is to run and fetch, scour and flush. I'm only a mother. I have no feelings. Cut me and I wouldn't bleed. Only Betty Crocker flour would ooze from the wound. 'Press this, Mom.' 'Don't wait up, Mom.' 'Eat without me, Mom.' 'When is washday, Mom?' 'Where are your car keys, Mom?' 'Happy Mother's Day . . . what's-your-name.' "

"You're ready," interrupted Mother. "These threats are guaranteed to make them feel lousy."

I grabbed the book from Mother's hand and read some of the threats at random.

"You go steady at fifteen and I'll play you a tape of a labor room at the rush hour."

"May you break your leg while dancing on your mother's grave."

"I'm sick of waiting up for you to come home. May you carry your first born eleven months and know what it is to wait."

"I hope your son calls you at Christmas . . . collect."

"So don't get your hair cut. It'll grow into a noose and choke you to death while you sleep."

"Show me a son who talks back and I'll show you a mother taking a bus to the Industrial School to visit him on weekends."

"Just wait till you have children of your own. Never mind why I am smiling. Just wait."

I put the book down. "These are pretty ridiculous, Mother," I said. "I know when I was a youngster I was pretty easily deceived, but kids today are pretty sharp."

"They'll believe," said Mother, nodding her head slowly,

her eyes closed. "Incidentally," she said, her eyes snapping open, "that book is valuable to me. I want you to return it as soon as you are finished."

"I will," I said lightly.

"I mean it," said Mother. "If you don't return that book, may you become the oldest woman in North America to become pregnant."

My head jerked up and my eyes flashed wildly, "MOTHER! YOU WOULDN'T!"

*"Shh. He's getting PSYCHED UP to mow the lawn."*

"When a teenage group gather in someone's home for a committee meeting, a formal or informal party or a casual get-together, one or two parents should be in the house. The host parents have an obligation to the parents of the guests to be nearby and to be in charge. All of this is ordinary social courtesy."

DR. BENJAMIN SPOCK,
(A *Teenager's Guide to Life and Love*,
Simon and Schuster, New York, 1970)

"SLUMBER *party?* When does their slumber begin?"

"It's my house," said my husband, "and I don't know why you and I are cooped up here in our bedroom like prisoners."

"Because our teen-agers are giving a party."

"Now I know how parents felt in Germany in World War II when their kids turned them in to the Gestapo for watching 'Hogan's Heroes.' You'd think they were ashamed of us."

"They are," I said. "Now be still and play the game. Do you want to buy Park Avenue or not."

"I don't know why you couldn't handle the group yourself," he sniffed.

"I told you I am going through my post-natal depression period."

"You've been going through that for the last fifteen years. Besides, I wanted to be at Kiwanis tonight. They're showing a movie, *Birth of a Ball Bearing* with no scenes censored."

"It won't hurt you to play Father for one evening."

"How many kids are supposed to come?"

"It's not definite. Anywhere from twelve to three hundred. It depends on how the word has spread."

"That's just wonderful. You know about the party. I know about the party. The New York *Times* knows about the party. But does Ben Grauer know?"

"Probably."

"I'm a fool for asking, but what do we feed all those people?"

"We don't. We just back up a truck of soft drinks and open drums of potato chips and pretzels."

"What time is it?"

"Five minutes before eleven," I said.

"I've got five minutes before I put on my baggy sweater and walk through the room looking like Fred MacMurray."

"You'll do fine."

"I feel like a fool," he mumbled. "What do I do if I see someone dancing too close?"

"If they're dancing too close, they're engaged. All the others dance alone."

"Do I look all right?"

"You look fine. Remember now. Under no circumstances are you to smile at your own children or give a clue that you live here. Just amble through and make sure everything is going smoothly. I'll roll the dice for you while you're gone."

He returned in twenty minutes. His shoulders sagged, his mouth was drawn and his eyes haunting and searching.

"Well, how are things going?" I asked.

"Would you believe there is a drummer in our living room who is a King Kong look-alike?"

"Yes. Pay Community Chest $50."

"And do you know where the wood box is on the porch? Well, there's a Volkswagen parked next to it."

"You own two utilities now and one railroad."

"And a wild red-haired kid is talking with Defense Secretary Melvin Laird on our telephone!"

"You just passed 'Go' dear, collect $200."

"It's not enough," he said, cowering in the corner.

# 5

## The family that plays together gets on each other's nerves

My husband looked up from his paper one evening, clicked his fingers and said, "I've got a tremendous idea. Let's take an instant vacation."

"A what?" we asked.

"An instant vacation. One that is spontaneous. No preparation, no planning. Just go. We'll get up tomorrow morning, throw a few clothes in a paper bag and a few goodies in the cooler and take off to Pollution Lake. Would you all like that?"

"We'd love it," they all shouted.

"Good. Then it's settled," he said, snuggling down with his paper.

"Oh, this is going to be exciting," I said. "We've never done anything impulsive before. One of you kids get on the phone and call the vet. Tell him we'll drop the dogs off on our way out of town tomorrow. I'll put a note in my mailbox to stop the mail and one in the milkbox to turn off the milkman for a few days. Oh, and I'd better get hold of my egg man."

"Do you suppose Frank could take my paper route?" said my son. "And maybe take care of the hamster and the tropical fish?"

"I suppose so," I mused. "Call him and when you're finished I have to use the phone to call Elsa and tell her I won't be able to drop those five hundred coat hangers for the Scouts off on Sunday. Maybe on the way out of town I'll drop them off at Fanny Flack's house. Oh, it is fun being impulsive." I grinned.

"Mom, what should I do about my dental appointment?" asked my daughter.

"Call your friend, Carol, and have her call the dentist for you first thing in the morning. Tell her it's important or we'll have to pay for the visit if we don't cancel. Listen, someone get in the car and run out for some mayonnaise for the potato salad. I'll get the cake in the oven while you're all taking baths. And don't forget to get the sleeping bags out of the attic and aired and the cooler off the shelf in the garage."

"We have a turtle collection in it."

"Then get them out."

"Want me to unplug all the electrical stuff?"

"Don't do that until just before we go to bed. Listen, while I am thinking of it, get your father's shirts. On the way out of town, we'll drop them off in the laundry slot. There's nothing worse than beginning a week without any shirts."

"Mom, I was going to the library tomorrow to return my books."

"No problem. We'll drop them off at the library on our way out of town. We have to deposit a check anyway and it's right down from our bank."

"Okay, and what about someone to cut the grass?"

"Oh, for crying out loud," interrupted their father. "How much can the grass grow in forty-eight hours? You are all making a big deal out of this. It's supposed to be spontan . . ."

"And it is a great idea," I said. "I hate calculated things. They never turn out. But an instant vacation. Snap it up with the laundry, kids. While it's drying I'll get out and buy new underwear."

"HOLD IT!" said their father. "I know I'm a fool for asking, but what do we need with new underwear?"

"Can you imagine for a minute," I said, "that I would put this family in a car on the highways with raggy underwear? Instant vacation or not, I have my pride. Can't you see having an accident and a patrolman telling the press, 'The ones with the new cars with all the fancy gadgets are always the ones with safety pins in their shorts.' I'd die of humiliation. There are certain moments in a person's life when they should definitely have new underwear like when you get married, graduate, go into the Army or on a vacation. Maybe you want to be known in the ward as the 'Multiple fracture with tacky underpinnings,' but not me. I'll be back in a jiffy. Do you want me to pick up film while I'm out? Sun lotion? A road map?"

"What about the key to the house, Mom?"

"We'll drop it off at Grandma's on the way to the post office. I wrote your sister, dear. You know how she calls the police when she calls and we don't answer. Have I forgotten anything?"

"That is the most incredible question I have ever heard," said my husband.

"Good, then carry on. I'm off to the beauty shop. Luckily Elaine could work me in tonight. You impulsive devil you," I said, tweaking my husband's cheek, "you'll make gypsies of us yet."

"I know the PERFECT spot for our vacation this year!"

For years, my husband and I have advocated separate vacations. But the kids keep finding us.

We have always said if we could just mail ourselves to where we are going, we might arrive in a gayer holiday mood. But it's all the miles in between that makes traveling as giddy as the Nuremberg trials. (We once picked up a hitch-hiker who wrote us a check to let him out.)

Although each vacation spot is a new, exciting experience, the trip by car is rather predictable.

First, there is the blessing of the car, followed by Captain Daddy's "Give 'Em Hell" speech.

"All right, gang," he says, resting his foot on the front of the bumper, "you're probably wondering why we're gathered here today. We're about to embark on what can be a wonderful vacation together. That depends on you.

"First, I want to make a few remarks about the car. You'll notice it has a floor in it. That is for your feet. At no time, repeat, no time do I want your feet resting on my shoulders. A good driver is an alert driver and I cannot be at my best with a pair of yesterday's socks in my face.

"Second, we will not play car roulette at any time during the trip. There is nothing more frustrating than for me to look through my rear-view mirror and see bodies hurling through the air like the Flying Wallendas. As your captain, I will make window assignments each morning. If there is any quarrel with these assignments, feel free to file a grievance.

"May I also remind you this car is not a trough. Any candy wrappers, banana peelings, stale bread, apple cores, broken straws, paper cups or breakfast rolls must be wrapped and thrown away or buried. I will not tolerate another fruit-fly assault like last summer.

"Third, transistors must be turned off while you sleep. Also the occupants of the car will not be subjected to more than ninety-nine choruses of "Ninety-nine Bottles of Beer" in a twenty-four-hour period.

"And last, there will be no reading of *Mad* magazine, *Sports Illustrated* or *Mag Wheels Digest* while we are touring breath-taking mountain ranges, historic monuments or indescribable cathedrals. Remember, you are going to have a wonderful time if I have to break every bone in your bodies. We are ready to start our motor. Good show."

Once Captain Daddy's speech is out of the way, we are in for five hundred miles of the Disaster Lady.

The Disaster Lady is our teen-ager daughter who didn't want to make the trip in the first place and who threatens to join a convent the minute the car slows down. Her fatalistic approach to a vacation makes it as much fun as diarrhea.

The car is barely out of the driveway before she lifts her head in a dramatic jerk and whispers, "Did you hear that? I thought I heard a knock under the hood. Cecily Ainsworth's dad had that same knock under his hood and the car blew up at the end of the driveway."

If she isn't predicting hurricanes as far inland as Indiana, she's telling you an amusing story of a shark that showed up in some freak way at the lake where we plan to stay.

When you are half a day out from home, she will stir restlessly in the back seat and yell, "Mom, did you remember to unplug your coffeepot and your iron? The last time I saw them they were on." Or, "Daddy, did you get a confirmation on the hotel room? I wonder if it's one of those places where you have to bring your own linens? I sure hope someone remembered to take the cat next door."

Occasionally, she will unplug the transistor from her ear and sigh, "Gee, that's too bad."

"What's too bad?" we ask.

"About the weather."

"What about the weather?"

"The extended forecast predicts two solid weeks of rain where we are going. But I don't mind really," she adds.

I'm almost afraid to ask, "Why not?"

"Because I was exposed to German measles thirteen days ago anyway."

In between Captain Daddy and the Disaster Lady, we have Happy Mouth.

Happy Mouth is the eleven-year-old who is one of the best testimonials to Planned Parenthood I can think of. There is something disgusting about a kid who wakes up happy and goes steadily uphill the rest of the day.

"Hey, do you want to hear the poem I read on the last rest-room wall?" he chirps.

"No," says the car in unison.

"It said, 'Violets are blue, roses are red, If you can read this, you're standing on your head.'"

"That's enough."

"There was a phone number underneath it."

"We don't want to hear about it."

"Can I call it when we stop?"

"No."

"Can I plug in the electric back-scratcher I bought at the last souvenir shop?"

"No, you'll run the car battery down."

"Can I take a picture of your teeth?"

"No."

"Anyone want to play Monopoly?"

"No."

"I'll roll up all the windows so the money won't blow around."

"Mom, will you hush him up?"

Happy Mouth may be put down on the average of once every three minutes, but he is undaunted. "Hey, this looks like a neat restaurant," he exclaims.

I grimace. "Are you kidding? This place will have to be cleaned before they can condemn it. Let's move on to something else."

"I want to eat here," shouts Happy Mouth. "There's a real neat dog inside, see him?"

"I should," I say dryly. "He's sitting in a booth."

"Aw c'mon, Mom."

"Okay," I relent, "but let me give you one word of advice. This place is a filthy dump. I bet they haven't had a customer since the septic tank backed up. We'll all be fine if we order something safe like cheese or peanut butter. Remember now. Something safe."

Happy Mouth is the first to order. "I'll have the roast turkey and dressing." He grins. Then, "May I use your rest room?"

The waitress blows an enormous bubble and pops it. "You walk past the juke box and turn and go through those two big double doors. You walk through the kitchen and out of the back into a gravel parking lot, then walk through that field about an eighth of a mile down the road."

"Isn't that the service station?" I ask.

"Right," she says.

Happy Mouth is absolutely jubilant when he gets back. "You should see the kitchen."

"I don't want to talk about it," I say, picking at my cheese sandwich.

"It's got a stove with big pots on it and a neat fire extinguisher on the wall."

"It's probably a stomach pump," snarls my husband.

"And the dog out there is real neat."

All eyes at the table focus hard on Happy Mouth. He senses our animosity. "Guess what?" he says cheerfully, "I didn't sit on the toilet seat."

Another fun occupant in the car is the Teen-age Grumbler. Nothing, it seems, is as much fun as he anticipated. He came on the trip with a change of underwear and a single word in his vocabulary, "Gross."

The tours are gross, the statues are gross, the motels and the food are gross, the girls are gross and the weather and the towns are gross. You get the feeling if he had been present while the Red Sea was being parted, he'd have whipped a pocket comb out of his shirt, yawned and said, "That's gross."

Efforts to introduce him to scenic phenomena of the world are in vain. "Would you look at that?" gasps his father. "Those faces carved in the side of a mountain are fantastic."

The Grumbler speaks, "They're gross."

"No, they're Roosevelt, Washington, Lincoln and Jefferson," says his father. "Look here, boy, I don't think you have the proper attitude for this trip. Here we have driven 1750 miles to show you a breath-taking view and you slouch in your seat and clean your fingernails with a matchbook cover."

"I saw a breath-taking view already yesterday," he grumbles. "When do we eat?"

"We ate yesterday," snaps his father and drives on.

If you did not know the background of the Grumbler, you would vow he was sired by a Bank Americard, born in a jet and weaned on Wall Street. Throughout the entire trip, he spews out his displeasure. "That swimming pool isn't heated." "Can't we get a motel with a phone in the bathroom?" "You can't get a decent TV picture in this cabin." "That stupid drugstore hadn't even heard of the *Mag Wheels Digest*." "They only have three kinds of soft drinks at this gas station." "Make him keep his feet on his side of the car." "I've been keeping tab, Dad. This is your 87th wrong turn, your 18th detour and your 467th profane word."

His father turns his head angrily and opens his mouth.

"That's 468th," he says. "That's gross."

Naturally, I have saved the Family Mother of the trip until last. Upon her frail shoulders rests the responsibility of dispensing discipline, maintaining order, keeping track of the gas and oil mileage, reading road maps and of course getting Captain Daddy to make pit stops with some regularity.

"Don't you think we should stop and get a bite to eat?" I ask.

"Why?" answers the captain. "We just got rolling."

"We got rolling at five this morning," I say. "It is now two-thirty in the afternoon and my vision is beginning to blur."

"You exaggerate," he said. "I wanted to make Goose Fork by four. If we stop you'll all want to go to the bathroom, stretch your legs and get out of the car to eat and that will blow another twenty minutes."

"I feel like I am in a getaway car. We are only human. We have a body that requires food and rest. Our muscles must be exercised or they become useless. We have plumbing that must function. We are mortal. We bleed like anyone else."

"NOT ON THOSE NEW SEAT COVERS," he yells over his shoulder.

"That was just an expression," I say. "Frankly, I don't understand you at all. Why don't you get hungry once in a while? Are you sure you aren't pilfering food from somewhere like the fat guy in *The Diary of Anne Frank?*"

"Really," he snorts, "if you are going to make such a big deal about it, look for a place to eat. When you see one, just yell."

"There's a plaaaaaaaaaaaaaace. . . ."

"Where?"

"Back there."

"I can't stop on a dime, you know."

"Not going seventy miles an hour you can't."

"Look," he growled, "you pick out a beanery the size of a flea's navel and expect me to see it and drive at the same time. Besides, it looked like a hole in the wall."

"I thought you didn't see it."

"I could smell the grease when I went by. Believe me, I know when they fry the shrimp and the French fries in the same vat."

"Oh, really."

Two hours later, we are still looking for a place to eat. Family Mother has her head wedged in the no-draft peering into the darkness for a lighted sign. The children are sprawled out on the seats to conserve energy as their stomachs bloat.

Finally, Mother rummages in her handbag. "I'm in luck,"

I shout. "Here are three breath mints, one for each child. Here is a sticky coughdrop for me and here's a piece of chocolate for Daddy."

Daddy smiles as he devours the square of chocolate. "This should hold us until we get to Goose Fork," he smiles.

"Don't count on it," I say, taking a deep breath. "I just fed you a laxative."

From the back seat came three voices.

"When laxatives are old, they loose their effectiveness," said the Disaster Lady.

"That's neat. I'm going to buy some when we stop and use them as tricks," laughs Happy Mouth.

"You're all gross," snarls the Grumbler.

# 6

# Different schools of thought

*"This report card is terrible!*
*I'm ASHAMED of you!"* *"Your hair is DISGRACEFUL!*
*And those clothes! I hate to*
*admit you're a member of this*
*family!"*

*"Go, Hank, go! Way to go, boy! THAT'S MY SON!"*

*"Why don't you grow up?"*

"My teacher didn't say a THING about my hair. His is longer."

"But this IS our homework! We're taping the history of rock music for Humanities Class!"

"We're having a '50s dance, Dad, and we're supposed to dress in freaky getups from 'way back. Can I wear one of your suits?"

"Hi, Dad!"

"My counselor recommended Penn or Purdue, the coach's advice was Michigan, I won a scholarship to Syracuse, my best friend picked Southern Cal, and I like Arizona State. . . . But, I'm going to Ipswich College because that's where my father graduated from."

# 7

# Sex is only a three-letter word so how can it be dirty?

"That's not the way we learned it in Sex Ed, Dad. Mrs. Thompson said that . . ."

"There is no need for you to be embarrassed about S-E-X," I told my daughter. "Sit down and I will tell you all I know about it. First, Lassie is a girl. Second, I lied. Sensuous lips do not mean fever blister. Third, I did not conceive you by drinking the blood of an owl and spitting three times at a full moon. Here is the bra and girdle section from the Sears catalogue. If you have any questions, keep them to yourself."

I don't suppose that was too technical, but a friend of mine overdid it. She bought books and charts depicting the reproduction cycles of chickens. Together they studied mating, fertilization and a racy chapter on chromosomes. Her daughter knew more about chickens than any young girl has a right to know.

One day, her mother walked out on the front porch and saw a rooster perched on the porch swing and liked to have had a heart attack.

Anyway, two weeks after my "talk" with my daughter she brought home Leroy.

Leroy was big for his brain. I couldn't look at him without remembering why the dinosaurs disappeared from the earth.

During the two years he was to live with us I can remember only one expression he used. He would come into the house and say, "You look like a drowned rat." (I always looked up and smiled only to discover he was talking to the dog.)

The first time my husband noticed Leroy, he was polishing off a loaf of toast, and a half gallon of milk.

"Who's that?" asked my husband.

"It's Leroy," I answered.

"He's a sex maniac," he said.

"How can you tell?"

I looked the same way the day I stopped thinking of Annette Funicello as a Mousketeer."

"Don't worry about it," I said.

"What do you mean, 'Don't worry about it?'"

"You haven't lost a daughter. You've only gained a disposer with teeth."

We saw a lot of Leroy, which is the greatest understatement since Noah called the weather bureau and got a recording predicting light showers and drizzle.

He arrived in time for breakfast, returning after school, spent the entire evenings, plus weekends, holidays and summers.

They never seemed to do anything together except eat and drink. One day I was passing through the kitchen when Leroy leaned over close to my daughter's ear. I held my breath. This was it. Was he going to nibble on it? Blow into it? Proposition it? I leaned closer, straining to pick up a few words. He spoke, "You got anything to settle my stomach?"

I know enough about sex to know that when bicarbonate enters the room . . . love flies out of the window.

"Hi, Beautiful!"

"What do you think of Wayne?" I asked my husband.

"I think he's a sex maniac," he said in a loud whisper. "He reminds me of a fella I went to high school with. In the yearbook he was voted the Senior Most Likely To."

"To what?" I asked.

"That's the kicker. You were supposed to fill in the blank yourself."

"Oh, good grief. He seems like a nice boy."

"Then why is he pawing our daughter?"

"He's not pawing. They're just holding hands."

"That's all they do. What would happen if they unclenched hands? Would they bleed to death?"

"You make too much out of it. He's an athlete."

"I'll just bet he is."

"I mean a football athlete. Did you know he got a letter this year?"

"So did Hester in *The Scarlet Letter*," he snapped.

"You're being dramatic."

"Why don't you offer them a cold drink to cool them off?"

"I offered them a cold drink and some cookies. They didn't want any."

"We're in trouble."

"We're not in trouble," I said. "Just relax."

I was whistling in the dark. Actually I was quite concerned for the health of both of them. They paled from sitting indoors. Both had lost weight. (At least with Leroy she got a square meal), and they were very awkward getting in and out of coats with their hands clenched together.

"Why don't you kids go to an RX movie or something?" I asked one evening.

They continued to stare into each other's eyes and a faint, "No, thank you" came back.

"Don't either of you have to wash your hair or something?"

Neither twitched a muscle.

"Anyone want to go out on the porch and breathe in and out?"

Silence.

Finally, several months later, my daughter bounded into the house.

"You look different," I said.

"Like how?" she asked.

"I don't know. Like something's missing. I got it. You're not wearing Wayne this afternoon."

"Oh HIM," she said.

"What happened?"

"He was a drag. All he wanted to do was sit around and talk about himself. Did you know that Wayne has eight red veins in his nose and when he has a cold they swell up?"

She noticed.

"TELEPHONE!" I yelled to my daughter.

"Who is it?" she yelled back.

"It's Bear."

"I got it," she yelled. "Hang up."

"Him again?" snarled my husband.

"Shhh. What's the matter with Bear?"

"He's a sex maniac, that's what he is."

"How can you tell? You've never even seen him."

"That's the point. How come he never comes around to the house? Every hour of every day that phone rings and he's calling. Bear could be a recording for all we know. Besides, can't you just get a picture of a guy named Bear?"

"I visualize Bear as a big, lovable teddy bear who eats out of picnic baskets."

"Funny," he said rustling his paper, "I see him as a big, grizzly with sharp teeth, strong arms and hairy feet."

Whatever Bear was, he was to remain anonymous.

When the phone rang, my daughter would snatch it and run into a closet, shut the door and whisper into the receiver until we threatened to detonate her.

"What in the world do you find to talk about?" I asked.

"Bear is deep," she said.

"Why doesn't he ever come to the house to see you?"

"He's shy."

"Then you have seen him?"

"Of course, I've seen him."

Bear bothered me . . . or the thought of him did. One night I had a dream that Bear and my daughter were getting married. She was a vision in filmy white as her father escorted her down the aisle. At the end, she was met by a representative of the phone company who joined her hand with a receiver with Bear on the other end.

She was attended by six Princess phones in assorted colors and six black wall phones. During the ceremony, an electronic system played "How Dry I Am."

The reception was even weirder. Daddy and I gave them a chest of dimes and quarters and a phone directory from each of the fifty states. Our daughter left the reception alone. She was going to rendezvous with Bear in a phone booth in Ft. Lauderdale.

I didn't tell anyone about the dream. It was too ridiculous. But the next night I dreamed again. This time my daughter was in tears. "I am getting a divorce from Bear," she sobbed. "I am charging him with harassment. It was terrible. Every time he wanted me to pass the butter, he'd run to the phone and call me up. I nearly went crazy running back and forth to the phone. Of course, there's the child to consider. Do you want to see your grandchild, Mother?"

"Oh yes," I said eagerly, reaching out to snatch the blanket from her. "Then deposit a dime," she said, throwing back the covers to reveal a small pay phone.

I know it was only a dream, but it was upsetting. I had a talk with her. "Look, either Bear materializes before our eyes or we will cut off his phone privileges. This is too ridiculous. You spend more time on a telephone than a storm-door salesman."

Later, my husband mumbled, "Phones are wonderful instruments, but I wouldn't want our daughter to marry one."

I knew then that when Bear called I would hang up.

"Surely you don't think Barney is a sex maniac," I said to my husband.

"And why not?" he asked.

"He's too cheap," I said.

"Just because the boy redeems our old pop bottles and dries out our charcoal and saves it in a bag is no reason to condemn him."

"It's not just that. Haven't you noticed how before every holiday he picks an argument so he won't have to buy our daughter a present?"

"You're imagining things."

"Look," I said, confronting him with a sheaf of papers, "I've kept track."

Palm Sunday: A jealous rage over Elliott Gould that lasted until the day after Easter.

Two weeks before the Prom: Made snide remarks about girls who shave their legs.

Eve of Memorial Day barbecue: Said he had to stay home and wash his hair and she should do the same.

Pre-Birthday fight: Decided he was too immature to go steady and was breaking his mother's heart.

July 3: She laughed when he said he was going to grow a beard and he cut out.

Pre-Labor day weekend: He argued she had a wart on her shoulder and she said it was a mole.

Two days before football tournament: He said if she really cared for him she wouldn't mind taking a bus and transferring twice.

A week before Christmas: He had to study for his draft physical.

Three days before New Year's Eve: He steamed her by suggesting her best girl friend resembled Jim Nabors.

Eve of their first anniversary of going steady: She caught him holding the drinking fountain for a cheerleader.

February 13: Argument over whether or not horned toads bleed through the eyes when they die.

"I repeat. That's insane," snarled my husband. "You take a mere coincidence and turn it into a case for a Philadelphia lawyer. Frankly, I like the way he goes around turning off the garage lights and folding the aluminum foil off the pizza for future use."

At that moment, our daughter came into the room and slammed a book down on the table. "Barney and I are finished. It's total this time."

"What happened?" I inquired.

"He said the Women's Lib movement was made up of women who looked like Russian pole vaulters and not one of them could make the center fold of *Popular Mechanics*. And I told him to split."

My husband turned to me, "Make something out of that, will you?"

I grabbed the calendar. "Aha. What did I tell you? Tomorrow is Ground Hog's Day and Barney isn't taking any chances."

Bufford had black curly hair, a devilish cleft in his chin and three more teeth than Bert Parks.

He also had the subtlety of a blonde on a bar stool holding an unlighted cigarette.

"Hi, Beautiful," he'd say, slipping his arm around my waist. Then with a double take (that killed vaudeville) he'd say, "Oh, good grief. I am sorry. I thought you were your daughter." The whole bit sounded like a commercial for break-fast cereal, but I always fell for it.

"I like that boy," I told my daughter. "He has charm, breeding, intelligence . . . taste. . . ."

"He also has twelve arms," she said.

"Oh, come now. Any boy who invites his girl friend's mother to a drive-in can't be all bad," I rationalized.

"In separate cars?" she asked incredulously.

She was right, of course. He had conned me into giving him a set of my car keys. ("I hate to bother you when you're relaxing.")

We always ate in the dining room when he was there. ("Don't fence with me. You did manage the Nixon's dinner parties, didn't you?")

I found myself dieting to see if he would notice. ("Didn't I see you on the February cover of *Seventeen?*")

One day he took me quite off guard when he said, "This is a big house. I figured out how you could make an apart-ment out of it just by adding a stairway."

"Why would I want to do that?" I asked.

"In case a young married couple was still in school and needed free housing until they both finished."

That evening my husband found me rummaging in a trunk in the attic. "What are you doing?" he asked.

"I'm through messing around," I said. "I've got to bring out the big ammunition on sex education. The bra and girdle section of Sears just isn't doing it."

"You mean?"

"*Poultry Management*," I said flatly.

*"Remember Joey Mackin and Ann Simons from my class?"*

*"They got MARRIED!"*

# 8

# Games teen-agers play

"Listen to this next one, Laurie. It's by The Who."

# Hide and don't seek mother

It is upsetting to many parents that their teen-agers introduce them to their friends as encyclopedia salesmen who are just passing through . . . if they introduce them at all.

I have some acquaintances who hover in dark parking lots, enter church separately and crouch in furnace rooms so their teen-agers will not be accused of having parents.

The first time I realized my children were ashamed of me was at a PTA Open House. One of the teachers asked my son, "Is your mother here?" Instinctively, he jammed me into a locker, threw his body in front of it and said, "No, she couldn't come this evening. She's playing pillowcase bingo at the church."

I was indignant. "Why did you say that? Have I ever laughed with cottage cheese in my mouth? Have I ever done my Gale Storm impersonations in front of anyone but family? Have I ever worn my loafers and Girl Scout socks to anywhere but the A&P and back?"

He didn't answer. He just smiled and pretended he was giving me directions to the gym.

If it will make parents feel better, girls in their teens often go through their "Our Gal Sunday" syndrome. It is far more romantic to imagine they were found on the doorstep of two old coal miners and will eventually find happiness with a virile English rock singer than to say, "I was born of Wanda and Louie Fish in a hospital in the suburbs of Cleveland."

Boys of this age go through their Sabu syndrome. They do not want to face up to the fact they were conceived by any other way than without original sin, so they prefer to believe they emerged from a seed in the jungle, fed by werewolves and later adopted by Jon Hall. (Or whoever was Tarzan that year.)

As a parent, I am going through a syndrome myself. It's called Joan of Arc, which means I am sick and tired of being treated like a dog with mouse breath.

I'm sick of scrubbing and washing, running and fetching, scrimping and sewing, hauling and cooking only to have them say four words to me all year: Wait in the car.

Last summer, I drove my daughter and son to the swimming pool. As my daughter and I prepared to emerge from the bathhouse, my daughter stopped.

"Where are you going?"

"Whatya mean where am I going? I am in a bathing suit. Am I dressed for a flu shot?"

"You go first," she commanded.

"Why, aren't they friendly?"

"Mom, no one goes to a swimming pool and sits with their mother."

"It's the bathing suit, isn't it?" I asked. "I should have shortened the sleeves."

"It's not the suit," she sighed.

"The varicose veins then. You're ashamed of my legs."

"The bathrobe covers them," she answered.

"What then?"

"It's just that the first thing you always do when you get inside is go in the water."

"I'd feel ridiculous swimming without it," I snapped. "What are you supposed to do at a swimming pool?"

"Other people's mothers don't go in the water."

"I suppose you're referring to Beverly's mother. I personally know she wears a girdle under her bathing suit and has enough foam rubber in her bra to keep eighteen seamen afloat in a tidal wave."

"She's got a neat tan," said my daughter.

"She's the type who tans when she hangs up Christmas tree lights," I snarled. "Besides, I don't trust a woman who sits around the pool reading the *American Journal on Tooth Decay*."

"Look," she said flatly, "I'm going to sit with some of my friends."

"Wonderful," I said. "When I am ready to go I'll flash my compact mirror into the sun and spit three times into the wading pool."

As I smoothed out my towel, I saw my son stroll by.

"Hi, Junie," I said cheerfully.

"Mom!" he said between clenched teeth. "The guys will see you. And don't call me Junie."

"It's your name, isn't it?"

"Other guys' mothers just say, 'Hey, you.'"

"I'll watch it."

"Boy, I bet they'll think I'm some creep talking to my mother."

"Why don't you tell them I'm a far-sighted movie fan and thought you were Paul Newman."

He made his exit.

It must have been several hours before I felt a shadow over my towel. It was my two teen-agers.

"Hey, Mom, we want to get something cold to drink. Where's the money?"

I brought myself up to one elbow, pulled my dark glasses down to the bridge of my nose and scrutinized them coolly, without recognition. "Whatsa matter, kids, lose your mother?" I said crisply and returned to my sun bathing.

That's one for St. Joan.

"Bill and I were just sitting in the car rapping."

"You were WHAT?"

"Talking."

# Twenty questions

Next to having my teeth cleaned without a sedative, my second favorite thing is playing Twenty Questions with my teen-age son at one in the morning. It is like carrying on a conversation with a computer with a dead battery.

"Is that you, Roger?" I shout from the bedroom.

"Who do you think it is?"

"What time is it?"

"What time do you think it is?" he answers.

"Did I hear the clock strike one?"

"What clock?"

"The one in the hallway. Did you have a good time at the dance?"

"Dance?"

"You know, the one you went to. Was it jammed?"

"Who told you it was jammed?"

"No one told me," I shouted. "I'm asking. I suppose you got a pizza afterward?"

"How did you know?"

"I can smell it. A pizza sinks into your pores. You can smell it until the next shower."

"You want me to take a shower at this time of night?"

"No. I said when you eat a pizza it sinks into your pores, which you can smell until the next shower."

"What's that got to do with the dance being crowded?"

"Nothing," I sighed. "Do you want anything to eat?"

"On top of the pizza?"

"Then you did have pizza. Did you see Marcia?"

"Marcia who?"

"YOUR SISTER, MARCIA."

"Was I supposed to?"

"You mean both of you were at the same dance and you didn't talk to one another?"

"What's to talk about?" he asked.

"Is that the clock dinging again?"

"What clock?"

"The one in the hallway. Did you let the dog out?"

"Why?"

"I thought I heard something scratching."

"Want me to check it?" he queried.

"Would you see if it's Marcia?"

"What would she be doing scratching on the door?"

"Is it the dog then?" I asked.

"Is that something to call your daughter?"

"What are you talking about?" I asked.

"What are you talking about?" he responded.

"Did you hang up your clothes?"

"Can't I do it tomorrow?"

"Do you know how much I spend in cleaning bills because you don't hang up your clothes?"

"How much?"

"Don't be cute. How late is it?"

"How late is what?"

"The hour. I think you are trying to keep the time from me, aren't you?"

"Why would I want to do that?"

"Because it is late," I said.

"Who said it was late?" he asked.

"Didn't I just hear the clock chime?"

"What clock?"

"Roger! Exactly what time is it?"

He was asleep. He had tricked me again. I had had my Twenty Questions and he had responded with his Twenty Questions. I was wide awake.

My husband rolled over restlessly. "Is that you babbling?" he asked.

"Who do you think it is?" I snapped.

"What time is it?" he yawned.

"What time do you think it is?" I retorted.

"I don't really care," he said and drifted off.

I shook him by the throat. "Wake up! You've got eighteen more questions to ask or you're out of the game!"

"I don't have TIME to clear off the table! They want us bus boys there by FIVE!"

# Parental squares

The saddest teen-ager I ever knew was Stuart Stark, whose parents bridged the generation gap.

I was so sorry for the kid I could have cried. His mom and dad would go around saying things like, "Groovy, wow, uptight and hey, man." They dug their son's records, ate the same breakfast cereal, grew sideburns (not his mother) and protested everything their son protested.

Not only were they a drag to both generations, but they took away Stuart's inalienable rights to play Parental Squares with the rest of the guys.

Parental Squares is a take-off on the old "Can You Top This" game. One boy tells how square his parents are and the next one will try to top him. The first liar doesn't stand a chance. (Not to mention the parents.) It goes like this.

"My dad is so square he still uses words like 'doozy, neato and drip.'"

"That's nothing," interrupts a boy. "We were in a restaurant the other day and my dad called a waitress 'toots.'"

"Listen to this. My dad picked me up at football practice the other night and was wearing knee shorts, dress shoes, white socks and an elastic stocking up to his knee."

"YOUR DAD WEARS SUPP HOSE!"

"Not only that. He has a picture in his billfold of him during the war with his arms around the Andrews Sisters."

"Who are the Andrews Sisters?"

"Who knows? But once I put a fingerprint on it and he almost clobbered me."

"My dad's so square," contributed another voice, "he sleeps in pajamas."

"Mine's so square he hoses down the lawn mower and dries it off so it won't rust each time he uses it."

"Mine saves old anti-freeze from year to year."

"My dad thinks he's a hippie if he doesn't shave on Saturday morning."

"Mine wants me to grow up to be just like the guys in the King Family."

There was a silence before the next round. Poor Stuart just sat there in silence. Then they were off again.

"Do any of your dads wear a belt around their slacks?"

"Are you kidding? I'm surprised my dad gave up wooden buttons on his trousers for zippers. He's so conservative he didn't buy a pullover sweater until last year."

"Has your dad talked with you about sex yet?"

"It was pitiful."

"I feel sorry for 'em."

"Yeah. My dad got so goofed up he had a sunflower seed making time with a blue jay."

"I know what you mean. My dad was so embarrassed he spelled out N-E-C-K-I-N-G."

"I got the squarest dad of anyone here. He was on the phone the other night and said—are you ready for this?—Okey dokey."

"My dad's squarer than that. The other day I said the meat was 'tough' and he made me apologize to Mom."

"Speaking of moms," said another, "does your mom get shook if you wash your hair before you go to bed?"

"My mom's worse," said a small voice. "She washes her hands every time she pets the dog."

"I don't believe it," they giggled. "You should see my mom. She wears a hairnet when the convertible top is down."

"Oh no. What about mine? Every time my hair grows down to my eyebrows she says the same dumb thing, 'I'm going to buy you a dog license.'"

"Does your mom try to stuff a hot dinner down you when you've just had three hamburgers and a double malted after school?"

"Yeah, and does she always tell you how you can't study, listen to the ball game, talk on the phone and chew gum all at the same time?"

"Look, you guys. My mom is really square. When my gym shoes get a hole in 'em and the sole flaps, she throws 'em away."

"Mine's worse," said a tall boy in the rear. "I gotta win the game with this one. My mom is so square that when I said to her, 'Why don't you let it all hang out and you'll feel better?' she sent me to my room, called Grandma and cried for fifteen minutes."

"Parents sure are weird," said one boy. "Wanta play another round?"

"Neh. Let's go play some ball."

Poor Stuart. He doesn't play ball well either.

"*Mother, is it okay if I wear your flowered shift?*"

# TV keepaway

From September 2 to August 31, the kids have control of the TV set. This means we view the complete football, basketball, baseball and hockey schedules, golf opens, bowling and chess tournaments, tennis matches, boxing bouts, track meets, car, stock and horse racing, ski, skating and soap box competitions.

On September 1 from 9:30 A.M. to 11:15 P.M. I can watch any program I want . . . provided it is not pre-empted by an interview with a toothless hockey player's dentist, an aerial replay of the fannies of the Green Bay Packers' defense, a pregame talk with a dog who has disrupted every Cincinnati Reds' home game since 1937, or a documentary on how left-handed bowling shoes are hand crafted.

It is difficult to single out one sport over another, but if I have to name one in my separation suit, it will undoubtedly be football.

Football is the only televised game I know that can be played over the International Date Line and instantly replayed, stop-action played, and slow-motion played in the East the day before it is played in the first place.

It is the only game I know where if you bring in thirteen channels you can turn the dial from 8 A.M. to 11 P.M. and always find a game that is just starting.

It is the only sport I know that has more bowls than the men's room at Ft. Dix.

The object of TV Keepaway is to drive me crazy. Each

viewer drapes himself across the floor, the tables and the sofa. They speak approximately six words a game (none of them to me).

If food is served they will guide it blindly into their mouths, chew and swallow it. If the world were coming to an end, they wouldn't go until after the roundup and final word from Johnny Unitas.

Naturally I have battled TV Keepaway for years. Only last week did I find the answer. Halfway through the game I announced, "How would all of you like for me to serve you dinner here in front of the TV?" No one moved.

"Right on," said one.

"Hey, hey," said another.

"Way to go," said a voice mechanically.

The hands reached out. There was nothing there.

"First," I said setting up the projector and placing a screen at the far end of the room, "I have some film clips of last week's meal that I know you'll want to see. There's the pot roast being lateraled to Ralphie and the pear and cottage cheese salad that you'll notice is a little offside the plate. We were a little raggy in our passing, but now we know where we made our mistakes."

"Come on, Mom. . . ."

"I have a few notes here on tonight's dinner and a few spot interviews with the butcher, our next-door neighbor, Doris, who made the cheesecake, and of course we'll have a couple of you kids comment on what you can expect from the meal tonight."

"Shhhh," they said, signaling for quiet.

"We're going into tonight's meal with a few injuries," I said, "nothing serious. Both our ends are stuffed from predinner junk like potato chips and dip and cookies, so I may have to play them only for a quarter but . . . Oh, and here's our dog, Lucy, who is going to tell us how she feels about the menu tonight."

"Are you finished?" snapped the kids.

"I have barely begun," I said. "I have my predinner lineup to introduce, an interview from the Claxsons who are scouting us before they have us to dinner at their house next Friday and some vital statistics on each member of the family.

"Now, this little casserole I call, 'Instant Replay.' We had it Saturday, Sunday and here it is again on Monday. Here it is in slow motion. Now stop action. Here's a different camera angle. We'll see how much yardage we can get out of it tonight. One of you may even get it down."

"Can't we eat?" asked one of the boys, rolling over on his side.

"Right after I tell you what I've got lined up for half time. I have 384 black olives that spell out Bombeck on a playing field of pizza, a recording of the Galloping Gourmet sharing with us his biggest thrills in the kitchen and a peek into the second half of the meal, plus Table Scrap résumé, Leftover Scoreboard and Belches from the Stands."

"You win," they said, shuffling to the table.

I owe it all to my defense.

# 9
# Teen-age diseases

# Virgin feet

The other day my son's guidance counselor asked, "What do you want your boy to be when he grows up?"

"A pedestrian," I said.

I know I'm a fool for hoping. My son has suffered from virgin feet since he was nine months old. Just after he took his first step, he slumped to the floor in a heap and mumbled, "No, na, knee, noo" (Meaning: Is that all there is to feet?).

Since then he has been wheeled about in buggies, strollers and wagons, supported in papoose-back packs, bicycle baskets, grocery carts and car seats, slung over hips and shoulders and transported on sleds, escalators, gocarts and automobiles.

In all that time he has never had his shoes half soled. Never grown a corn. Never worn a hole in his socks. Never gotten wet feet and had his socks fade. Never tripped over a shoe lace.

The other night he stood in front of me impatiently.

"What's the matter," I asked. "Is the Garbage Can Car Pool running late?"

"I am waiting for you to run me over to the school," he said.

"What for?"

"Practice."

"Practice for what?"

"Track. I am running the mile."

"How far is it to school?"

"About a mile."

"How long does it take you to run a mile?"

"About five minutes, forty seconds," he said proudly.

"Then run it. It would take me that long to find my car keys."

"RUN IT! You've got to be kidding. I can't run a mile to school, then run another mile cross country."

"Why not?"

"It's dumb. It's like going on a Boy Scout hike and not riding in a truck."

"Look," I said, "we've got to have a talk about your virgin feet."

"What about them? They look great."

"They should," I snapped. "They're brand new. They've been propped up on sofas and chairs and tables and covered with $20 shoes for the last seventeen years. Now I want you to start using them again."

"For what?"

"For walking. Think of it, boy. This could open up a whole new world if kids started to walk again. Imagine, walk-in movies, walk-in hamburger emporiums, walk-in banks, walk-in sit-ins."

"I can't do it," he whined.

"Of course you can. You simply stand up straight for balance, put your weight alternately on one foot and then the other and extend one foot at a time in front of you."

He stood up slowly and tried it. "It feels awful," he said. "Couldn't I get a motorcycle or a golf cart until I get the hang of it?"

"You'll never get well if you don't try," I said. "Today I want you to walk all the way to school and back."

Later that afternoon, he came limping back from track practice.

"What happened?" I asked.

"I tried walking," he said falling into a chair. "About halfway I got a piece of gravel in my shoe and I leaned down to take it out. A bicycle plowed into me, cut my knee and bruised my leg. I lost my shoe in a ditch and got a sprained ankle when I fell trying to find it. A car stopped to help and got sideswiped. I was lucky to get out alive. No wonder there aren't any old pedestrians. If you ask me, feet will never catch on."

"Have I ever lied to you?" I said, putting my hand on his shoulder.

"Yes. The time you told me the tooth fairy liked to be paid yearly by check to keep her income tax records straight."

"What about the time before that?" I persisted.

# Money deficiency

My son did not show signs of a money deficiency until he opened his small fist in the nursery and found it was empty. He leaned over to the kid in the next crib and said, "Hey, bub, you wanta buy an ID bracelet practically new?" He has never been without funds since.

When he was three, he was selling our financial statement to neighbors. When he was six he was underselling the Avon lady. By the time he was nine, he was pulling his teeth and peddling them to the tooth fairy faster than his gums could heal.

One Christmas morning, after he had received $200 worth of toys and baubles, he approached his father and said, "I want to talk about my allowance."

His father smiled, "What about every week if I gave you a shiny dime in return for emptying the garbage, cleaning your room (which is almost the same thing) and clearing the table each night for Mother?"

"You don't understand," he said. "I am not applying for the Peace Corps. I am talking about a guaranteed weekly salary of $1.50, with fringe benefits, option to negotiate biannually and 6¾ per cent interest on all money borrowed back by you and Mom."

Oh, how I hated to borrow money from that kid. It was like doing business with the Mafia. When a loan had not been repaid he would circulate through our small dinner party, walk up to his father, kiss him on either cheek and place a small, white carnation in his buttonhole and announce in a loud clear voice. "You have until 11 P.M. to repay the $3 you borrowed for pizza last Thursday."

We'd laugh, of course, saying, "Aren't children too much?" but I wished we had enough to pay him everything we owed.

The real crisis came one day in high school. He came home and said, "I have to have another increase in my allowance."

"I've been meaning to have a talk with you," said his father. "Your mother and I have decided we can no longer afford a teen-ager. We are paying you to shine your own shoes, pass English, take a laxative, keep your feet off the coffee table, close your mouth when you eat, stand up straight, be pleasant to your aunt Clara, feed your own hamster, eat a good breakfast, change your shirt and let us use our own phone. The next thing you know you will ask us to pay you to breathe."

"What are you suggesting?" asked our son.

"I am suggesting that you think about a job," said his father.

"Doing what?" he asked.

"That is up to you," said his father. "But if I were you I would begin to take stock of myself. At your age you should be able to contribute something unique to the job market. Think about it . . . perhaps you could do something mechanical."

"Come to think of it," he mused, "I was the only guy at camp who could light a match on his zipper."

"Or maybe something musical," said his father. "A lot of boys today are making a bundle. . . ."

"As a matter of fact, there's a group of us in study hall who can do the Hail Mary in belches." He grinned.

"Or something in an office. Your mother has an orderly mind."

"Yeah. I did have the idea to sleep with all my clothes on to save time in the mornings."

"Or maybe something in law enforcement. Have you thought about that?"

"Sure. Did I tell you I can hang my head out of the car window and make a noise just like a siren? Sometimes three or four cars pull off the highway."

"Perhaps sales is your answer. Maybe you have a hidden talent for selling things."

"Remember the garage sale Mom had and I sold the garage in the first five minutes?"

"Look boy," said his father irritably. "What exactly are your talents to date?"

"I ate twenty-two hot dogs once, packed fifteen boys and a fat cheerleader into a Volkswagen, recited *Hamlet* in pig Latin, did a great impersonation of Warren G. Harding and made a Christmas tree out of x's in typing class."

"That's it?" asked his father, his shoulders slumping.

"What ya expect? I'm only a high school boy."

"Do it again," said his father.

"Do what?"

"Breathe in and out. It isn't worth ten bucks, but everyone has to start somewhere."

*". . . Plus half of next week's allowance is $4.50, minus the change from Colonel Sanders makes it $3.75 and the $.60 I paid the paper boy brings it to $4.35."*

*"HE flunked freshman math?"*

# Convenient hearing

"*Tell it like it is, Mom.*"

The first time I observed my son with a case of Convenient Hearing, I thought he had been smoking old gym shoes.

I had called him six times to come to dinner. There was no response. Finally, I went directly to his room. He was sitting on the register in a fetal position. The record player was going full blast (Mr. Wonderful and the Electric Pimples). The television set was up to its aerial in decibels. He had a transistor cord in one ear and a telephone receiver in the other. He was teasing a yapping dog with a sock between his toes.

I pulled all the plugs, hung up the phone, silenced the dog and demanded, "Why didn't you answer me when I called?"

He looked up slowly, made a peace sign with his fingers and said, "You know I can't hear you with a war on."

What I had suspected was true. My son heard what he wanted to hear with maddening inconsistency or regard to an individual's sanity. He tuned on or tuned out when he felt like hearing.

There were many incongruities.

He could not hear the phone ring when he was leaning on it and you were in the shower.

If it was a girl calling for him, he heard it before it even rang.

He could not hear the dog scratch when he wanted in or out.

He could hear his buddies "lay a patch" twenty minutes away from the house.

He could not hear you ask him to take out the trash when your lips touched his ear.

He overheard your discussion of his report card when you talked in a whisper in the northeast corner of the garage.

He could not hear his alarm clock in the morning.

He could hear football plays whispered in a windstorm by a quarterback with a lisp and all of his teeth missing.

My neighbor Maxine was puzzled by our case of Convenient Hearing.

"How do you communicate?" she asked one day over coffee.

"We don't," I said. "My son has only spoken four words to me all year."

"What were they?"

"It was last April. I was separating some eggs for a cake. As I dumped the yolk from one shell to another, I miscalculated and the egg slid down the counter top, along the cupboard and onto my new kitchen carpet. My son was standing there watching. He looked at me and said, "Way to go, Mom.""

"That was it?"

"I was thrilled," I said. "I didn't think he even knew my name."

"I don't see how you can raise him when you don't talk," she sighed.

"There are ways," I said. "There's the old bumper-sticker-with-the-message trick. I hang homemade posters and stickers around his room reading 'HELP THE ECONOMY—TAKE A LEFTOVER TO LUNCH!' or 'STAMP OUT POLLUTION IN YOUR AREA—SEND YOUR GYM SHOES OUT OF STATE.' Of course, there's the ever-popular, 'DON'T LET YOUR MOLARS BE DROPOUTS: SEE YOUR DENTIST AT 1:30 THURSDAY.'"

"Oh good grief," she said, "does it work?"

"Most of the time. Of course, we have to get drastic on occasions and buy time on local rock stations to get through to him. This is how he found out we moved last April."

"I don't see how you have the patience to talk all the time to a boy who only listens at his own convenience."

"The beautiful thing about Convenient Hearing," I said, grinning, "is that it can be contagious. I can catch it too, you know. Like the other day, I was vacuuming the kitchen. The dryer buzzer was going off, the washer was pulsating, my favorite soap opera was on television and the disposer was grinding up chicken bones. My son came out and yelled, 'Hey Mom, you got $2?'"

I didn't move a muscle.

"Mom, did you hear me?" he shouted. "I need $2. Where's your purse?"

Finally, he unplugged all my appliances and put his face in mine. "Are you deaf?"

I made the sign of the Women's Liberation fist and cross and said, "You know I can't hear you while I'm being liberated."

# Prom fat

*"No dinner for me. I'm on a DIET!"*

Prom Fat is not a disease for all seasons. It manifests itself in teen-age girls two weeks before the prom. Not three, not one, but two weeks.

It is only then that the female species drops her elastic jeans, shinnies out of her bulky sweater, stands in front of the mirror and cries, "What happened?"

Her concern turns to hysteria in the fitting room as she shops for her prom gown. "It's no use," said my daughter, slumping to the floor. "I've looked everywhere and I can't find it."

"Find what?" I asked.

"My waist. It's gone. It was there last fall when I marched with the drill team. I remember. I tucked my blouse in it at that spot and my skirt had a waistband on it."

"It's here somewhere," I said, turning her around slowly. "We just have to find it. Try sucking in."

"I am sucking in," she said.

"This is ridiculous. All we do is look for the narrowest part of your body."

"That's my bust."

"Oh. Well then, bend over and I'll mark the crease."

"It's no use," she said, pulling on the jeans. I have a clear-cut case of Prom Fat. Let's buy the size 7 and I'll diet down to it."

In the two weeks that ensued she was to try the following "local" diets.

### CINDY'S MIRACLE DIET

A soft pretzel every three hours (mustard optional)
No water. Repeat. No water.
("What happens when you drink water?" I asked. "You
float around the world in eighty days.")

### LUCILLE'S EAT LIKE A FLY DIET

Sugared dougnuts (all you can eat)
Jelly buns (all you can eat)
Cakes and cookies
Any leftovers you can pick up.
("Flies exist on this," said Lucille, "and you never saw
a fat fly, did you?")

### ELSIE'S EAT AT SCHOOL PLAN

Eat in the school cafeteria for five days. This not only
eliminates your consumption of lunch at noon, it destroys
the taste buds for the other two meals.

### IRENE'S DESPERATION DIET PACKET

1 breath mint every three hours
(An 8×10 glossy of Mama Cass pasted on the refrigerator
door.)

BARBARA'S BANANA DIET

8 bananas a day
8 glasses of water
(A spare tire hanging from a tree in the back yard to swing from.)

It was two days before the prom. True to her promise to herself, my daughter had shed eight pounds. She looked like Vincent Price, but she had indeed conquered Prom Fat.

On the night of the dance, she ate only her eight bananas and drank eight glasses of water. It worked. The ball gown slid over her hips with ease. The waist had returned. The jeweled belt encircled it like slim fingers.

The next morning I went to her room for the details.

"How did it go?" I asked excitedly.

"It was the most wonderful prom I have ever seen," she said. "There were little jars of soaps and perfumes around the table. There was an attendant who gave you a towel when you washed your hands and when the door opened the music was fabulous."

"What do you mean when the door opened?" I asked cautiously. "You sound like you're describing a rest room."

"I am," she said, "I was there most of the evening. What with the water and all. Besides, I felt faint."

"You mean you spent your entire senior prom in . . . the john?"

"Would it make you feel better," she said, "if I told you I had the smallest waist in the room?"

# 10

# The rise and decline of the parental smarts

"You don't know how many votes this state has in
the Electoral College?
Gosh, Mom, ANYBODY knows that!"

There are several theories on how parents can survive the intelligence of their teen-agers.

1. They can bury them at twelve and dig them up again when they are twenty. (Some feel this is too soon.)

2. They can leave town and bequeath the kids to a recording that says, "Same to you, fella."

3. They can up the cocktail hour to ten-thirty in the morning.

There was a time when the respect and trust my children had for me would have made you sick to your stomach. They believed I could blow on a red traffic light and make it turn green. They believed I told Louis Pasteur, "Keep the refrigerator door closed, dingdong, or the milk will sour." They believed I could knit a broken leg just by blowing a kiss on it. I was riding the crest of the Smarts. Then I reached thirty-five and something happened.

One morning I woke up and didn't know the batting average of Johnny Bench or the formula of the rocket-fuel used in the Apollo 11. I didn't know who invented the folding chair or how to say, "My zipper is stuck," in French.

I overheard my children having a conversation about me one afternoon in the kitchen just after I had written a note for my youngest admitting him to class.

"Bet I know what Mom wrote on your note," smirked my teen-age daughter.

"Bet you don't," he challenged.

"Bet I do," she retaliated. "I'll bet she said you had an upset stomach."

He peeked in the note and then looked astonished.

"That's right," he said. "How did you know?"

"You cluck," she said. "For the last ten years we've had nothing else but upset stomachs."

"How come?" he asked innocently.

"Because," she grimaced, "Mom can't spell diarrhea."

"Just a minute," I said coming into the kitchen, "that is just not true."

"Then how do you spell diarrhea?" asked my son.

"Diarrhea is not on trial here," I said. "You have questioned your mother's intelligence. I know a lot of big words like enzyme, psoriasis and Platformate."

"You're out of it, Mom," said my daughter. "The world is changing. Schools are changing."

"I suppose you think I went to a school where they made license plates," I said sullenly.

"No," she said. "It's not the type of school you went to. It's what you were taught. I'll bet you don't even know what an enrichment program is," she chided.

"Are you serious?" I laughed. "Fred Fronk used it on his lawn last year and he's the only one in the block without crab grass. Of course, I offered to send our dog over. He could tell him a thing or two about enrichment."

"Mom, that's exactly what I am talking about. When you went to school you had only one teacher. We have teams of them. We have a new math . . . in the city experiences . . ."

"I know all about the in the city experiences," I said. "Joan Fontaine had one of those with Joseph Cotten on the late show two nights ago."

"That's another thing," she said. "You had no foundation at all for sex education. I cannot possibly imagine how you and Dad managed on your wedding night."

"Are you insinuating I went to my wedding bed armed only with a white apron, matching headband and recipe for divinity fudge?"

"I am insinuating that you couldn't have been too sophisticated about sex when you insisted they mail your marriage certificate in a plain, brown envelope. I worry about us sometimes, Mom. Lately, we can't even have a meaningful dialogue to initiate the feedback which is so grossly needed."

I walked to the utility room. Kids sure could make you feel rotten. She made me feel as if I wasn't important . . . as if my life was meaningless and drab . . . as if I had mentally deteriorated . . . as if housework did not stimulate me. I grabbed a dryer full of socks and said aloud to myself, "Black with black, green with green, gold with gold, brown with brown, one white, two white, a bluey here, a bluey there and three left over until next week."

I stopped short. Maybe I was out of touch. Last week when someone mentioned anthropologist Margaret Mead, I not only thought she was a foot doctor, I recommended her to three of my friends. And the week before that at a party when someone mentioned Taylor was touring Vietnam, I asked, "Is Burton there with her?"

Was it possible I was not maturing mentally with my teen-age children? Anything was possible with a woman who fed socks two by two into an airtight washer and came out every week with three odd ones left over. I had to try to keep abreast of the times. It wouldn't be easy. I would have to make an effort.

That evening my daughter came into the house and shouted, *"Bonjour, Maman. Comment ça va?"*

"Volkswagen and Maurice Chevalier to you too," I answered, grinning.

"What have you been doing all day?" she asked, opening the refrigerator door.

"I'm reading *Forever Amber* again. This time I'm going to finish it."

"Good," she said. "By the way if you'll promise not to go into convulsions, I'll tell you something funny that happened at school today."

"I promise." I giggled, anticipating a meaningful dialogue and feedback with my teen-ager.

"Well," she smiled, "you remember Debbie Smirkoff? Well, she came to class late today (giggle) and Father Sullivan was subbing for Mrs. Tarkeny (nose snorts and uncontrollable laughter)."

"Oh that is funny," I said.

"That's not the funny part," she said, doubling over and wiping tears of laughter from her eyes. "Father Sullivan looked at Debbie and said (this is too hysterial for words!), he said, 'Well, Debbie, where's Hank?' Everybody broke up!"

I sat there waiting for the punch line.

"Didn't you get it, Mother?"

"Of course I got it," I said. "I'm ready to burst on the inside, but you made me promise not to laugh."

"I don't think you got it at all," she said. "If I have to explain that Hank and Debbie are steadies and wherever there's one, there's the other, then it just isn't funny."

"You think I didn't know that?" I asked defensively.

"I think you ought to get out more. Like Biffy's mother, Barfy. She's on a thousand committees and even keeps a calendar to tell her where to go next."

"Why doesn't she ask me?" I mumbled.

"I mean it, Mother, you're becoming stagnant."

"That's not true," I said. "I am going out this afternoon."

"You're kidding. In that outfit?"

"What's wrong with this outfit?"

"When you bend over I can see your girdle. You should wear pantyhose like everybody else."

"I've tried. I can't seem to get a pair to fit me. The only ones that came close were a pair for women 6 feet 2 inches or over, and then the heel bagged at the back of my knee."

"Then maybe you should take off a few pounds," she suggested. "I read the other day where women when they reach forty don't burn energy like they did when they were young. Biffy's mother, Barfy, has an exercise program. She says she would no more miss her exercise program than she would miss putting on her eyelashes in the morning."

"I'll jog to the refrigerator from here on," I said.

"Wicky's mother, Wheezie, is a standing," she said, peeling a banana.

"A standing what?"

"She has a standing appointment at the beauty shop. Everyone thinks she looks like Ali McGraw."

"Oh yes. She's the one with the flat stomach who must have carried her babies in a shopping bag for nine months. Listen, I'm leaving now to go to the meeting of the Jolly Girls."

"Is that the group of girls you went to high school with?"

"Yes, why?"

"Honest, Mom, I'd think you could get involved in some meaningful projects. What do you do at these meetings?"

"First, we answer roll call with our favorite dessert. Then we dispense with the medical round-robin . . . who's pregnant, who's menopausal, who's in surgery and who had varicose veins stripped. We talk about having Paul Newman come and speak to us. He never comes, but it gives us something to hang onto. Then we break for chip dip and a sip of sherry."

"What a waste," she said. "How can you turn your back

on what is going on in the world today . . . like ecology?"

"I'm doing them a big favor, dear, by not getting involved. Remember? I'm the one with the Astro-turf door mat that died."

"What about politics?"

"They don't need me. I've got four bumper stickers . . . all losers on my Edsel."

"Then what about the liberation of women. Doesn't it bother you that pioneers such as Betty Friedan and Kate Millett are out working on your behalf? What will you say when your grandchildren ask what you contributed to your sex?"

"I'll say, 'Honey, your grandfather gave at the office.'"

"Have you burned your bra?" she persisted.

"I scorched it once on the ironing board."

"Have you ever felt remorse that you bore one and one fourth too many children?"

"Many times."

"Then you should pick up the banner of Women's Rights and carry it to the steps of the Capitol!"

"Could it wait until I empty the garbage on the back porch? If I don't it's going to attack me."

Her shoulders slumped. "For a while I thought we were having a meaningful dialogue and feedback," she said.

"It's me," I said sadly, "I blew it."

"I, Mother, not me," she corrected. "You should watch your grammar."

"I'll be home early," I said. "The church is having a conflab this evening."

"Confab!" she said, her eyes rolling back in her head. "I saw it in the church bulletin."

"Conflab," I insisted. "I saw the women."

As I lugged the garbage off the back porch I couldn't

help but hope that my daughter ended the war, adjusted the economy, restored equality, solved pollution, balanced the budget, erased poverty and disease, saved the schools and rendered justice for all before she reached the age of thirty-five.

After that, she won't be able to function as a person, speak correctly, dress herself, laugh, reason, comprehend or spell diarrhea.

"We can teach you French, Spanish, German, Italian. . . . But, I'm sorry, we have no course in Teenagese."

# 11

# Stone age versus rock age

"Sorry, sir, that album has been rated R and cannot be sold to anyone over eighteen."

"Timmy used the car last! Before you turn the key, turn down

. . . the radio."

I have the rather unique distinction of being the only mother in our block to be held captive for a week by two teen-agers and a Woodstock album and to survive.

True, I am not the same woman I was before the ordeal, but they tell me in time I will be able to take walks in the park and pass a wall without pressing my face in the corner.

In the interest of parents everywhere who are concerned with how today's music will affect them, I kept a diary of my seven days of confinement.

It all began on the evening of June 16. My husband was out of town. I was alone with the kids when my face felt feverish, my legs began to ache and my eyes felt as if they were being held in place by thumb tacks. A call to my family physician confirmed my suspicions. "You are sick," he said. "I want you to go to bed and stay there for the next seven days. You have a couple of teen-agers in the house. Let them take care of you." (My doctor also writes humorous one-liners for Henny Youngman and Morey Amsterdam.)

"I am going to bed," I announced to the kids. "I will call you if I need anything."

I might just as well have announced, "I am Jack the Ripper and look at the neat penknife I just got with my new boots." No one missed a beat. One son had his face in the TV set. Another was clicking his fingers in time with a transistor wedged in his ear. My daughter was rigid and glassy-eyed in the middle of two stereo speakers.

Around 11 P.M., the Tower of Babel subsided and I drifted off into a deep sleep.

On the morning of June 17, I awoke to the sound of screeching and banging that nearly took the hair off my head. "What is that?" I asked, sitting up. "Anybody? Do you hear me? What is that?"

Finally, a shadow crossed my door and I threw a lamp at it for attention. (I saw Joan Crawford do that once in a movie when Bette Davis was trying to drive her crazy.)

"What's up?" asked my daughter.

"That noise," I yelled, "what is it?"

"Isn't that neat?" she asked. "It's a new stereo tape. Shifting gears with a bad clutch. Wait'll you hear the flip side. It's a muffler dragging in a quiet zone with a police siren in pursuit. If you don't want to hear that, maybe you'd like to hear the 'Don't Let 'Em Goad Ya into Cambodia Rag?' "

"I have a headache," I said. "Is it possible to turn the volume down a bit?"

"I want you to hear a new group," she said excitedly. "Sweat and His Anti-Perspirants."

"No, really. What about juice and coffee?"

"I don't know them," she pondered. "What label do they record under?"

I turned my face to the window and bit my finger.

Tuesday, June 18. The beat goes on. Fourteen hours of guitar. My head is splitting. I have started to discipline myself by reciting my multiplication tables backward and forward, the alphabet in Greek and the words to "Hut Sut Ralston on the Rillera" and a "Bralla Bralla Suet."

I never realized it before . . . but there are no words spoken around this house. I see people pass the door, lips move and teeth flash, but I never hear a spoken word. Only guitars. Only guitars. Only guitars.

Wednesday, June 19. I awoke in the middle of the night in a cold sweat. Two guitars were fighting over me. I tried to get out of bed, but I couldn't move. One guitar was playing the hysteria of a woman who couldn't get the restroom key from a service station attendant. The other was playing "Happy Days Are Here Again" on a guitar with two strings. No matter who won, I lost. I rolled and tossed and finally sat up in bed screaming.

My daughter rushed to my side and said, "Gosh Mom, you're all uptight. You need something to soothe you." She flipped on a transistor whose decibels nearly paralyzed me, put it under my pillow and left. I spent the night sitting up straight in bed and listening to amplified belches by the Sickies.

Thursday, June 20. I began to reason if I understood young people's music, maybe it would not set my teeth on edge. I threw my lamp against the door again to summon my son.

"Did you want me, Mom?" he asked.

"Yes, what am I listening to?"

"'Happy Interlude.'"

"I know that. It's the only lyric in the entire song. But what does it mean?"

"It's the story of a boy whose father walked out on his mother, an unemployed Avon lady. He is raised strictly Establishment, but one day is busted from his job of writing cigarette ads because he is not smoking the sponsor's product. One weekend, he buys a guitar, writes a hit song, meets a girl who is a loser and finds his father who also hates the war. They live together in Canada."

"Who, the father?"

"No, he's with the State Department."

"The girl?"

"No, she commits suicide."

"The mother?"

"No. I told you this is a happy song. He goes to Canada with the guitar. Want me to turn it up so you can hear the words better?"

"No, please. Maybe if you have a glass of water."

"They must be a new group, but if you really wanta hear 'em, I'll check 'em out."

Friday, June 21. I know now I will never get well. That is not their plan. I am a virtual prisoner surrounded by drums, guitars and vocalists who sound like bullfrogs in labor. I can't remember things any more. Like whether or not I am married. Or if I know how to type. Or if my teeth are my own. I caught myself humming, "Go Tell Aunt Rhodie Her Old Gray Goose Is Dead" and then laughing a crazy little laugh. My daughter came into the room today with a new record.

"What happened to the one you played all day yesterday? 'Happy Interlude?' "

" 'HAPPY INTERLUDE!' " she exclaimed. Then she threw back her head and laughed. " 'Happy Interlude' was written yesterday morning, hit the charts by eleven o'clock, was in the top ten by three in the afternoon and as of nine o'clock last night was a Goldie Oldie. Really, Mother, you've got to keep current with music or you die."

"The thought did cross my mind," I said.

Saturday, June 22. This is my sixth day of listening to Woodstock and assorted rock groups. My cold seems better. I cannot hear the wheezing in my chest any more. Come to think of it I can't hear the phone, outside traffic, doors slam or the dog bark. My husband returned home today. He came to my room and asked, "How can you stand all that noise?"

I smiled. "What boys? Are they fighting again?"

"Not boys, noise," he reiterated

"Well, they certainly should pick up their toys before someone breaks their neck over them."

"Are you all right?" he asked, leaning over.

"Fright? I suppose I am. It's this cold. For the last week I haven't even combed my hair. I'll get it," I said, grabbing the phone.

"Get what?" he asked. "The phone didn't ring."

"A lot of people do that," I said. "They just let it ring twice and hang up."

"I don't believe it," he said slowly, his eyes widening. "What have they done to you?"

"Would you face me as you talk?" I asked. "If you comprehend what I am saying, squeeze my hand twice."

He shook his head. "You poor devil. I never knew you were up here in this room with that racket coming from all three bedrooms."

I watched his lips but couldn't make them out. "I'll get it," I said, lifting the phone. He sat there at my bedside with his head in his hands.

Sunday, June 23. Something is wrong. I awoke this morning to a deafening silence. Where is Joan Baez? Arlo Guthrie? The Jefferson Airplane? The drums? The twangs? The "Oh Bebbie's, the yeah yeahs and the uh uhs."

"We are going downstairs today," I read from my husband's lips.

"Why don't you come right out and tell me," I shouted. "I am deaf. I will never hear Lawrence Welk play 'Yellow Bird' again. I will never hear Lester Lanin ask the musical question, 'Night and Day.' The hearing. It's gone, isn't it?"

"Nonsense," he said, "I just sent the kids out for the day and pulled the plugs on the stereos. In a few days you'll be back to normal again. After all, you've been through quite an ordeal. Just lie here on the sofa and I'll get the doorbell."

I shrugged. "Who are the doorbells? They couldn't be much if they're not on the charts."

"Turn up the volume! It's the mini-bike solo!"

# 12

## "Why don't you grow up?"

"I'm not CRYING, dear. I was just getting rid of a few of
these old things and some dust got into my eye."

"Why don't you grow up?"

If I said it to them once I said it a million times. Is it my imagination or have I spent a lifetime shutting refrigerator doors, emptying nose tissue from pants pockets before washing, writing checks for milk, picking up wet towels and finding library books in the clothes hamper?

Mr. Matterling said, "Parenting is loving." (What did he know? He was my old Child Psychology teacher who didn't have any children. He only had twenty-two guppies and two catfish to clean the bowl.) How I wish that for one day I could teach Mr. Matterling's class. How I would like to tell him it's more than loving. More than clean gravel. More than eating the ones you don't like.

Parenting is frustration that you have to see to believe. Would I have ever imagined there would be whole days when I didn't have time to comb my hair? Mornings after a slumber party when I looked like Margaret Mead with a migraine? Could I have ever comprehended that something so simple, so beautiful and so uncomplicated as a child could drive you to shout, "We are a family and you're a part of this family and by God, you're going to spend a Friday night with us having a good time if we have to chain you to the bed!"

And a plaintive voice within me sighed, "Why don't you grow up?"

Parenting is fearful, Mr. Matterling. You don't know how fearful until you sit next to your son on his maiden voyage behind the wheel of your car and hear him say, "My Driver's

Ed teacher says I've only got one problem and that's every time I meet a car I pass over the center line."

And you worry. I worried when they stayed home. ("Suppose I get stuck with my son and have to feed him on my Social Security check?") I worried when they were gone. ("If the stuffed animal is missing from her bed, that's it. She's eloped!")

I worried when they talked to me. ("Mary Edith started taking WHAT?") I worried when they didn't talk to me. ("This is your mother and what do you mean Mother who?")

I worried when they dated a lot. ("They're not meditating in the Christian Science reading room until 2 A.M., Ed.") I worried when they didn't date. ("Maybe we should try a sixteenth of an inch padding.")

I worried when their grades were bad. ("He won't be able to get into karate school with those marks.") I worried when their grades were good. ("So swing a little. You wanta spend the rest of your life reading William F. Buckley and basting your acne?")

I worried when they got a job. ("She looks so tired, and besides it could bring back her asthma attacks.") I worried when they didn't get a job. ("Mark my word, he'll take after your brother, Wesley, who didn't get a paper route until he was thirty-three.")

And a tired voice within me persisted, "Why don't you grow up?"

Parenting is pain, Mr. Matterling. And disappointment. The first time I leaned over to kiss my son good night and he turned his back to the wall and said, "See ya." The first time I sat in the pouring rain for four quarters (and a thirty-minute half-time Salute to Railroads) and got chewed out for being the only mother there with an umbrella.

The first time they hit me with, "I'm not going to Grandma's. It's boring." The first time they ignored me on Mother's Day and explained coldly, "It's your fault. You didn't give us our allowance this week."

The first time they left the house and forgot to say, "Good-bye."

And the anger and the resentment came, Mr. Matterling. You forgot that part. The nights when I Freudianly set the table for two. The days when I felt like a live-in domestic. Days when I felt like sending Betty Friedan a cigar and the kids to my favorite charity. (Or my unfavorite charity.) Days when I beat myself to death with my own inadequacies. What kind of kids am I raising who would let a hamster die from starvation? What kind of kids would snicker during the playing of "The Star-Spangled Banner?" What kind of kids would tell you with a straight face they inherited a world less than perfect? What kind of kids would have a water fight in church . . . WITH HOLY WATER YET!?

"Grow up, won't you?"

And the days of compassion. These were the most agonizing of all. When the tenderness I felt for my children swelled so that I thought I would burst if I didn't cradle them in my arms.

This half child, half adult groping miserably to weigh life's inconsistencies, hypocrisy, instant independence, advice, rules and responsibilities.

The blind date that never showed. The captaincy that went to a best friend. The college reject, the drill team have-nots, the class office also-rans, the honors that went to someone else. And they turned to me for the answer.

And the phone was ringing. I was worming the dog. My husband had to be picked up in ten minutes. There was cake in the oven, a brush salesman at the door and I mumbled some tired chestnut about Abe Lincoln and his thousand failures but how late in life he won the big prize. And then, almost sanctimoniously, I admonished, "That's part of growing up and why don't you?"

And there were joys. Moments of closeness . . . an awkward hug; a look in the semidarkness as you turned off the test pattern as they slept. The pride of seeing them stand up when older people entered the room and saying, "Yes, sir" and "No, ma'am" without your holding a cue card in front of them. The strange, warm feeling of seeing them pick up a baby and seeing a wistfulness in their faces that I have never seen before. And I said to myself . . . softly this time, "Why don't you grow up?"

I shall never forgive Mr. Matterling for not warning me of the times of panic. It's not time yet. It can't be. I'm not finished. I had all the teaching and the discipline and the socks to pick up and the buttons to sew on, and those lousy meal worms to feed the lizard every day . . . there was no time for loving. That's what it's all about, isn't it? Did they ever know I smiled? Did they ever understand my tears? Did I talk too much? Did I say too little? Did I ever look at them and really see them? Do I know them at all? Or was it all a lifetime of "Why don't you grow ups?"

I walk through the house and mechanically shut a refrigerator door that is already shut. I stoop to retrieve a towel that has not fallen to the floor but hangs neatly on the towel rack. From habit, I smooth out a spread that is already free of wrinkles. I answer a phone that has not rung and with a subtlety that fools no one, I hide the cake for dinner in the oven.

And I shout, "WHY DON'T YOU GROW UP!"

And the silence where once had abounded frustration, fear, disappointment, resentment, compassion, joy and love echoes, "I did."

*"Didn't Grandma used to be taller?"*

ENJOY EVERY STAGE AND EVERY AGE .

# THEY ALL PASS TOO QUICKLY!

# I LOST EVERYTHING IN THE POST-NATAL DEPRESSION

*Illustrated by Loretta Krupinski*

To Bill, who said,
"Whatya been doin' all day?"

# Ironed
# Sheets
# Are a
# Health
# Hazard

Before you read this book, there are a few things you should know about me.

I consider ironed sheets a health hazard.

Children should be judged on what they are—a punishment for an early marriage.

There is no virtue in waxing your driveway.

Husbands are married for better or worse—but not for lunch.

Renaissance women were beautiful and never heard of Weight Watchers.

Mothers-in-law who wear a black armband to the wedding are expendable.

Missing a nap gives you bad skin.

Men who have a thirty-six-televised-football-games-a-week-habit should be declared legally dead and their estates probated.

For years, I have worked at being a simple, average housewife. I am ready to face the facts. I'm a loser. Excitement for me is taking a Barbie bra out of the sweeper bag. Fulfillment is realizing I am the only one in the house who can replace the toilet-tissue spindle. Adventure is seeing Tom Jones perform and throwing my hotel key at his feet (only to discover it's the key to my freezer).

Would it shock you to know that as an average housewife I have never been invited to an aspirin lecture? You know the commercial I'm talking about. There's this ratio-balanced roomful of people sitting around finding out everything they've always wanted to know about aspirin but were afraid to ask.

"Can I drive a car after taking aspirin? Can I take aspirin with other medication? What are the ingredients of aspirin?" I worry about me. I don't want to know anything about aspirin.

After twenty-three years of marriage, you would have thought that once during that time some stranger would have called and asked me what laxative I use. My kids never tell me what the dentist said. My husband never smells his shirts and smiles. We rarely spend an evening sitting around reading the ingredients on dog-food cans. And I can't tell you when was the last time my husband offered to shampoo my hair.

I was telling my neighbor, Mayva, how commercials had evaded me and she said, "You ninny, let me see your handbag."

I opened it to reveal the usual collection of women's junk.

"That's your problem," she said. "You'll never get into a commercial traveling like that." She opened her purse. In it was a large bottle of Milk of Magnesia ("You never know when you are going to sit on a park bench with someone who needs a coating on their stomach."), a package of breath mints, a pound of Mountain Grown coffee, a hair spray, a bottle of dishwashing detergent, a compound to soak your dentures, a can of floor wax, a room deodorizer, and two rolls of (whisper) toilet paper.

"If you want to be a normal, average housewife," she said, "you've got to be ready for 'em."

Yesterday, I knocked on Mayva's door. "Guess what?" I said. "It worked. I almost got in a commercial. I was in the supermarket and I was approached by this man who wanted to know what laundry soap I used. I opened my handbag and showed him this big box. He was pleased as punch. He said, 'What would you say if I told you I'd give you *two* boxes of an inferior brand for this one?' I told him I'd say, 'You're on, Barney!' "

"You blew it," said Mayva softly.

"I'm afraid you're right," I said.

I suppose I should be depressed, but I have a theory there are some things in this life you cannot control. It's psychological defeat. No matter what you do you cannot win.

Take my son. The other day I dropped him off at the tennis court and as his opponent walked over to introduce himself, my son froze. After the boy left, he slumped to the bench, holding his head between his knees. "Did you see him, Mom?" he asked miserably. *"He was wearing a sweat band."*

I could have cried for him. Any fool knows sweat bands always finish first. I wanted to comfort him, but in my heart, I knew the outcome. He was psychologically defeated.

I know. I was defeated for the title of Miss Eighth Grade Perfect Posture when I saw Angie Sensuous was a finalist. Angie was never carried in a fetal position. She was born sitting upright.

I knew I had blown the presidency of the Forensic League when I walked out on the stage dragging a piece of toilet tissue on my left shoe. I knew I could never shape up when I walked into the YWCA exercise class dressed in faded pedal pushers and knee-length Supp-hose when the rest of the class had leotards.

Don't ask me how you know. You just do. Your dog will never get well when you take him to the vet and all the other dogs have rhinestone collars and leashes and yours has a fifty-foot pink plastic clothesline around his neck.

You know your day is lost when you go into town and the elevator operator takes you straight to the basement budget store without asking.

You know instinctively that you will never get a hundred-dollar check cashed when the button falls off your coat. I always loved Fannie Flagg's remark that she could have won the Miss American pageant, but she got the wicker chair in the bathing suit competition. She knew.

I try, but somehow I am always the woman in the wrong line. Lines are like a foreign language. You have to know how to read and to translate them. What looks to me like a thirty-second transaction invariably ends up as a ten- or thirty-minute wait.

I am always behind the shopper at the grocery store who has stitched her coupons in the lining of her coat and wants to talk about a "strong" chicken she bought two weeks ago. The register tape also runs out just before her sub-total.

In the public rest-room, I always stand behind the teen-ager who is changing into her band uniform for a parade and doesn't emerge until she has combed the tassels on her boots, shaved her legs, and recovered her contact lens from the commode.

In the confessional, there is only one person ahead of me. A priest. Now who could be safer following a priest into the confessional? Anyone but me. My priest has just witnessed a murder, has not made his Easter duty since 1967, and wants to talk about his mixed marriage.

At my bank the other day I cruised up and down a full five minutes trying to assess the customers. There was the harried secretary with a handful of deposit slips. I'd be a fool to get behind her. At the other window was a small businessman with a canvas bag of change. I figured he had probably drained a wishing well somewhere and brought three years of pennies in to be wrapped. In the next line was an elderly gent who seemed familiar with everyone. He was obviously going to visit his money and his safety deposit box.

I slipped in behind a little tyke with no socks, dirty gym shoes, and a Smile sweatshirt. He had to be a thirty-second transaction.

The kid had not made a deposit since the first grade. He had lost his passbook. His records were not in the bank's regular accounts but were in the school section. He did not know his passbook number or his homeroom teacher's name, as she had been married near the beginning of the school year. Each of 2,017 cards of the school's enrollment had to be flipped. He deposited twenty-five cents.

He hesitated as he looked at his book, noting he had made fifteen cents in interest. He wished to withdraw it. As he was only old enough to print, he needed his mother's permission. His mother was called on the phone, which took some time, as she was drinking coffee at a neighbor's home. She said no.

He then wanted to know if he could see where they kept his money and if he could have one of the free rain bonnets they advertised. He asked directions to a drinking fountain and left— twenty-three minutes later.

I am psychologically defeated when I try to take one of those tests in a magazine to find out if I am a fit housewife and mother and I can't find a pencil in a six-room house. And when I do finally tally up my score, I discover I am not suited for marriage and motherhood, but have the aptitude and attitude for being a nun who drops out of the convent to sing and tap dance and make hit records.

Sometimes I don't know what's the matter with me. I find myself sitting around admiring weak kings. I don't seem to have the confidence that working women do. For example, the idea of taking a simple test to renew my driver's license was enough to make me drink my breakfast out of an Old Fashioned glass for a week.

I was standing in this long line at the Department of Motor Vehicles recently when I noticed the woman in front of me. She seemed just as frightened as I was. Her face was ashen, her eyes fixed, there was no pulse, and she dragged her feet like bowling balls.

I turned to the woman behind me. Either she was (a) wearing petite pantyhose that were crushing her kidneys or (b) she had just got word that her visiting mother-in-law had broken her hip and couldn't be moved for three months.

Me? I was terrified and suspicious of the whole outfit. In fact, I regard the test as a concentrated effort on the part of the Department of Motor Vehicles to get me off the road. I have taken enough tests in my time to look for the hidden words like "always" and "everybody" and "never."

Despite the fact that I had studied up on how many flares I would need to light up my tandem axle truck on an interstate highway at dusk, I was posed instead with the following questions:

"An elderly lady is crossing at an intersection against the light. Does the driver of the vehicle (a) stop suddenly to allow her to cross the street, thus snarling traffic behind him; (b) honk his horn and proceed with caution; (c) swerve and try to miss her."

I must have read that question fifty times. If I stopped, I might cause eight rear collisions behind me. Legally, I had an obligation to keep traffic moving. But if I honked the horn, the pedestrian might have a heart attack, and I would have to live with that the rest of my life. On the other hand, if I swerved, I might just pull into another line of traffic, causing an accident.

I pondered the question a full ten minutes before I asked the officer, "How old is the lady?"

"That's irrelevant," he said.

"I don't suppose you want to tell me where she is going?"

"That's also immaterial," he said.

"Does she have a son in Kansas who hasn't written her in three months?"

"What's that got to do with the question?" he asked irritably.

"Because I've just decided to run the old lady down and keep traffic moving!" I said.

The woman in the pantyhose leaned forward painfully and said, "Me too, honey."

There is absolutely nothing more horrifying to me than to go to a banquet and be separated from my husband and become a victim of the Long Banquet table. You've seen them. They're long, cold tables with 150 chairs lined on either side. Your instructions are to be seated in man-woman, man-woman style. Had I known this was going to be the case, I would have developed the body for it. Too often I have turned to the man on my left only to find him engaged in conversation with a cleavage on *his* left. As I turn to the man on my right, he too is terribly busy talking with a cleavage on *his* right. Looking across the table, I find an empty chair.

For some unexplained reason, it's always the other end of the table that's wild and raucous, with screaming laughter and a fella who plays "Holiday for Strings" on water glasses.

It's not easy having a good time by yourself. Especially if you're boring to begin with. After you eat the four salads around you, clean your silverware, count your fillings with your tongue, clear your throat, correct the spelling of your name on your place card and clean your glasses, it's downhill all the way.

Occasionally, someone about six people down on the same side of your table will wave and you will lean forward dragging your necklace through a mound of mushrooms to wave back.

"How's Sully?" she will pantomime.

You cup your hand over your ear and shrug your shoulders to express deafness.

"How's Sully?" she repeats slowly.

"Wonderful," you shout back.

It is only after you are looking down your bra and wondering how you are going to get the mushrooms out delicately that you realize you have never heard of Sully and besides she was talking to the man sitting next to you.

Any real conversation at a long banquet table is impossible. I have discovered I can say to my dinner partner, "Did you know Ho Chi Minh wore Supp-hose?" and he will look over your head and answer, "Tell Mary. She's perfectly marvelous at faking. Never had a lesson in her life."

I cannot think of anything clever to help stamp out the long banquet table. Yet, I do not want to simplify the problem. If we are ever to survive as a nation, ever to laugh and walk free in the sun once more and help conquer mental health in this country, we must find a way.

I always wish I were one of those women who could let the phone ring and say sorta flip-like, "If it's important, they'll call back."

A friend of mine (?) actually convinced me one day that I could save hours by not answering the phone when it rang. "Try it once," she said, "And you'll never break your neck to answer

the phone again." The phone rang . . . and rang . . . and rang
. . . (I began to perspire) and rang . . . and rang . . . (I paced
the floor) and rang . . . and rang . . . and then, there was
silence.

"You see?" she said. "There's nothing to it. And look at all the
time you saved."

As soon as she left, I called Mother. "I'm sorry I didn't answer
the phone when you called, but . . . What do you mean you
didn't call?"

I dialed my husband's number. "What do you want? I know
I called you, but I am only returning your call, which I didn't
answer when it rang. Oh, you didn't?"

Mayva's cleaning woman said Mayva had gone to town with
her mother-in-law and couldn't possibly have called me.

My mother-in-law in Florida said it was sweet of me to check
in, but she had not placed a call to me.

My publishers in New York said they were fine and it was always nice hearing from me but no one had contacted me that
morning.

The program director of "Happy Bucks for Homemakers" said
that a call to my number that morning had not been made and
that the jackpot still stood at forty dollars.

The principal at the school said they had been meaning to
call me, as my son had been playing in the johns again, but did
not get around to it.

I called my sister to ask if she wanted me and she said . . .
never mind. I phrased the question badly.

I called watch repair only to get a curt, "Madam, we did not
place a call to you, nor will we until your watch is ready to
be picked up."

Through conscientious dialing, I discovered my bank hadn't
called, nor had my insurance man, my Avon lady, any member
of the baseball car pool, or my friendly magazine salesman.

Nor did Sylvia Porter . . . the Governor of Ohio . . . Pauline
Frederick, Roy Rogers, or Dinah Shore. Finally, as I was dialing
in the darkness, my husband sat up in bed and shouted, "For
crying out loud. Put that phone down. What would the President
want with you?"

I guess what I'm saying is I fear change of any kind. Like there was always some comfort in the fact that although murder, rape, robbery, and prostitution have been on the rise in this country for some time, I could always depend on one law remaining, the tags on pillows that read, DO NOT REMOVE THIS TAG UNDER PENALTY OF LAW.

You could walk in the most elegant homes in the world, sink up to your supporters in carpet, drink coffee from bone china, and have domestics falling all over themselves, but there was always that one common denominator: a limp tag flapping under the chair like a piece of dirty underwear.

As a bride, I imagined all sorts of things would happen to you if you ripped the tag off your pillows. The IRS would fine you, Senator Joe McCarthy would put your name on a pinko list under the glass on his desk, and you would be blackballed from joining the VFW. There was some rumor that you would not bear children for seven years, but I doubted that.

One night my husband had a few drinks and threatened, "You know what I'm going to do? I'm gonna go in and rip the DO NOT REMOVE tags from the pillows on our bed." He didn't know what he was saying and a neighbor and I had to physically restrain him.

The other day I read where the Department of Labor, together with the Upholstery and Bedding Advisory Board, have reworded the tag to read,

THIS TAG NOT TO BE REMOVED EXCEPT BY CONSUMER.

Frankly, I don't know what the world is coming to. Today the pillow tags. Tomorrow, we'll be opening asparagus right side up.

Oh, I'm not lily white by any means, mind you. I've done some pretty rotten things in my life. Once, I deliberately left the cover of a matchbook open while I lit a match. Another time when I thought no one was looking I sprayed whipped cream on my strawberries without first shaking the can. In moments of anger, I've even taken the cellophane off lampshades and purposely screwed on lids in the opposite direction of the arrow.

But ripping the DO NOT REMOVE tags from pillows. That's something else. After I read the story, I went to my room and

shut the door. I pulled down the spread of the bed and held the pillow in my arms. Sliding my fingers along the seam I felt the tag. Gently, I wrapped my fingers around it and ripped it off.

At that precise moment, I heard a bolt of thunder, the cat ran under the bed and I saw small feathers oozing out of the seam where I had ripped the label.

I fell to my knees. "Bless me, Ralph Nader. I have sinned."

The world seems to be moving so fast. I know you're not going to believe this, but there has not been a how-to book on sex published in fourteen days. The little fact has made quite a difference in our Wednesday night bridge club. Last night, not one person made mention of the word sex . . . or for that matter even thought about it.

"How's your mother?" asked Maxine breaking a thirty-minute silence.

"Fine," said Mildred, "I finally seduced . . . rather induced her to go to town with me and check out the spring passions."

"You mean fashions," said Maxine.

"That's what I said," said Mildred. "The clothes were a drag, but we did enjoy lunch at a new place on Main Street. If you're interested, they have wonderful David Reuben sandwiches there."

We all looked silently at Mildred who stopped talking and rearranged her cards. Another half hour passed.

"An amusing thing happened to me at the supermarket yesterday," said Maxine. "I was in the express line when I realized I was down to my last sensuous . . . I mean cent."

"What did you do?" asked Mildred.

"Wrote a sex, what else?"

"You're lucky you had your sexbook with you," I said. Twenty minutes went by.

"I hope no one is on a diet," said Fern, our hostess. "I'd hate to contribute to anyone's . . . what is it they call fat people?"

"Obscene," said Mildred.

Ten minutes later, the silence was interrupted by Maxine. "Heavens, what time is it?"

"Eight-thirty," I said dryly.

"Time sure flies when you're having fun," she said.

"Well, it certainly is refreshing to sit around and talk about worthwhile things other than sex," said Mildred. "I have discovered a new dimension to me."

"Well, are we going to talk or play cards?" asked Fern. "Come on Mildred, it's your turn to bed."

"That's bid," I corrected.

"Whatya expect in fourteen days," snarled Fern, "a miracle?"

The sex thing does bug you sometimes. It used to be so simple. Now you have more manuals than a hydraulic truck. Last year, when I became old enough to buy *Cosmopolitan* without a prescription, I was intrigued by their sexy horoscopes. I would read through Aquarius, Gemini, Taurus, and Capricorn and literally blush at what was in store for them.

However, when I reached my own zodiac sign, it was always the same. "A new hair color could get you a cab. From the 10th to the 15th, it might even get you mugged (on a slow night). Stars born under your sign: Minnie Pearl, Wally Cox and Walter Hickel."

This month I opened the magazine and was thrown into shock. My sign read, "Mr. Sex and Vitality will come into your life around the second of the month."

On the morning of the second, I was quivering at what I knew would happen. Arising early, I fixed breakfast, sent the kids off to school and sat down to wait for Mr. Sex and Vitality. At ten, the doorbell rang. It was the garbage man telling me he had a rule about picking up more than five cans. I couldn't question his vitality, but how sexy can a man be who smells like cantaloupe and wilted lettuce at ten in the morning?

At eleven-thirty, as I was eating lunch, the phone rang. The voice at the other end wanted to make a house call and talk to my husband and see if we would like to spend our retirement managing a motel. He didn't sound sexy or vital, but then anyone who could get so worked up wrapping all those bathroom glasses in see-through bags . . .

That evening I stayed dressed just in case Mr. S and V rang my chimes.

"What are you dressed up for?" asked my husband. "You going bowling or something?"

"My horoscope said Mr. Sex and Vitality would enter my life today."

"That reminds me. Did you take my suit to the cleaners?"

"You wanta nibble on my ear or something?" I asked.

"Are we out of chip dip?" he asked absently.

Within minutes, he was dozing in the chair, his paper on his chest, his can of beer balancing precariously on the arm of his chair.

I wondered how Wally Cox, Minnie Pearl, and Walter Hickel made out.

# I Gave
# Him
# the Best
# Year
# of My
# Life

People are always asking couples whose marriage has endured at least a quarter of a century for their secret for success.

Actually, it is no secret at all. I am a forgiving woman. Long ago, I forgave my husband for not being Paul Newman. Those are the breaks. I realized, being mortal, he couldn't possibly understand my dry skin, boot puddles on my waxed floor, hips that hang like saddlebags, and a house that holds for me all the excitement of a disposal plant.

How could he appreciate that my life is like a treadmill with stops at tedium, boredom, monotony, and the laundry room. That is why he comes bounding in each evening with a smile and a report of his day. Last night, for example, he munched on a stalk of celery and said, "I've had quite a day. Worked like a son of a gun this morning with Fred. Then we got in the car and toured an installation north of town. Suddenly I remembered it was Sandy's birthday. You remember Sandy, don't you? (I remember Sandy. She was the one who burnt her bra and five engine companies showed up.) So, we treated Sandy to lunch. By the time I got back to the office, it was time to wrap up. I'm late because I stopped off at John's to see his new boat. What did you do today?"

"I fired my deodorant," I said. When he left the room I mumbled, "Paul wouldn't have been so unfeeling."

"Who's Paul?" asked my eleven-year-old.

Now, trying to explain Paul Newman's mystique to an eleven-year-old is as futile as explaining Dr. Wernher von Braun to Goldie Hawn.

"Paul Newman," I said patiently.

"The guy in *Butch Cassidy and the Sundance Kid?* He rode a neat horse in that picture."

"What horse?"

"How come you're smiling and looking funny?" he asked.

"Like what?"

"Like when you find a quarter in Daddy's chair."

"It's Paul Newman," I shrugged.

"Would you like to be married to him?"

"It has nothing to do with marriage," I said.

"You mean you'd like him to be your friend?"

"I wouldn't have phrased it quite that way."

"He's about as tall as Daddy, isn't he?"

"Daddy who?"

"Boy, ladies sure act silly over movie stars."

"I don't know if I can explain it or not," I said slowly, "but Paul Newman to a tired housewife is like finding a plate of bourbon cookies at a PTA open house. It's putting on a girdle and having it hang loose. It's having a car that you don't have to park on a hill for it to start. It's matched luggage, dishes that aren't plastic and evenings when there's something better to do than pick off your old nail polish.

"Paul Newman, lad, is not a mere mortal. He never carries out garbage, has a fever blister, yawns, blows his nose, has dirty laundry, wears pajama tops, carries a thermos, or dozes in his chair or listens to the ball game.

"He's your first pair of heels, your sophomore year, your engagement party, your first baby. Good grief, boy, he's the Eagle on its way to the moon. Don't you understand that?"

"I don't think so," he said. "Anyway, his horse was pretty neat."

As I passed the window, I saw my reflection. Flats. Head scarf. Daughter's windbreaker with 71 and two stripes on the sleeve. Mixi skirt (long and short). Who was I kidding? With the kind of day I had, I'd settle for the horse.

Like most women, I work at marriage, trying to keep alive the excitement and stimulation that made me marry in the first place. I convinced my husband that I have a friend who, every Friday, carries on a clandestine luncheon with her own husband.

She drives her car into town and he drives his. They meet at some obscure little restaurant, get a table in the rear where they hold hands and stare lovingly into one another's eyes. In the parking lot after their tryst, they kiss good-by and she whispers, "I'll try to make it next Friday."

He laughed until he snorted, "How bored can a woman get?"

"So bored she would meet Walter Brennan without his teeth . . . at McDonald's and go dutch."

"Who do you know who is that desperate?"

"Me," I said. "Every woman has to romanticize her marriage. Why don't we do it?"

"I'd feel like a fool," he said. Then, sensing my disappointment he added, "Okay, I'll meet you at Ernie's Eats next Friday."

I dressed carefully, feeling a bit foolish, yet with a certain sense of wickedness. I parked the car and ran to him. He looked at me intently. "What are you thinking?" I asked softly.

"Did you bring your American Express card? If you didn't we'll have to go to the Beer and Bloat Palace across from the office. They cash checks on Friday."

"You devil you," I countered, "you mustn't say things like that until we're alone."

"What happened to the fender?" he said. "Another parking meter run out in front of you?"

"We do have to stop meeting like this," I said. "Every week I say I am not coming, but when Friday comes I am helpless."

"Are your corns bothering you again? You don't look too good under the eyes. Like maybe you ought to get the load off your feet."

"It's eye make-up, precious. Just for you. Notice anything else different about me?"

"You sewed the button on your coat."

"The perfume, you madcap. I won't wear it again until you promise to behave yourself."

"What'll you have?" he asked, opening the menu. "Unless you're too much in love to eat."

"Are you crazy?" I asked, grabbing the menu. "Make it two

hamburgers, an order of onion rings, a double malt, and banana cream pie."

Naturally, I don't want any recognition or awards, but I've forgiven my husband for a lot of things during our twenty-three-year marriage.

1. I forgive him for not tanning. Actually, I have devoted my entire life to getting my husband tanned. I have basted him with oil, marinated him with lotions, tossed him on all sides, and broiled him to perfection. (Frankly, if I had spent as much time in the kitchen as I spent on him, I'd outdistance the Galloping Gourmet.)

It has all gone in vain. The other day I watched him inch his way out into the sunlight. He was swathed in six beach towels, a pair of dark glasses, and a pair of sandals that buckled to his knees.

"Did you lose your umbrella?" I asked dryly.

"I don't know why it bothers you that I am not tanned," he said, moving his chair to a shady spot.

"It bothers me because you don't look healthy. You look like a ninety-six-pound weakling would kick sand in your face at the beach and yell, "Yea Sicky.""

"When will you get it into your head that some people do not tan," he said.

"Everybody tans," I insisted. "It's just a matter of conditioning!"

"It's not a matter of conditioning."

"Doesn't it make you feel awful to go into a crowded room and have people ask, 'What happened?' "

"Look, just because I do not want to look like an escapee from an elephant burial ground . . ."

"Steve McQueen tans," I said, "and so does Paul Newman. And have you ever seen John Wayne sitting in the saddle with towels covering his arms?"

"What's that got to do with me?"

"They all look healthy. That's what it has to do. Wouldn't you like to walk down the street looking bronze and mysterious? Women would turn and say, 'Boy, does he look healthy.' "

"No."

"Just for an hour or so, let the sun do its thing. You stretch out and I'll pour three cups of oil over you and let you simmer."

From time to time I checked to make sure he was tanning evenly. Later, he came into the house and eased into his clothes.

"What did I tell you?" I laughed. "Already your clothes look better. You should see the contrast between that light shirt and your skin. And your eyes! I never knew they had color before."

Later, as we sat side by side, leafing through a magazine, I tried again. "I know you don't agree with me now, but believe me when I tell you, you are the healthiest-looking man in this doctor's office."

2. I forgive him for that performance he puts on every time he orders wine for dinner. Right away, he's Cesar Romero. First, he makes a circle with the glass under his nose. Then he tilts back his head like he is going to make Jeanne Dixon materialize. Finally, his tongue touches the wine.

The rest of us at the table sit there like idiots waiting for this man who doesn't know a vintage port from last week's Kool-Aid to decide whether or not the wine will meet with his favor or disfavor.

The waiter shifts his weight to the other foot. Finally, Cesar speaks, "A bit more please," he says extending his glass. As my eyes roll back in my head he says, "I've got to be sure."

"You have not the foggiest notion what you are doing," I accuse.

"Why would you make a statement like that?" he asks.

"Because I have that same look on my face when I squeeze melons in the supermarket and I don't have the foggiest notion what I am doing."

"For your information, my dear," he says, wiping a bit of the grape off his chin, "tasting wine is an old tradition that was once initiated to protect kings and queens from being poisoned."

"Where were you when the pot roast was served?" I ask.

As he sits there smacking his lips and wrestling with his decision, another question crosses my mind. How does the waiter know which one to have sample the wine for the rest of the group? The one with the reddest nose? Or the one who looks like he's going to pay the check? Or the Secret Service type who goes around protecting kings and queens?

"By the way," I finally say to my husband, "you've sampled half a bottle. Do you suppose it is safe for the rest of us to have a little wine with our dinner?"

"I sent that particular bottle back," he says.

"You're kidding. Why?"

"Why indeed. You're not fooling around with some little old lady who only tipples at the faculty Christmas party. I've had wine many times before in my home. I ordered them to serve us Lake Erie, 1970, and this time I want to see cork floating around in it!"

3. I forgive him for flunking Campfire in the Boy Scouts. It's amazing how a careless camper will flip a match during a rainstorm and seconds later the entire forest will be in flames.

We will give a party and my husband will "lay a fire," using thirty pounds of paper, a mound of brittle kindling, and a seasoned log with a guarantee stapled on the side. Within minutes, an entire party will be driven into the streets by smoke.

He's the only man I know who had a fireplace with a gas lighter go out on him.

"Why don't you forget the fire tonight?" I said, collaring him before a party.

"Nonsense," he said. "I've got the secret. I just have to use more paper and get it started early. That's the secret. Start it early and get a bed of hot coals. Then, just feed it logs all night."

At 6:30 P.M., he burned the evening paper which I had not read.

At 6:40, he emptied three trash cans into the fireplace and created another small flame.

At 7:05, he emerged from the garage with a wagon full of papers I had been saving for the last three months for the Boy Scout paper drive.

The guests began to arrive.

At 7:45, he burned all the calendars in the house, plus five napkins which he snatched from the guests.

At 7:50, he frantically tore the plastic bags off the dry cleaning in the hall closet and burned a drawerful of brown paper grocery bags I save for garbage.

At 8:05, with the living room snowing with flying fragments of soot, he began emptying shoe boxes and wedging them under the log.

At 9:00, he was reduced to lighting unpaid bills with a match and throwing them in on the smoldering log. I collared him, "Look, Smokey the Bear, will you forget about the lousy fire and pay some attention to your guests?"

"I almost got it," he said feverishly. "Just a few more pieces of paper. He ran to the cedar chest and emerged with the baby books, our wedding pictures, and our marriage license.

At 1 A.M., he grabbed me by the shoulder. "It's going," he said. "It's really blazing. Remember those cereal boxes with only a little cereal left? I threw it away and the boxes did it."

"Wonderful," I said, pulling the covers around my neck. "Now will you put it out and come to bed. We've got a big day ahead of us tomorrow. I'm going to have you committed."

Actually, my husband and I are different in many ways. Our sense of humor is different. I told an amusing story the other evening about Phyllis Diller in which an interviewer asked her if she was a neat housekeeper, like when her husband got up to go to the bathroom did she make his bed while he was gone. She replied, "Make it! I have it sold before he gets back."

My husband frowned and said, "Where would you find someone to buy a bed at that ungodly hour?" Then he retaliated by telling his dog story about the talking dog who played all the big night clubs and the talk shows. "Then one day he got sick and had to have an operation. After that, he couldn't get a job anywhere."

"How come?" asked a woman.

"Because all he did was sit there and bark."

The men howled with laughter until I thought they were going to be sick. The women sat there puzzled.

"Dear," I interrupted, "it wasn't because the dog just barked. It was because all the dog talked about was his operation."

"That's not funny," he said.

"It's not my fault," I countered. "It was your lousy joke."

"If it's my joke, then how come I can't tell it my way? Why would a dog rehash something so painful as an operation. You know what you are, you're sick. I bet if I said the dog sold his hospital bed before he got back to it, you'd have laughed yourself silly."

But being generous, I forgive him for his bad jokes and I even forgive him for being tall. I am 5'2", and he is just under 6'. According to him I get my kicks out of life by moving the car seat up to within three inches of the steering column and leaving it there.

"Okay, you win," he said, staggering into the kitchen and slumping into a chair.

"What are you talking about?"

"I am too weak to fight you anymore. My kidneys have been destroyed by a door handle. I have burns on my neck from being flogged with a shoulder belt. My head is bleeding from a clip by the mirror and I tore my pants on the left-turn signal."

"Is that what you were blowing the horn about?"

"I was blowing the horn because every time I exhaled, my belt buckle pressed against the horn."

"You are upset."

"Aren't you quick? Next year, you may even get tie shoes."

"There is no need for you to be sarcastic."

"That's easy for you to say. You have never tried to fold a pair of legs into a parachute and 'drop' into your own car before. Look at these," he shouted, putting his feet on the table under my nose. "Do you know what these are?"

"They are feet," I said softly.

"That's right. They were never meant to be folded, spindled or mutilated."

"Then why are they forked?"

"Because I have just rescued them from the jaws of the glove compartment. I thought perhaps if I crawled in from the passenger seat I could wind my legs around my neck and then unwind them under the steering wheel."

"What happened?"

"I was attacked by a sun visor and in the skirmish my foot was half eaten by the glove compartment."

"I don't leave the seat up on purpose," I began.

He jumped from his chair. "Oh, but you do. You have never really gotten over not marrying the Hunchback of Notre Dame, have you? Now, *he* could have fit in your mini-car, couldn't he? You'd like one of those cardboard cars whipping around with Barbie and Ken and Midge. Or Eddie Arcaro. You should have married a jockey. Or Mickey Rooney. What a twosome you would have made sitting on your pillows! Or Dick Cavett. Storing a picnic basket under your feet. Or what about that guy on top of the wedding cake?"

I think one of the real tests of a stable marriage is being married to a man who worships at the shrine of burnt food—the backyard chef.

Last spring, we decided to remodel our kitchen. We installed a stove that does everything but burp us, a refrigerator-freezer that coughs ice and defrosts itself, a line of counter appliances that makes humans obsolete, a dishwasher and disposer that eliminates leftovers, and shelves and storage to stagger the imagination.

On the day it was completed, my husband stood in the middle of this culinary carpetland, nodded his approval, then hit for the back yard, where he proceeded to cook our meal in a fetal position over a hibachi, using a bent coat hanger for a fork and a garbage-can lid to hold the salt and pepper.

Most men go through it. It is called the Back Yard Bicarbonate Syndrome, better known to most Americans as the "cookout."

The condition is usually brought about by the acquisition of a new grill, a fun apron that reads, BURNED IS BEAUTIFUL or a neighbor who delights and amazes his guests every weekend with dishes from his new Neanderthal Cookbook.

Somehow you cannot help but admire the courage of these virgin cooks who heretofore thought a pinch of rosemary was something you did when your wife wasn't looking and who considered aspic a ski resort in Colorado.

The big question is how to survive it.

When you are invited to a cookout be sure to check the invita-

tion. If it reads "7 p.m." assume that is the time of arrival. The time you are served may vary as much as forty-eight to seventy-two hours from then depending on:

(a) a confused host who puts the potatoes in the oven and turns on the clothes dryer for 60 minutes;

(b) an emergency visit from the local fire department that got a call that a tire factory is burning;

(c) a group of guests who are all members of the U. S. Olympic Drinking Team and are celebrating their victory over the Russians.

In order to survive a cookout you must also be aware of some of the old myths and clichés.

There's the perennial, "After all, what can you do to a good steak?" This line is often accompanied by a high, shrill laugh and a nudge.

The implication is that it takes very little skill to throw a good chunk of beef on the grill and get it off while still edible.

The answer to this question is obviously, "You can burn it."

Secondly, no cookout is complete without a large, furry dog who hangs around the grill all night. There is a myth that large, furry dogs never take the meat off the grill and run. Unless you have chased a dog through three back yards, a shopping center, and a sprinkler you might be lulled into believing this.

Next, there is the myth about "the couple that cooks together stays married together."

The other night I tripped over my husband who was hunched over his hibachi. "Is that you?" I whispered in the darkness.

"Who did you think it was?" he asked.

"I didn't care. If you hadn't moved I was going to eat you."

"Just a little longer," he said. "Are the guests getting hungry?"

"I think so. They are sitting around watching their stomachs bloat."

"It hasn't been that long."

"Are you kidding? It's the first time I've ever seen my finger-nails grow."

"Just a few minutes and the coals will be ready."

"Do you mean to say you haven't even put the meat on yet?"

"Give them some more hors d'oeuvres."

"It's no use. They're beginning to get ugly."

"Then go check everyone and find out how many want their steaks—rare, medium rare, medium, medium well, and well done."

I left and returned in a few minutes.

"Well?" he asked.

"Thirteen raws. Hold the horns."

"Very funny," he said. "How about the fourteenth guest?"

"He ate his coaster and said that would hold him."

"That tears it," he said. "That's the last time I waste my special barbecue sauce on this group of ingrates."

The survival of the cookoutee hangs solely, however, on how well he is prepared for the outing. Guests should never be without their Survival Kit which should be stocked with:

A flashlight to see what you are not eating.

Bright trinkets and beads to barter with the natives for bits of food before dinner is served.

A calendar to keep track of time.

Sterile face masks to keep from getting high on bug spray.

Dry matches for the host when he admits he was never a Boy Scout.

The other night, after the guests had gone and I was crawling through the grass, retrieving my silverware, my husband said proudly, "Well, it couldn't have been a complete disaster. Evelyn Weard just called and asked for my recipe for barbecue sauce."

I could hardly wait until morning to call Evelyn. "Is it true?" I asked. "Did you really ask for my husband's barbecue-sauce recipe?"

"I certainly did," she said excitedly. "You see, the other night when I dropped a bit of the sauce on my skirt, it didn't spot. In fact, it took a spot out. I made a batch of it this morning and would you believe it, your husband is a genius. His barbecue sauce kills crab grass, took a wad of chewing gum off the dog, the oil stains off the garage floor, and cleans chrome."

"Wonderful," I said. "Just keep it out of the reach of children."

"I know," she said.

My husband and I have produced three children, survived three wars, comforted one another at funerals, and dedicated ourselves to one another through sickness and in health. The other day, I backed out of the driveway, turned too sharply, and hit the side of his car. He was a perfect stranger.

"Where are you going?" I asked as he left his dented fender and bolted toward the house.

"Don't move your car," he said. "I'm going to call the police."

"*The police!*" I shouted. "For crying out loud, I'm your wife."

"This is no time for nepotism," he said stiffly.

I should have known better than to compete with a man and his car. For years, psychologists have been telling us that a man's relationship with his automobile supersedes even sex.

For you women who are skeptics, let me ask you a few questions.

Does your husband have an insurance policy on you that includes no-fault, comprehensive, and is fifty-dollar deductible? Or do you have the basic ninety-six-dollar burial policy that puts you on a public bus and takes you to the edge of town?

Do you have a guarantee for a complete oil change every six months and/or 1,000 miles, whichever comes first? Or do you only visit a doctor's office for major surgery?

Does your husband fly into a rage if he finds someone stuck a candy wrapper in your pocket or a piece of bubble gum on your instrument panel?

Has your husband ever patted you on your trunk and remarked what a beautiful trade-in you'd make?

Does he take you to a restaurant three times a week and instruct the waitress to "Fill her up"?

Does he care if the kids put their feet on your upholstery?

Does he object if your teen-agers drive you all over town?

Would he pay eight dollars to have you towed anywhere?

If you didn't start in the morning, would he stay home from work?

If you answered "No" to any or all of these questions, then you have a four-wheel corespondent in your divorce suit.

As the policeman surveyed our situation, he turned to my husband and said, "Sir, you are illegally parked. Your car should be at least fifteen feet from the edge of the driveway. Are there any witnesses to this accident?"

"Just my wife," said my husband smiling at me.

"I never saw this bum before in my life," I said.

After the policeman had gone my husband mumbled, "Joanne wouldn't have been so unfeeling."

"Who's Joanne?" asked our eleven-year-old.

"Joanne Woodward," said my husband. "I don't know if you'll understand this or not, son, but Joanne Woodward is like shaving at twelve, she's like going to buy a car and having the salesman take you directly to the convertibles. She's like having your mother-in-law allergic to you, and not having to have a belt to hold your suitcase closed.

"Joanne isn't mortal. She never wears hair rollers, never has chenille marks on her face, and never cleans a fireplace without gloves. She doesn't have to stand up to lose her stomach or talk about worming the dog during dinner. Joanne is. . . ."

"Does she ride a horse good?" asked his son.

"I knew you were too young to understand," he said sadly. "But I forgive you and I forgive your mother."

# Talk
# to Me—
# I'm
# Your
# Mother

For the first two years of a child's life you try to get him to talk. For the next ten years you devote your life to getting him to shut up. For the remainder of his life you try to get his lips moving again and sound coming from his throat.

Personally, I have always said if the Good Lord had meant for me to speak in the mornings, He'd have put a recording in my chest and a string in the back of my neck.

I don't understand people who can hop out of bed and synchronize their lips with words to form sentences and communicate ideas. I don't reach this point until after lunch.

I have a basic morning vocabulary of twenty words: "No. I don't care. It's in the dirty-clothes hamper. What's your name? Mustard or catsup? In your father's billfold." There have been no subtractions or additions in twenty-three years.

The other morning I shuffled to the kitchen and mechanically did my thing. My daughter said, "I need to buy. . . ."

"In your father's billfold," I interrupted.

"Where's my favorite V-neck sweater?" said a son.

"In the dirty-clothes hamper."

"Can I wear it?"

"No."

"Then I'll sit by an open window and probably die before lunch."

"Mustard or catsup?" I muttered, holding his sandwich.

"Catsup."

As I opened the sandwich and tried to force the catsup out, the phone rang.

"Hello," said my daughter. "Just a minute. It's for you, Mom."

I shook my head.

"She can't come to the phone now," she said tartly. "She's hitting the bottle."

"What's your name?" I asked my youngest. He told me and I scribbled it on his lunch bag.

"Wilma Whiplash called," said my daughter, pressing a message in my bathrobe pocket. "She'd like to meet you for lunch at the House of Chicken."

I nodded. And all morning I thought about Wilma Whiplash. Who was she? Had I met her and couldn't remember? Was she an old schoolmate? An Avon lady? A program chairman? An editor's wife? One of my children's teachers? A secretary trying to peddle underground pictures of the office Christmas party?

"I'm Wilma Whiplash," said a voice at 1 P.M. at the House of Chicken. "I know you don't know me, but I read your column in the newspaper and figured you'd be a scream at lunch."

"What's your name?" I asked dryly.

"Wilma Whiplash," she smiled. "Your dress is darling. Where did you get it?"

"In the dirty-clothes hamper."

"Ah . . . what are you drinking?"

"I don't care. Mustard or catsup."

"Where do you get all your wild ideas?"

"In your father's billfold," I said numbly.

I felt sorry for her, but it served her right.

Communication has always been a problem among families. We started off with one child who was misunderstood literally. From the day he uttered his first word to present day, no one seems to know what he is talking about.

For some unknown reason, I am the only one in the family who can translate. When he was a toddler, he stood for hours at his father's elbow, shouting, "Me no, na, noo noo," and his father would shrug and say, "What does he want?"

"Well, what do you think he wants?" I'd say irritably.

"He's either telling us the dog hates cold spaghetti, he hates the encyclopedia we bought for him, or he just swallowed his pacifier."

"He is trying to tell you he dropped a cookie down his drawers. I mean how dense can a father be?"

As he got older, things got worse.

"That kid has to have his mouth fixed," said my husband.

"What now?"

"He just told me he has to know all of his bowels by tomorrow because the teacher is having an English elimination."

"He's always had troubles with v's," I said.

"That isn't all he has trouble with. If he goes around talking like that, they're going to put him in a class where he makes recipe holders out of wooden blocks and clothespins all day."

"All he's ever tried to do," I sighed, "is imitate the rest of the family and he doesn't know how to pronounce the words yet."

"I'll say," said his brother. "He told the whole bus the other morning that you were a syndicated Communist."

"And he told everyone his teacher had hubcaps put on her teeth so they would look better," said his sister.

"And he told a client of mine on the phone the other night that I couldn't come to the phone because I was unapproachable. Really, something has to be done. At a football game the other night he yelled out, 'All we need now is one perversion and we win the game.'"

"What's the matter with that?" I snapped. "I told him myself one player had a mucilage separation in his shoulder and another was having trouble with his nymph gland and with the quarterback having a sensuous shoulder, we needed all the perversions we could get!"

You should have seen my family sit up and look at me. I guess it's because I don't lose my temper too often.

Then we have the other extreme of a son who speaks only four words a year. One day as I was separating an egg, the whole thing cracked and slithered to the floor. He looked at me and said, "Way to go, Mom."

My eyes misted. I didn't think he even knew who I was.

I have always been envious of the mothers of children who talk. What an insight they must have into the personality of their child. What good times they must enjoy . . . the intimate laughter . . . the first blush of a shared secret.

Our relationship is a lot like the President and Congress.

"What's that hanging out of your notebook?"

(Shrug shoulders)

"You're having your school pictures taken tomorrow? And what's this one? An insurance form for football? I didn't know you went out for football. What do you play? *When* do you play?"

(Grimace)

"Hey, here's one directed to my attention. They need someone to bake cakes for the ox roast. I think I could manage that."

"That's left over from last year."

"Oh. Here's one. 'Memo to: Revolutionary Troops. Cross Potomac tonight at 7:30 P.M. Bring money. Signed George Washington.' Thought I'd toss in a little humor there."

(Sigh)

"Look here. You're having an Open House. I think I'll go."

(Moan)

Now, if you think things at home are painful for the mother of a non-verbal child, you should try enduring Open House.

No sooner was I in the door than a mother accosted me and asked, "What do you think about Miss Barbie and Mr. Ken in the boiler room? I'm sure your son told you about it, didn't he?"

Then another one approached and said, "I would have known Mr. Brickle just from my son's description, wouldn't you?" (Lady, I wouldn't have found the building if there hadn't been a Boy Scout in the parking lot.)

Finally, "It's a shame you were too busy to come to the Booster's Awards. We thought since your son was on the team. . . ."

As I was ready to make my exit, my son's teacher put a hand on my arm. "I want to talk about your son's problem," she said.

So! It wasn't me. It was definitely a case of a poor, shy boy who couldn't express himself, so he lived in a world of silence.

"Your son can't seem to keep his mouth shut," she said. "He talks incessantly during class, shouts out the answers before there are questions, and is known to his classmates as 'Elastic Mouth.'"

"He's never been what you would call a talker," I confessed. "At home he talks in bulletins. Like the people on television where a husband says to his wife, 'Cold gone?' and she nods and replies, 'Fever's down. Cough disappeared. Feel great!' I mean when he comes home from school, I feel like Ironside interrogating a witness."

It's true. I always try to initiate a conversation by asking, "What kind of a day did you have at school?"

"Bummer."

"There are some doughnuts in the bread box if you want them."

"Dig it."

"Your brother took a bite out of one, but. . . ."

"Gross."

"Who was that boy I saw you walking with?"

"Hard man."

"You like him?"

"No."

"You don't like him. Why not?"

"Comes on strong."

We were having one of our exciting exchanges one night when his father came in.

"Will you listen to him?" I shouted. "If this boy doesn't start communicating, we're going to have to give him injections to keep his throat from drying up."

"He's no Buckley," shrugged his father.

"Are you kidding? I tried lying in the middle of the floor when he came home from school one afternoon just to see if the sight of my lying there unconscious would generate conversation. Know what he did? He leaned over my still body and asked, 'Did *Sports Illustrated* come?' "

"You are going to have to bridge the gap," said my son's teacher. "Cross over into his world and show him you care."

A few weeks later, I broke one of my own house rules. I entered his bedroom. (We were going to wait until he got married and then sell the house.)

He had a notebook before him and was picking his teeth with a ballpoint pen. "What's the greatest threat to man's environment?" he asked suddenly.

"This bedroom," I said, looking around in disbelief.

"People," he amended. "They're careless, and I am writing a paper on how we can help."

"Where do you keep your bed?" I asked, bustling around.

"In the middle of the floor," he said. "It isn't made because I am airing it."

"You've been airing it for three years," I said. "Why have you been sleeping with forty-eight copies of *Sports Illustrated*, a Dixie cup, a hubcap, and eighteen mismated socks?"

"Ecology is a personal thing," he mused. "It has to start with one person at a time. Every candy wrapper is important. Every bottle cap."

"Why are my eyes watering?" I gasped.

"It's the aquarium," he said. "The catfish just isn't doing his job."

I looked at the polluted bowl of water with the pump that gasped and gurgled. Other than the Cuyahoga River in Cleveland, it was possibly the only body of water to catch fire.

"Carelessness," he continued. "I think that's what it is all about. If you could just make people aware of how they are cluttering up our countryside."

"Are you saving those soft-drink bottles for anything?" I asked.

"There's a garter snake in one of them," he said offhand. "Now, where was I? Oh yes, clutter. How about, 'We must all band together and form groups to bring pressures against the Earth Molesters.' How's that?"

"Wonderful," I said. 'Did you know you have gym shoes under your bed that have rusted? A three years' supply of crumpled nose tissue in your sock drawer? A piece of green bread under your pillow? A pre-schooler under your clothes on your chair? A nest in your toothbrush and a towel on the floor of your closet that just spoke to me?"

"Mom," he said, "are you gonna help me with this paper on ecology or talk?"

I guess what it boils down to is that I don't trust anyone under thirty. I didn't trust anyone under thirty when I was under thirty. Particularly, I don't trust children. It isn't that they mean to lie, it's just that by omission or fancy mouthwork they spin some of the most incredible stories since Jack London.

One friend of mine was asked by her son one day whether he

could go on a chartered bus to New York to see a basketball game.

The request seemed reasonable. She asked all the usual questions. "Was it chaperoned? Were there others going? Was it a school function?"

She didn't find out until about fifty-five irate parents called her that her sixteen-year-old, newly licensed son was driving the bus into New York City. He failed to mention that small detail.

With teen-agers particularly, you have to touch all bases. You have to learn to speak and translate obscurity.

"May I go to a party Saturday night?" she will ask.

"Who is giving it?" asks the parent.

"One of the girls." (Your own daughter)

"At a house?"

"Yes." (Yours)

"Are the parents going to be there?"

"Probably." (Providing the parents can drive from Miami, Florida, to Cleveland, Ohio, in three hours)

"Who else?"

"Just some of the kids from school." (There are five schools in the entire district)

"How many?"

"Twenty or thirty." (Couples)

"I assume it will break up early."

"Definitely." (With a little help from the local police)

I could write an entire book on the incredible stories my children pass on to me as gospel. One told me about a boy he met at camp who was closely related to Howard Hughes. However (here comes the zinger), since Hughes had disappeared he didn't get his allowance, and for twenty-five cents he would swallow a fly. My son believed him.

On another occasion he told me of a classmate (seventh grade) who flew his own airplane and was hijacked to Minneapolis one weekend. My son believed him.

He approached me in the kitchen one day and asked, "What day is it?"

"Tuesday," I said. "Yesterday was Monday and tomorrow is Wednesday."

He cocked his head to one side and asked, "Are you sure?"

They say communication at the dinner hour is the most important part of child rearing. When our table began to sound like F. Lee Bailey's summation, we decided to do something about it.

"We are both at fault," I said to my husband. "Why don't we knock off picking at the kids while we eat. No chewing around about bicycles left outside to rust.

"No nagging about how they have the table manners of a weak king.

"No confrontations about report cards, dirty rooms, or bringing home the car with the tank empty.

"No harping about the garbage stacked up on the back porch, whose turn it is to do dishes, and who has the scissors in their room. We've got to stop criticizing them while they eat or they're going to have ulcers."

At dinner that night things were painfully silent.

"We had an amusing speaker at Kiwanis today," said my husband, "who spoke on nuclear survival."

The kids chewed in silence.

"You'll never guess who I met in the Cereal and Spices aisle today." They ate stiffly, only occasionally exchanging glances with one another.

"Anyone notice I defrosted the refrigerator?" I asked.

"Hey, has anyone heard what a five-year-old child said to Art Linkletter when he asked what animal she wanted to be when she grew up?"

Finally, one of the children spoke. "Don't you wanta know who broke the storm-door windows?"

"No dear, eat your dinner." I smiled happily.

"Aren't we going to talk about who left the lids off the garbage cans and the dogs got into them?" asked another.

"Absolutely not," said my husband. "This is no time to discuss unpleasantries."

"Aren't we even going to talk about who traded who on what night and whose turn it is to clear?"

"Not during a meal," I said softly.

As if on cue, all of them pushed themselves away from their half-eaten dinner.

"What's the matter?" I asked.

"We can't eat when you're sore at us," they said.

Getting through to kids is not easy for parents. Especially when they go into their "locked door" syndrome. Our entire house used to be open range. Anyone could graze anywhere and still be in plain sight. Now it has all the charm of a mental institution.

The other night I knocked loudly on the bedroom door.

"Who is it?" asked a voice.

"It's Mama."

"Who?"

"*Mama!*"

"Are you sure?"

"Yes."

"What do you want?"

"Open the door. I want to talk to you."

"Did 'he' send you to get his records back?"

"No. Unlock this door."

The door opened a crack and one eye peeked out. "Oh, it's you."

"You were expecting Donnie Osmond? Come to dinner." The door slammed shut.

Following a telephone wire, I traced the next child to a locked closet.

"I know you are in there. The telephone wire is warm. Come to dinner."

There was silence. Then a whispered voice said, "She's listening. I'll call you back."

The next one was a toughie. I found him behind a locked door in the garage playing his drums.

"Do you hear me?" I shouted. "It's dinner."

"Who told you I was here?"

"The neighbors."

"Is that all you want?"

At dinner I asked them, "Why do you feel you have to lock yourselves in your rooms? Surely, we can respect one another's privacy without bolts and chains. Getting this group to a dinner table is like cracking the First National Bank."

"Look, Mom," they explained patiently, "we are going through a phase of our lives when we need privacy. We have to have time to find ourselves . . . to find out who we are, what we are, and where we are going. Surely you can understand that."

Later that evening, I had locked myself in the bathroom, when a note slid under the door. It read, "I need a quarter. Where is your purse?"

I wrote back, "I am finding myself. If I don't know who I am, it's a lead pipe cinch I don't know where my purse is."

The experts say there is a time to talk and a time to be still. With teen-agers you're never quite sure. I was riding with my daughter, when suddenly, for no reason, she turned down a dead-end street. Cautiously I said, "You'd better turn around." She kept going, so I raised my voice and said, "There is a guard rail approaching us and I think you'd better turn around." She sat there frozen to the wheel until I finally shouted hysterically, "For God's sake, *stop.*"

She slammed on her brakes, turned to me, and said softly, "Can't we ever talk? You're always shouting at me."

Now that might not sound like a formal invitation to you, but to me it was like a Bird of Happiness chirping. "I've wanted to talk with you for a long time," I confided, "particularly about selecting a college. I've been noticing that you've been getting application blanks from schools behind the Iron Curtain and thought you might like a little help from Daddy and me in choosing a school."

"Why should you want to visit a campus?" she charged. "You're not going there."

"Indulge us," I smiled. "We are old people and we are highstrung. Your father and I just want to make sure there are alligator-stocked moats between the girls' and boys' dormitories and that the dorm mothers aren't smoking funny cigarettes."

"I wouldn't mind it if you just look," she sulked, "but you and Daddy will ask a million questions like, 'How much does it cost?' and 'How many ironing boards are there on each floor?' and 'How many students are there in each class?' Dumb stuff."

The first school we toured we liked. Academically, it was tops. She shook her head hopelessly. "That's easy for you to say. Did you see those five boys in the Student Union? Short. Short. Short. Short. Short."

The next school we visited also had some merit. (Also five iron-ing boards per twenty-five girls.)

"You're kidding," she said. "The ski slopes are a day away."

The third one had a poster of Fidel Castro in the administra-tion building, but other than that it seemed acceptable.

"No way," she complained. "The registrar had a burr haircut."

Other schools met with disfavor because (a) a chaplain made you write to your mother once a month; (b) their football team had a bad season; (c) Pauline Frack had been accepted and if they took Pauline Frack they'd take anybody!

"I wish you'd be more like Wyckies' mom and dad," she said. "They check out campuses but they don't bug anyone."

My husband and I had never toured a campus tennis court by flashlight, before, but at least our daughter was talking to us. She said, "Crouch a little more."

Her departure for school was quite dramatic. Not that she spoke a lot, but her actions moved us to tears.

As my husband and I walked through the gutted, bare rooms of our home, our footsteps echoed hollowly on the bare floors. Fi-nally, my husband spoke, "It's incredible, isn't it? It took us twenty-three long, married years to amass eight rooms of furniture, forty-three appliances, linens for five beds and an acceptable wardrobe, and now . . . it's all gone."

I nodded. "And to think she condensed it all in two large suit-cases and a zippered gym bag."

"I just don't believe it," he said, closing the doors on the bare linen closet. "The sheets, the towels, our electric blanket. All gone. Why don't you make us a cup of coffee?"

"Can you drink it out of an ashtray?"

"Forget it," he said, "I'm going to sit down and. . . ."

"I wouldn't," I cautioned. "She took that small occasional chair you used to sit in."

"And the TV?" he gasped.

"The first to be packed. Along with the transistor radio, the hair dryer, the make-up mirror, the iron, the electric skillet, your shaver, and your parka jacket."

"And I suppose the phonograph is. . . ."

I nodded. "College bound, along with the typewriter, the electric fan, the space heater, bulletin board, label maker, bowling ball, popcorn popper, and full set of encyclopedias."

"How will she lug all that stuff back to school?"

"I think she dismembered the bicycle and put it under her seat."

"What are we going to do?" he asked, looking at the barren rooms.

"If we looked better we might get on 'Newlywed Game' and try to win a washer and dryer."

"I think we've got enough Green Stamps for . . ."

"Forget the Green Stamps," I said softly. "She took them."

"We could take a trip and. . . ."

"If we still had luggage," I corrected.

"This is ridiculous," he snarled. "Why can't she go to college right here at home?"

"She wants to get away from our materialism," I said.

# One Size
# Fits All
# of What?

The women in the Mortgage Manor housing development just started a Watch Your Weight group. We get together every Monday for coffee and doughnuts and sit around and watch each other grow. Somehow, it makes us all feel better to know there are other women in the world who cannot cross their legs in hot weather.

The other Monday after I had just confessed to eating half a pillowcase of Halloween candy (I still have a shoebox of chocolate bars in the freezer to go), we got to talking about motivation of diets.

"When my nightgown binds me, I'll go on a diet," said one.

"Not me," said another. "When someone compliments me on my A-line dress and it isn't A-line, I'll know."

"I have to be going someplace," said another woman. "I know as sure as I'm sitting here if someone invited me to the White House I could lose fifteen pounds just like that!" (Snapping her fingers)

"I am motivated by vacation," said another one. "I starve myself before a vacation so a bunch of strangers who have never seen me before can load me up with food so that when I return home I look exactly like I did before I started to diet."

"Home movies do it for me," said a woman, reaching for a doughnut.

"You mean when you see yourself and you look fat in them?"

"I mean when they drape me with a sheet and show them on my backside."

Finally, I spoke up. "There is only one thing that motivates me to lose weight. That is one word from my husband. My overeating is his fault. If he'd just show annoyance or disgust or say to me, 'Shape up or sing as a group,' I'd do something about it. I

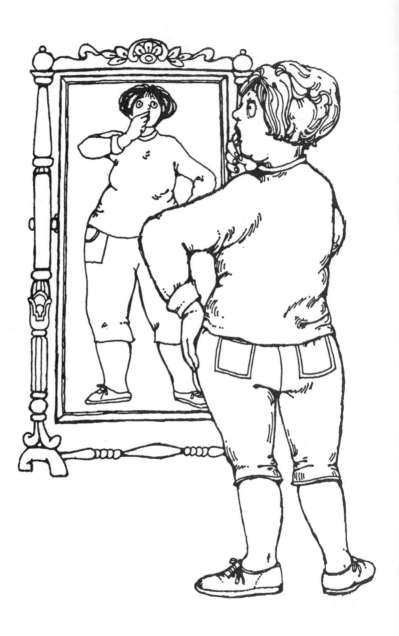

told him the other night. I said, 'It's a shame your wife is walking around with fifteen or twenty excess pounds. If things keep going on I won't be able to sit on a wicker chair. What are you going to do about it?' I asked, 'just sit there and offer me another cookie? Laugh at me. Shame me into it! Humiliate me at parties!' Sure, I'd get sore, but I'd get over it and I'd be a far better, thinner person for it. Just one word from him and I'd be motivated!"

"Diet," he said quietly from behind his paper.

"Fortunately, that wasn't the word. Pass me another doughnut, Maxine."

## WEIGHING IN

I have dieted continuously for the last two decades and lost a total of 758 pounds. By all calculations, I should be hanging from a charm bracelet.

Although I kid Weight Watchers a lot, it is the only organization in which I ever lost a great deal of weight. But I fought them.

Every Tuesday morning, a group of us had to "weigh in" before the lecture. Our ritual was enough to boggle the imagination. We got together a checklist of precautions before we actually stepped on the scale.

Bathroom? Check. Water pill? Check. Have you removed underwear, wedding rings, nail polish? Check. Set aside shoes, corn pads and earrings? Check. Are you wearing a summer dress beneath your winter coat? Check.

The first week I stepped on the scale and my instructor said, "You have gained." (Next week I cut my hair.)

The next week, she said, "You have lost eight ounces, but that is not enough." (I had the fillings in my teeth removed.)

The third week, I had dropped a pound, but my instructor was still not pleased. (I had my tonsils taken out.)

Finally, she really chewed me out. She accused me of not sticking to the diet and not taking it seriously. That hurt.

"I didn't want to tell you," I said, "but I think I am pregnant."

"How far?" she said coldly, clicking her ballpoint pen to make a notation on my card.

"Possibly three days," I said.

She glowered, "Any other excuses?"

"Would you believe I have a cold and my head is swollen?"

"No."

"How about I was celebrating the Buzzard's return to Hinkley, Ohio, and had butter on my popcorn?"

She tapped her pen impatiently on the card and stared at me silently.

"Lint in the navel?" I offered feebly.

"How about first one at the trough?" she asked dryly.

I learned quickly never to argue with a woman who had the scales on her side.

I saw my old instructor the other day and she eyed me carefully and asked, "When are you returning to class?"

"As soon as I have my appendix removed," I said, returning her gaze.

I'm not sure, but I think I heard her moan.

THINK FAT!

I am sick and tired of people saying to me, "Boy, do you have it made. A sober husband, three healthy kids, a house in the suburbs, and a little part-time job to keep you in pantyhose."

Well, let me tell you, my life is not all pretzels and beer. How would you like to get up every morning of your life and confront a seventeen-year-old daughter who is 5'6", weighs 110 pounds, refuses to eat breakfast, and insists, "I'm not hungry."

Every time she says it, it burns me up. I set two alarm clocks to make sure I don't miss a meal, and she says, "I'm not hungry."

My husband says I am suffering from repressed antagonistic rivalry that manifests itself in many strained mother-daughter relationships and simply means resentment, jealousy, and competition between us.

"Nonsense," I told him. "It's just heartburn from the cold cabbage rolls I ate before I went to bed last night."

The other morning as I forced down three pieces of bacon she left untouched, I had it out with her.

"Look," I said, "it's not normal to wake up in the morning and not be hungry. From the time you eat dinner the night before to the time you eat your lunch at school, it is sixteen hours. That's too long between meals."

"But some people don't need food."

"*Don't need food!*" I gasped. "I don't want to frighten you, but a buzzard followed you to school the other morning."

"I can't help it. It upsets my stomach when I eat."

"Do you know what you are doing to your mother?" I sighed. "Killing her. That's right. I don't know how much longer I can go on carrying you. When you were a baby I didn't mind eating your leftovers . . . the strained peas, the mashed squash, and the puréed lamb, but as you got older, the burden became greater. Having two breakfasts for the last seventeen years is beginning to show on me. I put on weight easily. Remember when I got a flu shot and put on three pounds from it? But, if you don't care what happens to your mother. . . ."

"The dog doesn't eat his breakfast and you don't yell at him," she said, slamming out the door.

You know something? With a little catsup, it didn't taste bad.

## FATTIES VERSUS THINNIES

If there is one person in this world I have absolutely no compassion for, it's a size five telling me she'd like to put on weight and can't.

It's like Zsa Zsa Gabor complaining to a spinster that they don't make drip-dry wedding dresses.

One of these frails nailed me in the supermarket the other day and charged, "Why don't you ever write about thin girls who are just as miserable being thin as fat people are being overweight?"

"Look, thermometer hips," I said, looking around nervously, "if the girls in TOPS see me talking to you I'll be dropped from their (excuse the expression) rolls. You're a no no."

"But why?" she whined. "How can we have peace in the world when fatties and thinnies can't communicate?"

I looked up tiredly. "What do you want from me?"

"Tell me how you put on weight," she said.

"This is ridiculous," I sighed. "I don't know how I do it. All I know is I gain weight when I have to eat my own words. I gain weight when I chew on a pencil. I added five pounds in the labor room."

"You must have some tips you can pass on to thin girls on how to gain weight."

"All right, here is the BOMBECK FLAB PLAN."

1. Go on a diet. There is no better way to gain weight than to call up everyone you know and tell them you are going to lose fifteen pounds by the time the pool opens on Memorial Day. You can sometimes add as much as two pounds a week.

2. Agree to go to your class reunion. As if on cue, your waistbands will grow tighter, your chins will cascade down your chest and you'll grow shoulders like Joan Crawford.

3. Read a cookbook before retiring. Rich recipes at bedtime are hard to digest and tend to turn to fat. They also tend to get you up in the middle of the night to fry doughnuts and make malts.

4. Sit next to stout people. Overweights are contagious. They always carry food on their body and have an overwhelming urge to share it. I have gained more weight in exercise classes, health spas, and centers than anywhere else.

5. Drastic measures: Get pregnant. Suffer a hangover (at least your head gets fat). Look into the new fat transplants. I have this chubby friend who is such a willing donor . . . in fact, I'll even throw in my Debbie Drake record.

YOU WANT ME FOR LUNCH?

In trying to rationalize my flab the other day it occurred to me that the high cost of dieting is keeping me portly.

Think about it. Did you ever see a fat Ford sister? Or an obese

Rockefeller socialite? Or a tubby in the White House? Face it. The good life begets a slender figure. The truth is they can well afford the dietary food products, the fresh fruits out of season, the imported fresh fish and the lean steaks.

They can absorb the cost of new wardrobes and extensive alterations to the old ones. But mostly, they can go the health and spa routes which cost anywhere from $2 to $1,500 a pound.

Actually, I have seen only one plush spa in my life. It was the Elizabeth Arden spa in Phoenix. A friend of mine was spending a week there and called me and said, "We'd like to have you for lunch."

"You are desperate for roughage, aren't you?" I said.

"I mean we'd like to have you as a guest," she said.

It's a beautiful, incredible place. To begin with, it is lousy with mirrors. (I had the good sense to take all mine down when I passed a mirror one day, sucked in my stomach, and nothing moved.)

All the dietees wear white terry-cloth robes and scuffs and wonderful smelling cream on their faces. They are massaged, pampered, exercised, sunned, and rested on a schedule that is carried around in their white terry-cloth pockets.

The lunch was simple. Cottage cheese, fresh fruit, and Ry-Krisp.

"I wish I could afford not to eat like this," I said sadly, "but I come from a home where gravy is a beverage."

"Don't be ridiculous," said my friend. "You could duplicate the spa in your own home . . . schedule and all."

At home, I slipped into my chenille duster with the button over the stomach missing and consulted my schedule in the pocket. At 8 A.M., I ate the leftovers from breakfast. At 9 A.M., I sat on the washer during spin which did wonders for my hips but dissolved my breakfast. At 10, I chinned myself fifty times on the guard rail of the bunk beds. At 11 A.M., I jogged to the garbage can, followed by luncheon at noon (cottage cheese) and beauty treatment at 12:30. (I rubbed hand cream on my elbows.)

I lasted until 1 P.M. By this time my bathrobe was hot and the cottage cheese had worn off. Then I saw it. A half of an

Oreo cookie in the carpet. I leaned over and popped it into my mouth and smiled my fat little smile. Money may make you thin, but you cannot buy ecstasy.


THREE SIZES FITS ALL

I have always admired women who can wear a one-size swim-suit. That is, either a size 12, a 14, or a 16. I wear all three sizes at the same time.

In the modern-day vernacular, I can't seem to get it all to-gether. My friends tell me exercise is the secret. It's not how much weight you carry, it is how it is packaged and distributed.

I stood in front of the mirror the other morning and assessed myself. Imagine if you will the state of Texas. I look terrific at Amarillo, but by the time I hit Dallas and Fort Worth, I begin to blouse, and don't really thin out again until Corpus Christi. (But after Houston, who hangs on to see Corpus Christi?)

I've exercised. I really have. Once I signed up for a course at the neighborhood YWCA. The classes were held in a church and because of the popularity of the class, we were put in the church proper. One afternoon the minister visited and paused long enough to see me in a pair of pedal pushers trying to touch my nose to my bent knee which was resting on a pew and said, "You are desecrating the altar." I transferred to cake-decorating class and licked my way to six additional pounds.

For a while I used to eat my dessert at breakfast while watch-ing a Swedish girl on television. She held me spellbound by winding her leg around her neck. I watched and listened to her for over a year and one day I wheezed, strained and gasped and finally got one of my ankles hooked over the other. I quit before I really hurt myself.

The idea of going to a spa really intrigued me. I thought how great it would be to splash around in the water and steam your pores and ride a bicycle to nowhere, but going to a spa is like having a cleaning lady. You can't go to a spa looking like you need to go to a spa any more than you can have a cleaning woman walk into a house that needs cleaning. Somehow, I just couldn't get myself in shape for a towel.

For the last year, I have watched my husband faithfully execute his Air Force exercises (which could account for the decline in enlistments). If there is anything in this world more boring than a man who exercises regularly, I have not met it.

"You should join me," he keeps insisting. "A few push-ups; a little jogging. It's good for the old body."

"Then why aren't your knees straight when you bend over to touch your toes?"

"I suppose you could do it better?"

"Sure, by letting my fingernails grow fourteen inches."

He's not fooling around with some amateur.

## WRINKLE CITY

All I said was my face was beginning to look more like John Wayne's every day of my life.

Then my neighbor said she had this book on body and facial exercises that you can do while you do your housework.

And the next thing you know, I got a box of homemade cookies from my bread man's wife. I don't understand it.

I guess it started the first day I began to exercise. I was on the phone, talking to my neighbor with my knees partially bent, my legs apart and as I talked, I slapped my thighs together. When the bread man walked by the window, I waved. He waved feebly, put a package of brown 'n serve rolls on the milk box and left.

Later that week in front of the picture window, I rolled my head slowly five times from left to right, then five times right to left. In between I would shake my head from side to side going faster and faster until everything was a blur. I thought I saw my bread man running toward his truck.

For my neckline, I was instructed to stick my tongue out as far as I could and try to curl the tip. As I did so, I noticed my bread man looking back at me with both his fingers in his ears and his tongue extended. He looked ridiculous.

The following week I worked on my chin, by throwing my

head back and biting into an imaginary apple with my lower lip protruding. I could really feel the chin and neck muscles pull and tried to tell my bread man so, but he stood at his truck, folded a coffee cake like a newspaper, and literally threw it into the bushes. That was strange.

I didn't see him again for a week. By this time, I had worked up to the face lift exercise. As I did the breakfast dishes, I winked with my left eye and at the same time lifted the side of my mouth. As I winked and smiled, winked and smiled, I looked up to see the bread man staring at me.

That was the last time I saw him.

His wife called and thanked me tearfully for being the single guiding force that cured her husband's drinking problem. That same afternoon, I found a box of cookies in my mailbox from her.

Yesterday, my neighbor came over with a new guide to beauty. She said for tired brains, just sit in a chair with arms loose at your sides and pretend you're floating on a white cloud in the blue sky.

Like I told her, "With crazy people running around like my bread man, I'm afraid to close my eyes."

## CREEPING UNDERWEAR

We have virtually erased bad breath in this country, stamped out dandruff, and done away with burning, itchy feet, but we have been unable to conquer one of society's most dreaded diseases: Creeping Underwear.

Everyone talks about Creeping Underwear, but no one does anything about it. Technical research has put powdered orange juice on the moon, yet on earth we are still plagued with pantyhose that won't stay up, slips that won't stay down and girdles that should contain a WARNING, WEAR AT YOUR OWN RISK label.

To suggest that Creeping Underwear changes a person's personality is the understatement of this decade. The other night I went to a movie, a fully confident, well-adjusted, stable, human being.

Two hours later, I was a totally different person. My slip had crept to my waistline to form a solid innertube which added about fifteen pounds to my form.

My girdle, in a series of slow maneuvers, had reached several plateaus during the evening. First, it slid to my waist. Upon finding this area was already occupied by a slip, it moved upward, cutting my chest in half and gradually moved upward to where it pinched my neck and caused my head to grow two inches taller.

The pantyhose were quite another story. They kept sliding down until I realized halfway through the movie that I was sitting on the label in the waistband and that if I dared stand up the crotch would bind my ankles together.

I tried to adjust these garments in a way so as not to call attention, but every time I bent my elbow, two straps slid onto my shoulder and bound my arms like a strait jacket.

My husband was the first to notice the change in my personality. "What are you doing sitting under the seat in a fetal position?" he asked. "Are you trying to tell me you do not like the movie?"

"I am suffering from Creeping Underwear," I whispered.

"You should have taken a couple of aspirin before you left the house," he snarled. "Now, get up here and sit up straight in your seat."

He didn't understand. They rarely do. Nearly 98.2 per cent of all the victims of Creeping Underwear are women. As I sat there I looked under the seat next to me and saw another woman in a similar position. "What are you doing down here?" I asked.

"I crossed my leg and was all but flogged to death by a loose supporter," she sighed.

"Do you think they'll ever find a cure?" I asked hopelessly.

"I hope so," she said. "Your tongue is beginning to swell."


GOOD-BY, GIRDLE

This generation must be doing something right. I read in the paper last week where a girdle factory shut down from lack of sales.

I regard the obituary of a girdle factory with mixed emotion. It's like having your mother-in-law move out because you have snakes in your basement. There is something good to be said for girdles. Maybe I'll remember what it is.

The problem with girdles is that they are designed under the law of redistribution. They really don't contain the flab; they merely reappropriate it. For example, when I put on a girdle, three things happen immediately: my stomach goes flat, my chin doubles and my knees inflate. So I always say, "What does it profiteth a woman to have a flat stomach if her teeth become loose?"

I have had some miserable experiences with girdles. One was with a miracle garment that I bought while carrying one of the children. It was expensive and rather complicated and came with some rather explicit instructions.

It read, "Welcome to the Constrictor 747. The Constrictor 747 is mechanically engineered to take inches off your waist and hips. When laced and hooked properly it will perform for 18 hours without adjustment. Before wearing, please familiarize yourself with the two pressure exits located over each kidney. In the unlikely event oxygen is required, the stays will open and automatically eject an oxygen mask. Please extinguish all fire material and place the mask over your face and mouth and breathe normally."

The Constrictor 747 was a great disappointment to me. I was wearing it one afternoon when a friend saw me and asked, "When is your baby due?"

"I had it two years ago," I said, and went home to give the Constrictor 747 a decent burial.

After that, I stuck with a little cheapie . . . a model called the Little Nothing Tourniquet. It was reinforced over the tummy, the hips, the rib cage, the legs, the seat, and sometimes the ankle. But it did the job. You may have seen it. When I started wearing shorter skirts, everybody saw it. It cut me just above the knees. One day my daughter said, "Gee, Mom, haven't you heard? This is the era where you let it all hang out."

And that, my friend, is what is closing girdle factories.

BOOTS! BOOTS!

I have no idea of the circumference of my legs. I only know they are bigger than a water glass, smaller than a furnace duct, and impossible to fit into the knee-length boots.

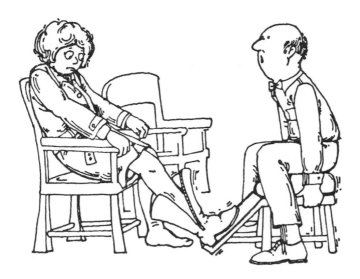

It is probably my own sensitivity, but I always imagine boot salesmen are the lowest in seniority. They are serving time in this department only because their father, who owns the store, wants to keep them humble.

My salesman was a leg watcher. (Not mine, however.)

"I would like a pair of boots," I said.

He scrutinized me closely, squinted his eyes, and appeared with a pair of Arctic boots that laced up to the knee.

"No, you don't understand," I said, "I don't want to get a construction job. I want a pair of dressy boots to wear with wools and jumpers."

With detachment, he went over to a display table and returned with a boot so long and narrow it had an echo. There was only one pair of legs in the world that would fit into that boot: Phyllis Diller's. (As a friend of mine once remarked, on Phyllis's legs, "The last time I saw legs that size they had a message attached to them.")

"Where's the zipper?" I asked.

"There is no zipper," he yawned. "They're the new easy-stretch pullons." He reached in to take out the tissue paper and got his arm stuck.

"Perhaps one with a zipper," I suggested.

He placed the zippered boot on my foot and began to ease the zipper all the way up to my ankle bone. Then it stopped.

"Thanks anyway," I said, "but . . ."

"No, no," he insisted. "It'll work. Just twist your foot a little and bear down." A crowd began to form.

"Really," I said, "it's no use. The boot is too. . . ."

"We can do it," he insisted. His pocket comb fell out and he ignored it. The blood rushed to his head and I feared for a nosebleed.

"Maybe if you took off those heavy hose."

"My nylons?" I gasped.

"Look, lady," he shouted, forcing the zipper, "suck in! Suck in!"

My leg throbbed. I spoke softly. "I appreciate what you are trying to do, but just bring me that pair over on the center table.

"Are you sure those are what you want?" he asked.

"They'll do fine," I said. I slipped easily into the ankle-length white boot with a stencil of Cinderella and a castle on the side. I may not be a fashion plate, but I'll be a smash at Show and Tell.

## DISCRIMINATION

As a woman who thinks a needle is something you take out splinters with and step on in your bare feet, I have always been annoyed with the inequality of alterations.

Why is it when a man buys a suit, his alterations come free, but when a woman buys an outfit of equal or more value, she pays extra?

I was with my husband a few years ago when he bought a $49.95 suit (with a vest, two contrasting pairs of slacks, a matching tam, and a set of dishes). Not only was it a cheap suit (the label said, "Made in Occupied Guadalcanal: Fashion Capital of the World") but it hung on him like an ugly blind date.

"I don't like the way it breaks across the shoulders," he said, twisting before his three-way mirror. "And the sleeves—I like them short enough to count my fingers. Maybe you can reset them."

"No problem," smiled the salesman.

"There's too much slack in the seat and the waistband seems a little loose . . . maybe a tuck or two."

"Of course," grinned the salesman. "Let me summon a tailor."

The tailor spent thirty-five minutes chalking up my husband's anatomy. The suit looked like a steer being divided for two freezers—all at no charge.

The other day I tried on a dress of comparable value.

"It bags a little in front," I said, looking sideways into the mirror.

"There are operations to correct that, honey," she yawned. "Or we'll alter it for three dollars."

"And the sleeves. They hang so long."

"That'll be two-fifty or you can roll 'em up and keep your elbows bent."

"I don't know," I pondered. "Maybe a knit isn't for me. It clings so."

"Tell you what," she said, "if you want to save two dollars, just block it yourself by stretching it over a chair for a couple of days . . . or a sofa depending on how loose you want it."

"How much to shorten it?"

"Four dollars," she said, "but it'll be worth it. This dress will look like it's been made for you. Here, let me help you with the zipper."

"How much for helping me with my zipper," I chided.

"I'll throw it in," she said. "I feel sorry for you."

PAJAMA TRYOUTS IN BOSTON

I knew when I got a pair of "at home" pajamas for Christmas, I could never wear them "at home." They were definitely not apparel to unclog a sink, paper-train a dog, or make pizza in.

They were pajamas to sit on the sofa and cough in. Or descend a stairway with a brandy snifter in your hand. Or pose for a magazine ad which read, "Erma Bombeck could afford any oven she wanted, but she chose a Kenmore."

That's why I took them out of town for a trial run to get the bugs out before bringing them into my living room.

The place was a reception in Boston. I shook them out of the suitcase, belted them, and took off.

In my own mind, I envisioned my entrance as having the same impact as you would have seeing Elizabeth Taylor jog. I imagined conversation coming to a hush, glasses paralyzed in mid-air, jealous hearts taking the caps off their suicide rings and a voice booming, "You and your sexy pajamas! You have our hearts, you she-devil; must you have our souls too!"

My entrance produced as much excitement as a paper-clip display in the lobby of the bunny club.

"You're late, luv," said one of my friends putting her arm around my waist. "Good Lord, what's that?" she asked, her fingers touching a lump around my waist.

"It's my slip," I said.

"Doesn't it bother you?"

"Only when I walk. Do you like my outfit?"

"You look like someone I saw in a movie a while back."

"Bette Davis? Katharine Ross?"

"No, Dustin Hoffman. There's something wrong with your cleavage."

"What cleavage?"

"That's what I mean. You're wearing your darts backwards. You know something? I think you've got this thing on backwards. Hey gang, come look at this. Would you say the zipper goes in front? Maybe if you wore a bathrobe over it. . . ."

I think the pajamas need a little work before I bring them into my home town for their big opening.

BE YOURSELF!

I was walking along a center aisle of a department store the other day when a representative of a cosmetics firm smiled and beckoned me over to the counter.

"You mean me?" I giggled.

She nodded. Then she leaned over, sized me up and whispered, "I can help."

I was overwhelmed with the way she looked and the way she smelled. There sure wasn't any peanut butter growing under her fingernails.

"First, dear," she said, "I want you to walk for me."

I felt like a fool. Stiffly, I swaggered out to handbags and back again. "Are you carrying your money in a knotted handkerchief tied to your knees?"

"Why? Am I walking funny?"

"A bit self-conscious perhaps," she said. "We'll work on that later. Now, we are going to create a new you. First, your shape. You can do all kinds of artificial things to change it. Don't turn your back on me, dear."

"I'm not," I said miserably.

"Oh. Well, all that can be fixed with padding. As for your hips and waist, there are cinchers to wear. Now, for the important parts. Do you do anything to your hair?"

"I put three rollers each morning on the side I slept on the night before."

"Perhaps a wig," she mused. "We'll just slip this one on for effect. Now, what about eyelashes?"

"Those fake ones make me drowsy."

"You weren't putting them on properly," she said authoritatively. "Now, we'll accent your cheek bones with a dark make-up making your face look thinner. You are rather sallow. We'll add this rouge to make you look vibrant and healthy. There now. Have you always worn glasses?"

"Only since college when I went steady with a parking meter my junior and senior years."

"I would suggest contacts. They really give the eyes a new dimension. And your nose. Are you happy with it?"

"It works O.K."

"I meant the shape of it. You know cosmetic surgery is very commonplace nowadays. You should have it bobbed and give your face a better profile. Of course you were planning to have your teeth capped."

She worked on me for over an hour. At the end of the session, I was laden with creams, liners, rouge, powder, nutrients, fake eyelashes, wig, waist cincher, padding, and suggested doctors to cap my teeth, fix my nose, and outfit me in contact lenses.

"Thank you very much," I stammered, "you've certainly been a help."

"Just one last bit of advice, dear," she said softly, touching my shoulder. "Be yourself!"

YOU LIED, SOPHIA

The beauty secrets of the stars never worked for me. I remember once Arlene Dahl suggested placing chilled cucumbers over each eye to relieve tension. My husband leaned over to kiss me hello, thought it was Daddy Warbucks and has had a twitch in his right eye ever since.

Dolores Del Rio, an older star who remains ageless, said she retained her youth by never smiling and creating laugh lines. Any mother knows it's not the laugh lines that create valleys of facial erosion, but the crying lines.

I suppose I should never have trusted Sophia Loren when she was quoted in a magazine article as saying, "All I am I owe to spaghetti." Just by looking at her I would never have thought that. Good posture? Maybe. A new baby? Possibly. A sixteenth-of-an-inch padding? Oh, c'mon. But spaghetti!

Spaghetti being my favorite food, her advice was easy to take. At least once a week, I would get out the big pot (not me, you fool, the other one) and begin the ritual that is called "spaghetti sauce." Then I would toss up the salad, rich with oil, load the garlic bread with butter, reverently face Sophia's picture on the wall and say, "This one is for you, Sophia."

As the weeks went by, it became obvious my sand was not settling in the same proportions as Sophia. While she was built like a cut diamond, I was taking on the shape of a pyramid. But I persevered.

"Well, Sophia," jeered my husband, "how are you and Marcello Mastroianni making out?"

"I had it for lunch," I said.

"It's funny," he said, "but I cannot remember Sophia walking around with a safety pin in her slacks."

"A sex symbol cannot be built in a day," I retaliated.

It wasn't until I began to think the "before" pictures in magazines looked great, that I realized the road to beauty is not paved with spaghetti. Sophia lied to me. It was all a hoax to make the women of America look like beasts, while Sophia slithered her way through movie after movie. (Like having ugly bridesmaids so you'll look good.)

Taking off "spaghetti," my friends, is like taking off no other food. You can run around the block and take off an eclair. You can do a few sit ups and dissolve lobster dipped in butter, but spaghetti hits your hips, takes roots and begins to grow again.

The other night as I sat nibbling on a piece of carrot, I watched Sophia in a movie with Cary Grant. I couldn't help but wonder . . . maybe if I left off the Parmesan.

*Put Down
Your Brother.
You Don't
Know Where
He's Been.*

My husband's idea of a fun vacation is sitting around watching a ranger pick his teeth with a match cover.

My idea of "roughing it" is when you have to have an extension for your electric blanket.

My husband is one of those idiots who leaves pieces of bacon out to attract bears to the camp site.

I once trapped a gnat in my bra and went to bed with a sick headache for a week.

"Face it," I said, "we are incompatible. I want to go to New York and see some theater and shop and you want to go to Murk Lake and watch mosquitoes hatch their larva."

He stiffened. "I am not going to New York and watch a bunch of lewdy nudies cavort around the stage."

"And I am not going to Murk Lake and watch men shave out of double boilers."

"I am not going to the city where I have to wear a necktie to bed," he continued.

"And I am not going to a camp ground where life is so primitive the animals come to watch us feed."

The point is we are incompatible on the subject of vacations.

"You don't understand," I said to my husband. "I don't ask much in this world. All I want is a few weeks where I could sleep in a bed where the alarm clock is on the opposite side.

"I want to go to the bathroom, lock the door, and know that when I look through the keyhole I will not encounter another eye.

"I want the phone to ring and have it be for me. I want to walk in a room and see all the drawers closed. I want to drink a cup of coffee while it is still hot.

"Don't you understand? I want to pick up my toothbrush and have it be dry."

He was silent for a moment. Then he said, "Why didn't you say so? We'll compromise. We'll go camping."

I know for a fact that a lot of families who travel together have a swell time. They play "Count the Cow" until they faint. They wave to "Out of State" license plates and sing gaily, "Getting to Know You" in two-part harmony. Our kids play a game called, "Get Mama." Or, "The Family That Camps Together Gets Cramps Together."

It's a 400-mile non-stop argument that begins when we leave the driveway and doesn't end until Mama threatens to self-destruct.

The players include a daddy who drives in silence, a mama who listens in silence, a daughter who keeps repeating, "Mom!" and two brothers who make Cain and Abel sound like the Everly Brothers.

Just for the mental discipline, I kept a record of the last "Get Mama" game. The kids argued for seventy-five miles on whether or not you could run a car a hundred miles in reverse without stalling. They used up fifty miles debating how workers in the U. S. Treasury Department could defraud the detectors by putting hundred-dollar bills in their mouth and not smiling until they got out of the gates.

It took them longer to resolve the capital of Missouri than it took to settle the entire territory. They argued about whether or not you could use a yo-yo on the moon. Whether hair would grow over a vaccination. Whether a gorilla if put at a typewriter could eventually produce a best seller. How come some daddies had wrinkles in their necks and others didn't. What size shoe Pete Maravich wore. And if a nun were allowed to become a priest, would you call her Father.

They threatened to "slap" 55 times, "punch" 33 times, said, "I'm telling" 138 times and whispered, "I'll give you one" three times. (That sounded ominous and I didn't turn around.)

As I sat in the front seat nervously knotting my seat belt into a rosary, I concluded our family would never make a TV series . . . unless it was "Night Gallery."

As I slumped against the door, one of my children yelled,

"Hey, Mom, you better push the button down on your door or you'll fall out."

If only I could believe that.

It does not impress me one bit that every year more than a million families embark on a camping venture.

I know that of those who make it back (some poor devils wander around for years looking for ranger stations, children, and ice-cube machines) a goodly number are disenchanted. Why you may ask yourself?

To begin with, few realistic camping guides have been written. Usually, they are small, shiny booklets with waterproof covers (this should tell you something) showing a family in a small, secluded paradise. Daddy is in a trout stream up to his creel in excitement. Mother is waving nearby from a pair of water skis. And the children are gathered around a campfire playing Old Maid with Gentle Ben.

It never rains on the covers of camping guides. Mother is never shown doing a three-week laundry in a saucepan. Dad is never depicted fixing a flat on a tandem trailer in Mosquito City, with three children dancing around, chanting, "We are going to miss 'Mod Squad' and it's your fault." It is never revealed that children often sit around for four days at a time crying, "Make him stop looking at me or I am going to bust him one."

There are all kinds of camping, of course. There are the primitives who sleep on a blanket of chipmunks under the stars and exist only on wild berries and what game they are able to trap in the zippers of their sleeping bags. There are the tent enthusiasts who use cots, ice coolers, matches, transistor radios and eat store-bought bread, but who draw the line at electricity and indoor plumbing. Finally, there are the wheelsvilles. They run the gamut from the family that converts the old pickup truck to a home on wheels to those who rough it with color TV, guitars, outdoor lounge furniture, flaming patio torches, ice crushers, electric fire lighters, showers, make-up mirrors, hoods over the campfire, plastic logs, Hondas for short trips to the city, and yapping dogs that have had their teeth capped.

It doesn't matter how you camp. The point is that a few practical suggestions could keep you from going bananas:

What to do when it rains. Rearrange canned foods, plan a side trip, write letters home, remembering to lie. Read all the wonderful books you brought and promised yourself to read. (*The Red Badge of Courage* and *The American Journal on Tooth Decay.*)

And rains. Pick grains of sand out of the butter, sit in the car and pretend you're going home, find out who really has gym shoes that smell like wet possum.

And rains. Send the kids out to find traffic to play in. Call in friends and watch the clothing mildew. Pair off and find an ark.

Otherwise camping can be loads of fun. Tips from my woodland log:

## How to bed down without hurting yourself or anyone else.

1. Don't kneel on the stove to let the cot down from the wall until all the burners are off.

2. If the table converts to a bed, make sure it has been cleared.

3. Whoever brought the guitar along sleeps with it.

4. If the wind is blowing southward, sleep northward of the person who bathed in mosquito repellent.

5. Place the kid who had three bottles of pop before bedtime nearest the door. Oil the zipper of his sleeping bag before retiring.

6. If you are sleeping on the ground, make it as comfortable as possible by using a rollaway bed.

7. Make sure all the cupboard doors are closed and traffic areas cleared before the light is extinguished. Statistics show that more campers are lost through carelessly placed ice coolers and clotheslines than through crocodile bites.

## How to live among our furry friends.

1. Forget Disney. Remember, not all bears have their own television series. Some of them are unemployed wild animals.

2. Never argue with a bear over your picnic basket, even though deep in your heart you know the green onions will repeat on him.

3. Any woman in the laundry room who tries to assure you snakes are as afraid of you as you are of them should be watched.

## *How to know when you are there.*

1. When you are reading the road map and your husband accuses you of moving Lake Michigan over two states.

2. When the kids start playing touch football in the back seat with a wet diaper and the baby is in it.

3. When not only starvation sets in, but your stomach begins to bloat and your vision becomes blurred.

4. When Daddy screams, "Stop kicking my seat!" and the kids are all asleep.

5. When you find a haven the size of a football field that you don't have to back a trailer into (even if it is a football field).

## *What to do when togetherness becomes an obscene word.*

No one, not even a man and a woman, can endure two weeks of complete togetherness—especially when they are married. Thus, being confined with two or three children in an area no larger than a sandbox often has the appeal of being locked in a bus-station rest-room over the weekend. Planning your activities will help avoid this.

1. Keep busy. Rotate the tires on the car. This gets you out in the fresh air and at the same time gives you a feeling of accomplishment.

2. Play games like "Look for Daddy" or "Bury the Motorcycle" (the one that runs up and down through the campgrounds all night).

3. Have a roster of chores. One child could be in charge of water for the radiator. Another could be in charge of killing that last mosquito in the tent at night.

4. Have family dialogues around the campfire. Suggested top-

ics: Who was the idiot who had to bring the ping-pong table and "Harvey, where are you getting the drinking water and what did you hope to find when you put a slideful of it under your new microscope?"

5. Make new friends (assuming your marriage is stable).

If it happens to be Be Kind to Campers Month (July 19–26), observe it by taking a camper to the city for a day.

Maybe other mothers make it to the water skis, but the closest I ever get to water is a laundromat. I have spent entire vacations watching my enzymes and bleach race their way to the dirt and grime in our underwear.

Commercials lie. They always make laundromats seem like fun places where you go around smelling each other's wash, comparing whiteness, looking for hidden cameras, and breaking out in acne at the thought of stubborn stains.

It's not like that at all. There are thirty-eight washes to every washer, sixty-three dryees to each of the three dryers (one of them is out of order) five Coke machines (all of them in order), no chairs, and a small snack table to fold your clothes on.

The "washees" are bustling, no-nonsense people. They stuff the washers, deposit the soap and coins, look at their watches, and estimate they'll be out of there in an hour.

The "dryees" are a bit more affable. They know with three dryers (one of them out of order), they must live as a community for an indeterminate amount of time, striking up acquaintances, laughing, talking, eating, and sometimes intermarrying.

I was lucky. I got in line for a dryer once behind a bearded boy who couldn't have owned more than two pairs of shorts, a T-shirt with the peace sign, and a fringed vest. I figured him for twenty minutes of drying time.

"Why do you suppose the dryers are heating up?" he asked.

"It's all that nerve gas they're dumping in the ocean," I said tiredly.

"Hey, man, I think you're right," he mused. "You come here often?"

"Only when I can slip away," I said.

We talked for another hour or so. Finally, it was his turn. "Hey, Mildred," he shouted across the laundromat. Mildred had four baskets of wet laundry, three children, and five rain-soaked sleeping bags. Her hair was in rollers the size of fruit juice cans. "Wait a minute," she said. "I want to dry my hair first." She started the dryer and stuck her head inside the door.

Later that night I decided to compromise with my husband and go to New York for a vacation.

"That's impossible," said my husband. "Who will sit with the children?"

"My mother," I stated firmly.

"You know how your mother feels about baby-sitting," he said. "After our first child was born, she had her phone and her address unlisted."

That's not exactly true. Mother loves her grandchildren. As she puts it, "I also love Smokey the Bear and Harry Reasoner, but I wouldn't want to sit with them on a regular basis."

She once told me she considered grandchildren a special bonus for having outlived her own children. "When you're a sitting sit-in," she declared, "you lose your role as a grandparent. Of course," she said, "if you get desperate you can call me at this number at a candy store. They know where to reach me."

I called the number. "Mom, I haven't had a vacation away from the kids since my honeymoon."

"What kind of a crack is that?" she asked.

"I told you I was desperate. Do you suppose you could sit with the kids for a few days?"

"They hurt me the last time," she sulked.

"That's my fault," I replied. "I should have told you that when you stand the baby up on your lap, he pushes his head against your chin and severs your tongue in half. Besides, the kids are older now. It'll be easier."

"Than what?" she asked cautiously.

"The problems of teen-agers are overdramatized," I told Mother. "Actually, there is nothing to sitting with them. First, I have hidden the distributor from the car in the flour canister. This will give you a warm, secure feeling when the announcer on TV asks, 'It's ten o'clock. Do you know where your children are?' They'll be tearing the house apart looking for the distributor.

"Second, don't worry about meals. They'll eat anything as long as it is in a carry-out bag.

"Third, keep a supply of dimes. You'll need them when you have to make a phone call at the gas station on the corner. Fourth, if you want them to wear something clean, put it in the dirty-clothes hamper. It's sneaky, but it's the only way you can get them to rotate their clothes.

"Fifth, you'll get used to the records, especially if you spend your evenings crouched in the utility closet next to the hot-water heater.

"Sixth, don't ever say you understand them. It breaks down the hostile relationship between you that it takes to understand one another. Now you know all there is to know about the children, I am off to the city."

"Hold it!" shouted Mother. "In case I need you where can I get in touch with you?"

"Here's the number of a candy store," I said. "I'll check in from time to time."

For years, I have tried to figure out the logic of parents who travel on separate airplanes. This is some decision. Do I want to be on the plane that doesn't make it? Or do I want to be left to raise three children alone on an educator's pension?

This is like asking a drowning man if he wants the leaky tire tube or the boat with the hole in it. Either way, you lose.

Frankly, I think it is a theory advanced by airlines to keep women from finding out what Joan Rivers has known for years: The Bunny Club in the sky is a man's world.

I sensed it when my husband and I boarded and I asked the hostess to hang up my white coat that was made out of a perma-wrinkled fabric. She folded it carefully and (excuse the expression) heaved it onto the rack above my head. When my husband boarded she snatched his attaché case out of his hand and started to hang it neatly on a hanger.

"Really," he giggled, "that's not necessary. I can put it under my seat."

"Let me do it, sir," she insisted.

She leaned over and I instinctively threw my shopping bag

over her sit-upon. Throughout the trip she was as obvious as a mal bag in the seat pocket.

"Gum? Drink? Pillow? Ice? Dinner? Oxygen? More coffee? Stereo? Magazine?"

"If you play your cards right," I told my husband, "she'll give you a pair of wings and let you drive the airplane."

"She's just being nice," he countered. "She's that way to everyone."

*Oh yeah? Then why did she tell me my seat was a folding chair on the wings?"

We were about twenty-five minutes in the air when we heard the Spanish voices. At first they were faint, but as more people became aware of it, conversation ceased and the voices became more distinct.

Our hostess had just emerged from another costume change when she heard it too. She walked slowly up and down the aisle and stopped at ours. My husband caught her eye and eased the attaché case out from under his seat. He opened it carefully. Through juggling, the switch had been thrown on his tape recorder which contained his Home-taught Spanish records.

"You are the bravest man," said the hostess, grabbing his arm. (What was so brave about apprehending a recording saying, "You are standing on my burro's foot"?)

The rest of the girls crowded around him as though he had just discovered a cure for cracked heels.

On the return flight, we'll be traveling on separate airplanes. I've thought it over. The two alternatives beat this.

I stood on the corner of Seventh Avenue and Forty-second Street in New York at last with my arms outstretched and said to my husband, "You are looking at a woman who has been liberated!"

"Put your arms down before someone puts a cigarette out in your palm," he said dryly.

"Really," I said, "do you realize this is the first time in years we have been on a vacation without the children? No more dried eggs on the dinner plates. No car pools. No telephone. No eating at 3 in the afternoon because of ball practice. We are free! Stand up straight, dear, and don't slouch or your spine will grow that way. What shall we do first?"

"Let's look for a restaurant," he said.

"Good idea. Take Mother's hand before we cross the street. You never know when some crazy man will try to crash a light. Where was I? Oh yes, being free. You know, some women are so child-geared they can't forget they are mothers. This is sad."

"What about this place?"

"It looks all right, but just to be safe order cheese or peanut butter. You can't go wrong with cheese or peanut butter. The men's room is over there. I'll watch your coat. Don't sit on the seat and don't forget to flush."

"Well, I'm back," said my husband. "Did you order?"

"Yes. Did you wash your hands?"

"Really now."

"Here we are. Don't forget your napkin. And don't talk with food in your mouth. They filled your milk glass too full."

"You don't have to cut my sandwich for me," he said irritably. "I'm quite capable of cutting it myself."

"Habit," I grinned. "Creature of habit. What was I talking about?"

"About being free of the children."

"Speaking of children, did I tell you what your son said when —did you kick me under the table? Now, what does Mama say about keeping your feet on the floor?"

"If God had meant for me to wipe my feet off on people, He'd have made them out of plastic," he said mechanically.

"Right. As I was saying. We have a whole week to be free of kids. Let's go out and do some shopping for them. I saw this four-foot African drum and a Chinese wastebasket with a red dragon on it that would be perfect. I mean if you buy something that fits in your suitcase, they might think we don't love them.

"Isn't it great being liberated?"

# I Lost
# Everything
# in the
# Post-natal
# Depression

In case you are keeping score, I missed being named Mother of
the Year by three votes (all cast by my own children), I was not
named to the Olympic Dusting Team, and I was laughed out of
the Pillsbury Bake-off. (My husband ate my Tomato Surprise and
said, "Why don't you flake off?" and I thought he said "bake
off.")

However, at the 1972 meeting of the doctor people in Passaic,
New Jersey, I was named as the woman who had the longest
post-natal depression period in the history of obstetrics.

After fourteen years, I was still uptight about toilet training,
upset because the stretch marks wouldn't tan, and depressed because I was still in maternity clothes.

My favorite story on motherhood came to me through the
mail. It involved a mother who had it all together. She was a
model of virtue, a paragon of womanhood. She had six children,
whom she counseled with great wisdom and patience. She was
never too busy to listen and to talk with in a cool, calm way that
was to be envied. She managed her house with quiet efficiency,
her personal life with equal stoicism, and she never appeared to be
frazzled or overwrought. She thrived on crisis and trauma, smiled
in the face of disaster, and through it all remained peaceful and
ever-smiling.

One day she was asked how she did it. She was silent for a moment, then she said, "Every evening after the children are in bed,
their clothes are laid out for the next morning, their lunches are
readied and the lights are out, I fall to my knees beside their beds
and say a prayer to God. I say, 'Thank you God for not letting me
kill one of them today.'"

Motherhood . . . thy name is frustration.

X-RATED HAIR

Five years ago if someone had told me I would be lending a hair dryer to my son I would have laughed until I got a stitch in my side.

His hair always looked like an unmade bed. The wind parted it. Five fingers combed it. And when birds began to make a nest, we had it cut.

Then one day, all of that changed. The nation went unihair and my son went with it.

It would be nice to report that by this time parents have become acclimated to long hair on their sons. They haven't. Everywhere I go, the first question is, "How long is your son's hair?" I regard the length of his hair as a graph to my parental control over him. In June 1971, I used the heavy-handed parental approach. I told him I did not go through eighteen hours of labor to give birth to a pre-historic Cro-Magnon. He compromised by having the barber wave the scissors over his sideburns.

In September 1971, I used the humiliation route by telling him he looked like Prince Valiant with a two-dollar permanent wave. He was flattered and borrowed my setting lotion.

January 1972 was the year of the direct approach. I set him down and asked him point blank what he was trying to achieve. He said his long hair stood for his individuality. I asked him to get his individuality trimmed as it was falling into his chili. He declined but said he would keep it out of his eyes, which produced an affliction whereby he would snap his neck and for a brief moment you had a clear view of an eyeball.

In March 1972, I decided to compromise. If he would get a haircut, I would let him in the house, reinstate him in the will, and let him put a yellow bug light in his reading lamp. He refused.

This month, I conceded defeat. I told myself that I had seen boys with longer hair (or were they girls?). I told myself that there were worse things than having a son with long hair—like having a tooth grow through your ear, or an eighteen-year-old who wasn't toilet-trained. I told myself I would have to get with 'it as this is a new generation and they must set their own style. After all, didn't I wear Mickey Mouse hair ribbons? I was in the middle of telling myself that it was a fad and that in a few years he would be as bald as a Marine sergeant, when he went by the door and snapped his neck so that I could see he was conscious.

"Hey, Mom," he said, "we're out of hair spray."

I bit my lip. I'd give it one more try. If chaining him to the bed and playing Wayne King waltzes in his ear doesn't work . . . then I'll adjust.


## MOVIE ROULETTE

Something has got to be done about the ratings of movies. No one understands who goes, who waits in the car, who is admitted over sixteen, under seventy-five, or who must be accompanied by Rex Reed.

The way a GP movie rating was first explained to me, it stood for "General viewing with parental consent."

After the first GP movie I saw, I figured it meant Bambi kept his clothes on but he cussed a lot.

Now, after seeing several GP movies with the children, I have come to the conclusion GP means, "Go, but Push the Popcorn."

Let me explain. *The Hawaiians* was a GP movie with Charlton Heston. I trusted Charlton. After all, hadn't he read the Bible on the "Ed Sullivan Show"?

When a woman faced attack on the ship coming over, I shoved our youngest into the aisle and said, "Get some popcorn." When Charlton crawled into bed with Geraldine Chaplin, I turned him around toward the exit and said, "Get more popcorn." As the hero stripped and climbed into a public bath with six or seven nudie natives, I yelled out to the lobby, "More popcorn and wait for fresh butter."

During the showing of *Patton* (which was also a GP, I sent that kid out for popcorn eighty-two times, plus I had him check the pay phones for possible dimes, make sure our car lights weren't on, and check the men's room for his father's Ruptured Duck discharge button from World War II.

My kids say they do more walking during a GP movie than the ushers and besides all the other kids have seen it and said there is nothing wrong with it.

I was reared in a house where my dad canceled *Liberty* magazine because they carried ads for trusses. I was reared in an era where *Gone With the Wind* made headlines because Rhett Butler's parting words were, "I don't give a damn." I was reared in puritanical times when you walked across the street to avoid passing in front of a burlesque house. (Now, they're closing burlesque houses because they can't compete with GP movies.)

I should love to blame somebody . . . anybody . . . for not building censorship into movies. It would be easier. But maybe movie makers are trying to tell us something. Maybe they are putting the responsibility of saying "yes" or "no" back to the parents where it belongs and has always belonged.

I can't tell you how "Donna Reedish" I felt the other night as Mother and I checked out a GP movie the kids wanted to see. The screen was dark and quiet. A couple giggled. I saw them kiss softly.

Mother leaned over and whispered, "Go out for popcorn, Erma." I stomped up the aisle, grumbling, "All the other mothers have seen it and said there was nothing wrong with it!"


THE IMPOSSIBLE DREAM

I never understood why babies were created with all the component parts necessary for a rich, full life . . . with the unfinished plumbing left to amateurs.

If it was a matter of money, there isn't a mother in this world who wouldn't have chipped in a few extra bucks to have the kid completely assembled, trained, and ready to take on long trips.

As it is, mothers stumble along trying to toilet-train their babies by clumsily running water to create an atmosphere and holding sea shells to their ear to suggest rushing water. I used to turn on every faucet in the house and showed slides of Lake Erie while the kid sat there unrolling johnny paper.

I even used to threaten them. I had one kid whom I vowed I would send to the Army with diapers. I threatened him with other things too: a bed with a hole in it, a bicycle with portable plumbing, and an alarm system that rang when wet and lit up a sign on his back that read, LOOK FOR THE RAINBOW.

The whole affair was pretty ridiculous. But then aren't we all when the most important thing in our lives is succeeding vicariously through our children?

Now I note that a new "training kit" has come on the market guaranteed to cut toilet training time up to 90 per cent. (With some kids that adds up roughly to two weeks before football practice.)

It's a little throne with a built-in music box. When the baby has performed . . . and not until . . . the music box rewards him with a little tune.

I first saw it in the bathroom of my next-door neighbor, Gloria.

"Hey, that's terrific," I said. "What does it play?"

" 'The Impossible Dream,' " she said dryly.

"Then, you're having some success with it?" I asked hopefully.

"Not really," she said. "Todd isn't too swift. The first time I put him on, he sat there frozen and scared like he had just been asked to fly the thing to Cuba. So I explained to him, 'Todd, if you do your thing you will hear music.' "

"Did he understand that?"

"Not a word. He sat there a couple of hours and finally I took him off, went to the kitchen, got a glass of water and poured it into the bowl. The music came out and Todd clapped his hands and danced around like he was seeing the circus for the first time. Then I put him on it again and he sat there for another couple of hours."

"Then what did you do?"

"I took him off and got another glass of water and demonstrated for him again."

"And he finally got the point and now is on his way to being trained, right?"

"Wrong. Every couple of hours or so, he gets a glass of milk and pours it over the potty and dances to 'The Impossible Dream.' "

"Do you think he'll ever be trained?"

"I don't know," she said, sadly shaking her head. "I only know how disappointed he's going to be when he throws a pitcher of water over an Army latrine and there is nothing to dance to."

OBJECTION SUSTAINED

You know the trouble with some women? They have no imagination. A neighbor was telling me the other day that her little boy, Jody, wanted to bring a bull snake home from his vacation.

"What did you tell him?" I asked.

"I couldn't think of a reason why he couldn't," she said, help-lessly shrugging her shoulders.

"Are you kidding?" I shrieked. "A few years ago, my son captured a small, slimy specimen in a Coke bottle and I could think of ten reasons for leaving him behind (the snake, not the boy).

"1. Snakes do not know their own minds. They may jump up and down and think they want to leave their mommies and daddies for a fun trip, but after two days away from home, it's split-up time. (Or spit-up time if they stay)

"2. You would get bored with one another. After all, what can a snake do? Can he chase a ball after you throw it? Can he walk to the shopping center with you on a leash? Can he walk into a crowded room and keep it that way?

"3. Snakes are a minority group. Face it. Do you want him to feel the pains of discrimination? Wouldn't it break your heart to have his admission refused at Bible School? Or leave him outside in a Mason jar while you were inside with friends?

"4. Snakes are difficult to paper-train.

"5. Snakes adhere to a diet of living things. What happens when he runs out of mice and begins to eye our meter reader?

"6. How would you know if he got a headache?

"7. How would you explain it to him if someone accidentally clobbered him with a rake?

"8. You would be forcing on him a monk's existence. How do you know he doesn't want to date and eventually have a family?"

"Did he buy it?" asked my neighbor, bright-eyed. "I mean did he realize that there were inherent differences between a boy and a snake?"

"Not until I hit him with reasons nine and ten."

"Which were?"

"9. If you put that snake in the car with your mother, she will have a heart attack and drop dead.

"10. Ask yourself, do you want to be a motherless boy roaming through life with a sex-starved, militant, maladjusted snake in a Coke bottle?"

"He chose you instead of the snake, right?"

"No, but he's thinking about it."

"GUESS WHO'S STUCK WITH DISHES?"

*Fiddler on the Roof* holds the all-time performance record for live theater. On Broadway, this is true.

In our home, the record is held by a little drama that unfolds every evening, called, "Guess Who's Stuck with Dishes After Dinner?"

During the past eleven years, the original cast has staged 4,015 performances, plus a matinee on Saturdays and Sundays. The curtain opens to reveal a family sitting around after the evening meal. The oldest child speaks.

"It's your turn," she says mechanically to her brother.

"No way," he says, turning to his brother. "I did them last night."

Little brother turns to the diner on his right and says, "I did them night before last."

"What did we have to eat that night?" challenges his sister, her eyes narrowing.

"We had chicken. I remember because I broke the disposer."

The daughter moves to stage left and shouts, "Then that proves it. We had casserole the night before which I left to soak so that makes tonight *your* night." (She whirls around and points a finger at larger brother.)

"No way," he says. "If you remember I traded you last Tuesday night because you had to decorate the gym."

"And what about that time five years ago when I filled in for you when you broke your arm and spent the night in the hospital?"

"I paid you back for that. Besides, I don't put large mixing bowls in the refrigerator with one prune pit in it to keep from washing, like some people I know."

"And I don't leave my garbage in the sink like other people I know."

Little brother at this point is making a quiet exit stage right when he is discovered.

"*Hold it!* It's your turn. I can tell by looking at you. You are laughing on the inside."

"I am not laughing. I think we should start fresh with the oldest and then keep track."

"You say that because you are the youngest."

"Big deal. I didn't get a watch until I was twelve." (No one has understood that line in eleven years.)

The audience, comprised of two adults, pushes away from the table and walks out of the theater.

"When did we have spaghetti last?" asked my husband.

"About three weeks ago," I said. "Why?"

"I found some on my plate."

"That's what happens when you try to make dishwashers out of sensitive performers."

E IS FOR EAT

The average life span of a refrigerator light is thirty-seven years, four months, and eighteen hours.

We have replaced three bulbs within the last two years. This is due to the fact that every fifteen minutes, the two giant doors swing open (one for the freezer and one for the refrigerator) and my son stands there motionless staring at the contents as though he is awaiting the second coming.

Seeing him look from one side of the box to the other, it always seems as though he should be saying something like, "I suppose you are all wondering why I have gathered you here," but there is nothing. Only cold, silent appraisal.

The other night, as I threw an afghan over my feet to break the chill from the open refrigerator, I yelled out to him, "Why don't you let those poor leftovers deteriorate in peace?"

"I'm looking for something," he said.

"And you're gonna get it," I threatened. "Now shut that door."

"There's never anything to eat in this house."

"Then how come we are the only six-garbage-can family on our block? Besides, you cannot possibly be hungry. You just got up from the table."

"That was an hour ago."

"Shut the door."

"Can I have an ice cube?"

"I suppose so," I said tiredly. Minutes later, I heard the blender going and went out to investigate. The counter top was spread like a Roman orgy feast with French bread, olives, lunch meat, cheese, dips, and a malt frothing in the blender. "I thought you only wanted an ice cube," I said.

"You can't eat an ice cube by itself," he said, sinking his teeth into a sandwich.

The other night after I had stocked the refrigerator to capacity just three hours before, I too succumbed to the lure of the refrigerator and thought I would open both doors and view the array of food.

To my dismay, I plucked two empty milk cartons from the top shelf, an empty olive jar, a butter carton with no butter in it, a long slice of cheese that was beginning to curl, a cake plate with only a layer of crumbs, the bone of a chicken leg, and a quart-size soft-drink bottle with a cap on it and a quarter-inch of soda in it.

My husband came up behind me. "You too? What's the big attraction?"

I was numb. "I can't believe he ate the whole thing."


FIELD TRIPS

My son entered kindergarten with a four-word vocabulary: "My mom can drive." Later, he added words like "anytime, anywhere, and distance is no object." But for the first year, he made it on those four.

His teacher, Miss Varicose, was quite concerned about him and asked me to come to school to discuss the problem.

"I'm quite puzzled over . . . by the way he never told us his name."

"It's Charlie," I said.

"Charlie seems to be on the outside of our little circle. He does not seek out friends. He never volunteers to answer questions, and at times his behavior is bewildering. For example, the other day I said to the class, 'I want you to line up against the wall, the boys in one line, the girls in another. We are going. . . .' At that moment, Charlie jumped up on the desk, waved his arms excitedly and shouted, 'My mom can drive.'

"'That won't be necessary,' I told him. 'We are only going to the lavatory.' I don't understand Charlie."

"Of course you don't," I said. "You have to know that Charlie was born on the tail end of our other children, all needing to be driven hither and yon. He was born in a car between helping deliver a Sunday-morning paper route and taking his sister to a Girl Scout cookie rally. He cut his teeth on a stick shift. He learned his numbers by reading the mileage gauge. The only primary colors he knows are red, green, and amber. His alphabet is limited to P, R, N, and D. That kid has spent so much time in a car that when we passed a house the other day, he wanted to know who stole its hubcaps."

"Then being raised in a car has had an effect on Charlie?"

"You didn't notice he holds his pants up with a seat belt?"

"No, I didn't."

"You are not the only one confused, Miss Varicose. Not only for having trouble understanding him, but for the mother image I have created. Most children think of their mothers as hot apple pie and the American flag. Charlie sees me as four wheels and a tank of Platformate. He thinks driving a car is the only thing I can do."

"How did it all begin?" asked his teacher.

"Well, it all began with my first child," I explained. "She came home from school one day bearing a mimeographed sheet of paper. It read:

## MOTHERS MOTHERS MOTHERS
## WE NEED YOU

The first grade of Bradford Primary will participate in a field trip on Saturday at the Stillwell Owl Sanctuary. We are in need of mothers who can drive. This will be an enriching experience for you.

## PLEASE PLEASE PLEASE

"Actually, it wasn't an enriching experience at all. Two of my little passengers entwined themselves around a soft-drink machine and refused to go on the nature walk. One child in the car confided he had chicken pox but his mother covered it up with make-up so he wouldn't miss the field trip. And a flock of owls mistook my car for a relief station and created a credibility gap at the car wash.

"By the time my second child entered school the word was out. 'My mom can drive,' became their battle cry. It brought them prestige, importance, attention. It brought me girdle creases that can only be removed by surgery. I had so many 'enriching experiences' that the family was eating plastic food and wearing plactic underwear. I took a group to the book bindery, the state gas chamber, the piano factory, the persimmon festival, the press room of a local newspaper, and an aardvark farm.

"One day after returning from a field trip through a steel mill (which was responsible for the fillings in my teeth melting down), my child brought me a mimeographed sheet. 'Guess what, Mom? Our class is going on a boat trip down the river to visit a polo score card factory. I told my teacher, "My mom can drive." '

" 'Not this time,' I sighed, removing my goggles and safety helmet.

" 'Why?'

" 'Really, dear, I mustn't be greedy. There must be thousands of other mothers out there in utility room land who have an enrichment deficiency.'

"His face fell. 'What can I tell my teacher?'

" 'Tell her I am having labor pains thirty seconds apart. Tell her my Mother won't sign my permission slip. Tell her anything.' "

"Did it work?" asked Charlie's teacher, leaning closer.

"No. I ended up driving eight boys and girls to the old Salt Line Pier where we joined forces with eighty other third-graders. The trip was like a Chinese fire drill. Fifty-eight out of the eighty children ate their box lunches before we got out of the school yard.

"Two little girls became nauseated on the boat and threw up in my handbag before we left the dock.

"A kid named Max had me hang onto his water skis which he brought along 'just in case.' Three sweaters, a pair of glasses, and the kid voted most likely to fall overboard fell overboard.

"Linda dropped her loose tooth down the john and became hysterical when the kids told her the tooth fairy couldn't swim.

"The class bully spread a rumor we were on the *Titanic* and had half the class in lifeboats singing 'Nearer My God To Thee.'

"One child swore he saw a ship nearby flying a black flag with Cyril Ritchard aboard. I spent the entire boat trip in the restroom throwing my body in front of obscene words printed in lipstick on the walls.

"When we landed at the factory site, we discovered we had a mutiny on our hands. Two thirds of the children voted to stay in the souvenir shop and buy alligators dressed as merchant seamen and sweatshirts proclaiming, SAVE WATER. TAKE A BATH WITH SOMEONE.

"The other third were bored and wanted to get back to school early so they could shoot baskets in the gym.

"On the trip home, I asked one youngster what he liked best about the trip. He said, 'The towel machine was neat.'

"So you see, Miss Varicose, 'My mom can drive' are the only four words Charlie has heard since he was born and those four words are driving me out of my tree."

"What do you suggest we do?" she asked.

"I was hoping you could work with Charlie and perhaps teach him a new word."

"Like what?"

"Like 'no.' "

"Isn't that rather drastic?" she asked. "I was hoping you might favor the tapering-off plan. You see, this Wednesday our class is going to the museum to see a film on *Birth of a Peat Bog.* No scenes censored. We need mothers to drive. As soon as Charlie discovered it was an enriching experience, he volunteered you. He has the mimeographed sheet telling you to pack a box lunch, wear flats, and be at the school by ten."

"Miss Varicose, what would you say if I told you I was going to put a seat belt around Charlie's mouth?"

"But . . . his pants would fall down. It would be a traumatic experience."

"Better traumatic than enriched."

# 40 Anonymous

This country is extremely age-conscious. That is why a new group has been formed called "40 Anonymous" to help people overcome the problem. Here's how it works. Several months before reaching age forty, birthdayees are invited to a group-therapy program.

There is a ten-minute film where Doris Day wrinkles her nose, moistens her lips, and smiles, "I'm over forty and I still have all my own freckles," just to get the audience in a receptive mood. Then a testimonial is given. The one I heard was from Sylvia X.

"I'm over forty," she said in a faltering voice. (Applause) "A few months ago I was depressed and morose and thought life was not worth living. I got a chill when the furnace blower went on. I refused to eat apples even though I had my own teeth. I nipped at Geritol in the mornings after the kids went to school. I sent sympathy cards to myself and refused to start any long novels. A friend suggested I come to a 40 Anonymous meeting. That night I heard Senator Thurmond speak. He was wonderful.

"I went home and practiced saying 'forty' in front of the mirror. I thought I was cured. Then one night I went to a party. Everyone there was under thirty. It was terrible. No one knew the verse to 'Shine on Harvest Moon.' They had never head of Lyle Talbot or Maria Montez. When I said Okey Dokey, they laughed.

"I went berserk that night and drew a mustache on an advertisement for 'Mod Squad.' A member of 40 Anonymous found me throwing rocks at a rock festival. 'Get hold of yourself,' he said. 'Just say out loud, "I am forty." '

" 'I am foooooffffffffooooorrrr . . . I can't do it,' I cried.

" '*You can!*' he challenged.

" 'It's no use,' I said, 'this world is for the youth. Everyone around me is younger than I am. My doctor carries his stethoscope in a gym bag. My attorney has to shave only once a week. My son's math teacher is still wearing braces. I rode a plane the other day with training wheels on it. Good Lord, man, don't you understand, I am older than Mickey Mouse!' "

Sylvia's voice broke. "Today 1 am proud to say I have learned to live with my problem one day at a time." (Applause)

That night I stood in front of my mirror and said, "My name is Erma X and I'm fffff. . . . I don't look it, but I'm ffff . . . some days I look . . . fffffoooo . . . last year I was. . . ." It was no use. I called 40 Anonymous. Sylvia came over and had a drink with me.

Actually, forty or any other age wouldn't be so hard to face were it not for the current trend of restaurants making a fuss over birthdays. This ranges anywhere from a drum roll and house lights to a group of waitresses in headbands and adenoids charging at you with a cupcake and a sparkler on top.

I have warned my family if they ever inflict a public birthday on me, I will impale myself on a flaming skewer. After age twelve, birthdays should be as private as hernia surgery. After all, they're as personal.

Philosophers and poets may be as cute as they like about middle age but the question remains, "*What* begins at forty?"

Your laugh lines turn to wrinkles, the dimples in your knees and elbows fill in, you need glasses to read billboards, you find yourself listening to every word of the commercials on motel management and when you at last figure your teen-agers are old enough to be told about sex, you've forgotten what it is you weren't supposed to tell them until they were old enough to be told.

There is little comfort in people like Elizabeth Taylor chirping, "I am not going to fight middle age or wrinkles or fat." (If I had Richard Burton sewed up my hip pocket, I wouldn't fight anything.)

If I sound bitter, it is because I am going through a phase of middle age known as the "Didn't we go to school together syndrome?" (DWGTSTS)

The DWGTSTS begins on the eve of your fortieth birthday and continues until no one wants to claim you as a contemporary. I have never had so many bald, paunchy individuals accost me and invite me to remember the good old days. (And those are the women.)

The other night at a restaurant a Sun City Freshman stopped

by our table and said, "Remember me? We were in cooking class together."

I looked up, shocked. When this woman was in cooking class, fire hadn't been invented yet. "It's Edna something or other, isn't it?" she persisted. "And you used to write for the school paper."

"You're thinking of Edna St. Vincent Millay," I said stiffly.

"No," she said, "your hair is a little different color, your teeth look different, you're wearing glasses and carry a little more weight, but I'd know you anywhere."

"What gave me away?" I asked my husband.

"The way your eyes lit up when the orchestra played 'Beer Barrel Polka.'"

It's occasions like that that make you swear off high school reunions. If you're keeping track I have just gone to my last one.

It's not fair to all those balding, aging, dissipated, frumpy, flabby, graying people wandering around trying to be cheerful, when I look so great.

I found myself walking up to classmates, saying, "What happened?"

Take poor Clara what's-her-name. Her memory is shot. She went around all night calling me Ernie. Serves her right for marrying old Charley . . . or was it Harley what's-his-face.

As for poor Iris Pick, I could have wept for her. Had three children, bang, bang, bang. They drive her out of her tree. Lucky my three are spaced better.

The real shocker was our valedictorian, Enis Ertle. She's absolutely out of it. If the President has been there she'd have gone up and asked, "What are you doing these days?" I told her I'd give her my copy of *Peyton Place* when I finished reading it.

And if anyone had told me my best girl friend, Wanda Weight, would be nearly white-haired, I wouldn't have believed it. My wig nearly fell off when I saw her. Everyone was saying my old boy friend, Leroy Katch, looked positively prehistoric. I couldn't find my glasses in the bottom of my handbag to see for myself, but I can't imagine they would lie.

As I told my husband on the way home, "It's incredible to imagine some of our classmates are grandparents."

"I know," he said quietly.

"Do you know what that means?" I asked. "It means some of them had to have their children when they were mere babies of. . . ."

"Twenty-five," he said.

"It's funny about the teachers though," I commented. "Miss Kravitz looked seventy years old when I had her for Social Problems. Tonight she looked only about fifty. You're quiet. Anything wrong?"

"Nevin Noose came up with a mouthful of false teeth. I nearly dropped my partial."

"Couldn't you cry for them?" I said sadly. "Poor devils fighting middle age. We shouldn't have gone, but I wanted to see them all again before they got too old to appreciate me."

People do approach milestones in their own particular way.

On my husband's fortieth birthday, he locked himself in his bedroom with a copy of *Playboy* magazine and made an obscene phone call to Ted Mack.

That's the way fortieth birthdays are.

I knocked on the door and pleaded, "Why don't you come out and show us your presents? I want to see what the kids got you?"

The door opened a crack and he said, "Come in."

"I know they got you a bottle of hair creme," I said, "but what kind? Torrid Torment? Show No Mercy? Shameless Interlude?"

"No," he said, shaking his head vigorously.

"What then? Frankly Intimate? Sextop for Pop?"

"Let me say it is something I can handle," he said, clearing his throat nervously.

"It's not one of those things you're going to have to fight your way on and off buses with, is it? Or Karate chop your own mother?"

"I know what I'm doing," he said. As he scooped his boxes, tissue and ribbon up in his arms, the box of hair creme fell to the floor. I picked it up and read the name "Resignation Hair Creme," and in small letters below it claimed, "For the man who has everything but hair. No sexy aroma. No tantalizing softness to run your hands through. No double takes from girls on the beach.

Resignation Hair Creme just keeps your head from getting chapped."

"I guess that's all the kids could buy without a prescription." I alibied.

"I guess so," he replied softly.

He moped around for several months after that. Then, along came the football season and George Blanda. For all of you who think football is a winter replacement for the summer reruns, George Blanda is the world's oldest quarterback. He is forty-four years old. At a time of his life when he should be sitting in the stands with a thermos of hot chicken soup, he is sparking the Oakland Raiders to some unbelievable victories.

Well, I can't begin to tell you what George Blanda did for my husband.

When George kicked a forty-eight-yard field goal against Kansas City for a tie, my husband kicked off his lap robe (he was sitting in the living room by the fire) and said, "I think tomorrow I'll jog to the garbage can and back."

When George kicked a fifty-two-yard field goal to win the game with Cleveland 23–20, my husband kicked his Geritol bottle thirty-two feet into the air. When Blanda whipped out a twenty-yard touchdown pass with only seconds to go to beat Denver 24–19, my husband ambled through the living room and announced loudly, "I am donating my Supp-hose to Goodwill."

George Blanda was Lydia Pinkham to my husband. Then the new neighbors moved in next door and we were back to where we started.

"What are they like?" I asked as he came back across the lawn.

"Young," he snarled.

"How young?"

"He can still get his car in the garage."

"What about his wife?"

"She was waxing the garden hose."

"What did you talk about?"

"Don't ask. I made the mistake of telling him I was in the Army. He said his grandfather was in World War II and they studied it a lot in college. I tell you, it was incredible. He had never heard of victory gardens, Senator Joe McCarthy, Glenn

Miller, Snooky Lansen, the twist, Ozzie and Harriet, Packards, the Brooklyn Dodgers, or Fred Allen."

"It won't be easy. Do they have any children?"

"No. He said he and his wife decided not to have any in view of the fact they were concerned with overpopulation and what do you call it?"

"Copping out?"

"No . . . ecology."

"Do they play bridge?"

"No. He said it was frivolous in this time of involvement, when everything else needed his attention. I don't want to frighten you, but I think he's going to take sex education out of the home and put it on the ballot where it belongs. And she's a feminist who is going to picket the Avon lady."

"What do they do for kicks?"

"I think they sit around and watch each other's hair grow."

"You're being unkind. We were that young once."

"I was born older than they are," he sulked.

"Why, I remember the first time my grandmother met you," I said. "When you turned your back she said to me, 'He's a funny-looking thing, but when he grows hair, he might look all right.'"

"I had a burr haircut. It was the style," he shouted.

"I know. And we didn't know anything about Tom Mix, Will Rogers, the League of Nations, the cakewalk, Gene Fowler, and the Reo Runabout."

"I suppose you're right," he sighed, "but when people start moving next door to you who have never heard of Fred Allen. . . ."

"There goes the neighborhood," I said sadly.

On my fortieth birthday, my family chipped in and bought me a tennis racket. I don't wish to sound ungrateful, but this is like buying the Pope a Mouseketeer beanie.

"When are you going to use it?" the kids kept clamoring.

"When it snows and I get another racket to put on the other foot," I said.

The truth is, I have never cared for sports that take me away from the table. (Besides, I tire easily and tend to black out when I spend an evening licking Green Stamps.)

But these obstacles were small compared to the prejudice I encountered when I ventured to the tennis courts with my brand-new racket and my old body.

There is no evidence to sustain this, but I have a feeling new tennis rackets secrete an odor that is detected within a fifty-mile radius by experienced tennis players. The moment you appear, men in white shorts hurry toward their cars, women in white tennis dresses sniff the air and mumble something about burning dinner, and even small children playing in their bare feet back off and say, "I think I hear my mother calling."

I found one young man trying to scale the fence and said, "Would you like to play a game?"

"Have you ever played tennis before?" he asked.

"No," I giggled, "what gave me away?"

"Your sweat band. You don't wear it to the armpits."

"But that is where. . . ."

"You wear it around the wrist. Listen, I gotta cut out. Some other time. . . ."

The next night I went down again and this time collared a twelve-year-old girl who tripped and fell as the rest of the players ran from the courts to their cars.

"What am I doing wrong?" I asked.

"First, you don't get a new suit if you hit the ball over the big fence. That's baseball. Next, you don't get an extra point if you hit the drinking fountain. And take the press off your racket when you play."

During the next few weeks, I worked like a demon to shake the new-racket stigma . . . playing with anyone I could trap.

The other day I ambled onto the courts and there was this tired-looking housewife in pedal pushers and a Howard Hughes sweatshirt.

"Have you ever played tennis before?" I asked.

She shook her head. "How can you tell?"

"You don't wear the sweat band around your ankle, dear. I gotta go. I hear the timer on my stove going off. . . ."

Actually, my physical shape isn't the only thing that bothers me about my twilight years.

A scientist in California has figured out that every day after thirty-five, the adult loses 100,000 brain cells which affect thinking and memory.

My kids would argue that the loss is considerably higher than this. Since age thirty-five, I haven't had an original thought, done anything significant and while others were making giant steps for mankind, I was making giant steps with the garbage.

To prove to you this is not an idle observation, I took the trouble to keep a diary for an entire week, during which time I scientifically dropped 700,000 brain cells.

Monday: Twelve-year-old working on an English assignment asked me who the Earl of Sandwich was. When I suggested he was the one who always carried his lunch to the castle, twelve-year-old shook his head and said, "I'll call up one of the guys."

Tuesday: Reached a high level of incompetence by absent-mindedly pouring powdered milk in dishwasher dispenser. Daughter suggested a companion to sit with me all day until Daddy could relieve her in the evening.

Wednesday: Heard a suspicious rattle in the car. Drove it into the service station where they discovered an aerosol can of de-icer rolling around near my spare tire. I am permitted to drive now only if accompanied by a teen-ager.

Thursday: Was called upon to determine the sex of our hamster, which I did without hesitation, claiming no mating was possible. Male hamster is now in maternity tops.

Friday: Missed taking my discarded chicken innards from the freezer and putting them in garbage, thus bringing the total of chicken innards in my freezer to 320 pounds.

Saturday: Mental deterioration noted as someone mentioned having a paternity suit and I said I hoped they didn't catch on because I don't have the legs to wear them.

Sunday: Family found me laughing hysterically over Tom Jones singing, "I Who Have Nothing." Family saw no humor in it and concluded I should be sent to a church camp.

The scientist from California is on to something. He has already figured out the brain drain is caused by aging, impaired circulation, and other causes. He has not figured out why thirty-five is the magic year for deterioration.

Even in the prime of my senility, I figured that one out.

At thirty-five, most parents launch their first teen-ager. After that, professor, it's Bananasville all the way.

As far as my memory is concerned, as I was telling my husband, what's-his-name, "I've got to do something about my memory."

"Why?" he asked.

"Why what?"

"Why do you have to do something about your memory?"

"Oh, I don't know. Just little things have been getting by me lately. Like letting your insurance policy lapse . . . and forgetting Christmas the way I did and the humiliating thing that happened to me at the airport last week."

"What humiliating thing?" he asked, putting down his paper.

"Well, I was saying good-by to your sister when I saw this man smiling at me and he looked so familiar and I was sure I knew him, but I just couldn't put a name to him. So, just to be safe I ran over and grabbed his hand, pumped it and said, 'Gosh, it's good to have you home again. We've all missed you. As soon as you're settled, call and we'll get together for dinner.'"

"What's the matter with that?"

"In the car coming home I remembered who he is. It is Mr. Whitlock, the man who cleans our septic tank every year."

"It could happen to anyone," he said sympathetically.

"I suppose so. But ever since I took a memory quiz that appeared in the newspaper last week I've been real concerned."

"What quiz?"

"It's good to know someone else has a rotten memory. Don't you remember? It's the article I clipped out just before you got the paper. Here it is:

"1. When you cannot remember where you parked your car in town do you (a) have total recall of your make of car, serial number, and license plates, or (b) take a bus home and pretend it doesn't matter?

"2. At class reunions, do you (a) use the Association Method to remember names (i.e., he is hairy and paunchy; ergo, his name is Harry Paunchy), or (b) do you squint at name tags upside down and say, 'Nayr Mot, long time, no see'?

"3. Do you (a) have specific places for your sewing basket,

office equipment, cleaning supplies, and cooking utensils, or (b) are you content to put in hems with Band-Aids and take down phone messages using a cuticle stick on wax paper?

"4. Do you (a) keeps tabs on your grocery shopping cart by re membering its contents, or (b) do you have to 'mark it' by forcing your twelve-year-old to sit in the basket in a fetal position?

"5. Do you (a) always remember the ages, sex, names, and grades of your children, or (b) do you have to stop and count backward or forward the year the cat came to live with you?

"6. Do you (a) always repeat the name of the person you are introduced to, or (b) repeatedly look perplexed and say 'Abigail *Who?*'

"7. Do you (a) always make a note in your checkbook of the amount of the check and to whom it was made out at the time you are writing the check, or (b) do you tell yourself that you'll do it later when you're not in such a hurry?

"You know what I think the trouble is?" I asked, folding the paper. "I share my house with four disorganized people. It isn't easy trying to keep everything in a place with everyone going in separate directions. For example, the other day I opened the tea canister and some clown had put tea in it."

"That's wrong?" asked my husband.

"That's wrong!" I shouted. "So where's my rice now? And speaking of boots, do you know how long it took me to find the kids' boots the other morning?"

"I can't imagine."

"Three hours. And just because some ding dong took them out of the soft drink cooler in the garage and didn't put them back. I suppose I could be like Doris you-know-who."

"You mean my sister?"

"Yes. She's so organized she makes me sick. I was in her house the other day and she had a pad and pencil right next to the phone. Can you imagine that? And when she wants a needle she doesn't have to have kids run through the carpets in their bare feet. She keeps them in a package with her thread. (The needles, not the kids.) And here's the zinger. She keeps her car keys on a little hook in the utility room so she always knows where they are.

Oh well, what can you expect from a woman who numbers her checks consecutively?"

"Don't you keep your car keys in the same spot?" he asked.

"Are you kidding? If it weren't for looking for my car keys I'd never know where anything is. Take the other day. I was looking for the keys in the trunk of the car where I always leave them and found my new sweeper bags.

"When I went to put the sweeper bags on the broom-closet shelf, I found my rain hat which I haven't seen in two years. And when I went to put the hat in the coat closet I discovered my checkbook, which had been missing.

"While returning the checkbook to the stove drawer where it belongs, guess what? There were the scissors I had been searching for during the last week. I returned the scissors to the bookcase where I hide them from the kids, and found my dental appointment, which I had been using for a bookmark. I always keep my dental appointment in my jewelry box, so when I dropped it in there, lo and behold, there was the freezer key."

"And where are the car keys?" asked my husband.

"Well, if you can't find yours either," I sighed, "maybe I'm not as bad off as I thought."

Minutes later the phone rang. As I replaced the receiver I said, "Hey, guess who's coming to dinner Saturday? Wilma and Leroy Whitlock. You wanta give me a hint? Who are *they*?"

# Who
# Packed
# the
# Garbage?

We had a couple of good years in our house, then it happened. The rooms shrank, the cupboards disappeared, and the schools and the shopping centers moved. The lawn spread, the closets diminished, and no one could find the garage that the buyer swore went with the house. "Maybe we could start looking for a larger house," I suggested.

"Indeed not," said my husband. "I am sick and tired of moving every time the ashtrays fill up. We stay!"

He would need a little convincing.

"Why am I sleeping with the storm windows?" he asked one morning.

"You devil, you noticed," I said.

"I noticed. Why am I sleeping with the storm windows?"

"It's a mistake," I said. "The boys are supposed to sleep with the storm windows. You're supposed to sleep with the bicycles. There's no storage space in this house."

"You're as subtle as bad breath," he said. "We stay."

"I love these advanced schools out here," I continued. "Did I tell you the primary grades are putting on *The Last Picture Show* for a Christmas pageant?"

"We stay," he persisted.

"I hope you're not in your safe office worrying around about us all day in a house with a front door that won't lock, a clogged-up flue, an overloaded kitchen circuit, and Smokey the Bear posting signs all over the attic.

"The front spigot is broken, the lawn is ridden with crab grass, two dining room windows are stuffed with paper towels, the front door snaps behind you like a trap, the bathroom tile is rusting, and I took the Sears catalogue out of the bathroom. When the wind whistles down the vent. . . ."

"Maybe we'd better start looking around. . . ."

"I've already written the ad," I smiled. "'Charming three-bedroom home in the suburbs you have to see to believe. Spacious rooms, storage, fireplace, two baths, many extras. Convenient to progressive schools and shopping center. Will sacrifice to family who promises to love it.' What are you doing?"

"I'm making a list of the things that have to be done. I had no idea the house was that bad. Where's your pride, woman? Do you want people to think we live this way?"

Later that night we read the ad. "I'll miss your homemade screens. Remember the night we almost named a mosquito in our divorce suit?"

"That was nothing compared to the day we hung wallpaper in the hallway. And your daffodil bulbs. Remember? You planted them upside down and they haven't surfaced yet."

"I love this kitchen. The trees are just beginning to look finished. We brought three babies to this happy house."

"I hope no one buys it," he said.

"Me too," I sobbed.

Our sentiment gave way to practicality a few days later. As you know there are two methods of selling one's house. You can try to sell it yourself or contract an agent to do it for you.

Real estate agents tell you if you attempt to do it yourself you will be badgered by phone calls, hounded by curiosity seekers, and driven crazy by Sunday lookers. They are right.

The first day our ad appeared we were badgered by eight agents on the phone, hounded by five agents who were curiosity seekers, and driven crazy by four real estate agents who were Sunday lookers.

We were also discouraged by our homemade tours. Lord knows we tried. I would gather a couple of live ones in the hallway (my husband threatened to start biting his nails again if I involved him in my little off-Broadway production) and give them a brief history of the house.

I cautioned them about staying with the guide and reminded them that the closets would be opened only upon a written request submitted twenty-four hours in advance of the tour.

Some groups were quite ugly. When I gestured toward the lavatory and announced, "This is the bathroom," one fat man with a cigar snarled, "You're kidding! I thought it was a mess kitchen with a crazy soup pot!"

Some women, I discovered, made a profession of touring houses for sale. It was something to do on grocery day, like trying on hats in the dime store or looking at trusses in the medical-supply house.

We finally put the house in the hands of our friendly real estate agents. From that moment the family was on red alert.

When the agent called to say she was bringing a prospective customer through, one child would empty ashtrays, gather all the dishes off the table, and dump them in the oven. (Later we found people look in ovens, so we stored them in the back seat of the car.) One would smooth the empty beds, put out fresh towels, and empty waste cans.

Another would cover the bird, tie up the dog, and douse the hamster cage with a strong deodorant. I would pull down the garage door, unscrew the bulb in the utility room, prop a few crummy plastic flowers in the bathroom, and as my last act on the way out . . . flush.

Satisfied that the house looked as if it had never been lived in, we scurried to the neighbor's spirea bushes where we stayed until the entourage left.

This went on for weeks. The strain was beginning to show on all of us. Then one night it happened. We showed the house with the kids in it . . . sitting on the sofa . . . with all the lights on. This was the night the house sold.

I felt a quiet giddiness and relief, like when you think you're pregnant and it turns out to be Asian flu. I was smiling out loud when my husband walked in.

"You know the garage that's been missing since we bought the house? I just found it under some junk. As they say in the ads, 'You have to see it to believe it.'"

If selling the house was traumatic, moving made me a prime candidate for the Mental Health poster girl of the month.

Once when I was a kid I remember the circus came to town. Within minutes of the finale, the big tent was hauled down and loaded on a train. Aboard were 15 trained elephants, 5 wild lions, 2 domestic bears, 12 dancing ponies and a singing prairie dog all

caged neatly in a row, and 250 performers and workers who waved good-by from the train as they pulled out of town.

It took me *three weeks* to make contact with my friendly moving representative.

He gave me a manual, *Everything You've Always Wanted to Know About Moving but Were Too Cheap to Ask,* that said there was nothing to it. In the foreword it said, "One out of every five families in the United States moves every year. (See page 117 for illustration.)"

I turned quickly to page 117, where a picture brought tears to my eyes. Mother was playing checkers on a moving box with her pre-schoolers. Dad, with a pipe in his mouth, was bouncing a beach ball to his son, while in the background six movers were earning hernias.

The manual continued, "Remember the three key concepts of a fun move: Planning, Organization and Ruthlessness with Your Discards."

"If you want to stand around and bounce a beach ball to your son on moving day," I announced to my husband, "you are going to have to plan."

"What does that mean?" he asked.

"That means I have already packed your golf clubs, electric shaver, books and clothes, with the exception of a pair of slacks, three shirts, and a change of shorts."

"But we're not moving for five weeks!"

"That's where organization takes over," I said. "You will note that each box which is packed has a number on it from one to nine. Each number corresponds with a master sheet on which each room in the new house is given a number. Thus, when the mover walks into the front door and says, 'Number Five, lady,' I will look up from my checkers game and say softly, 'That's the second bedroom on the right, down the hall.'"

"Where's the master sheet?" he asked.

"I'm not sure," I pondered. "It's either packed in a Number One box with unpaid bills and unopened fourth-class mail or it is stuffed inside an encyclopedia in a banana box that I got from the A&P. It will show up. Don't worry. In the meantime, we must work on being ruthless with our discards."

We had never been ruthless with our discards before. We discovered that when we ran across three boxes in the attic marked, RAIN-SOAKED HALLOWEEN MASKS.

"I say we can do without your attendance certificates from the third grade and your leather desk calendar from 1954," I said, blowing dust from a carton in the attic.

"Very well," he retaliated, "I say we can do without your broom with four straws and a dress form that hasn't fit you since you were ten."

"Okay," I growled, "it's out with your torn billfold with the autographed picture of Gale Storm."

"Then it's *out* with that box of baby things with the milk-stained bibs."

"Now, just a darned minute," I said. "Any mini-brain knows that you do not throw out baby clothes."

"Why not?"

"Because you're asking for it, that's why. I knew a woman who gave away her baby clothes and the next month she became pregnant."

"What's wrong with that?"

"She was fifty-three years old!"

During the next few weeks we were to devote every waking hour to disposing of our disposables. It took us a day and a half to lug all the stuff from the attic to the end of the driveway. It took our kids just twenty minutes to bring it all inside again. (The baby just sat in the middle of the floor in a Mouseketeer beanie clutching a consumptive basketball and looking hostile.)

Against my better judgment we even staged a garage sale that made Disneyland look like a mausoleum.

The whole idea was conceived by my girl friend Esther, who said, "You are a natural for a garage sale."

"Why do you say that?" I asked.

"Because you are cheap."

"I don't think you understand," I sniffed, "that spreading one's personal wares out in a garage for public exhibition is not only crass, it smacks of being tacky."

"I made thirty-two bucks off my junk," she said.

"Why didn't you say so?" I asked excitedly. "Get the card table and let's get started."

The garage sale began at 9 A.M. By 7:30 A.M., I had fifteen cars parked on the driveway, eighteen on the lawn, two in a ditch, and a Volkswagen trying to parallel park between two andirons in my living room.

They grabbed and bought anything that wasn't pumping water, cemented in the ground, growing from seed, or spit sparks at them when touched.

They bought cocktail toothpicks that were billed, "Like new" . . . radios guaranteed not to play ever . . . plastic flowers that had died . . . toothless rakes . . . buckets with leaks . . . books of German military commands . . . and a ukelele that only knew one song, "The World Is Waiting for the Sunrise."

At one point I tried to shove through the crowd with a package in my hand. A woman grabbed it from me and said, "I'll give you thirty-five cents."

"No, really," I stammered, "this isn't . . ."

"Forty cents," she said, grabbing it, "and that is my last offer."

It is the first time anyone ever paid me forty cents for my garbage.

By 4 P.M. I watched tiredly as a woman tried to coax my husband into her trunk.

"Esther," I said, "this is the most incredible sight I have ever seen."

"What's in that package under your arm?" she said.

"It's nothing," I hesitated.

"It's mildewed laundry," she shouted. "How much did you pay for it?"

"Thirty-five cents, but some of it still fits."

With the garage sale behind us, all that remained was the checklist the moving representative had given us.

"You want to read it aloud," I asked my husband, "while I confirm it?"

"I can't," he said. "You packed my glasses away five weeks ago."

"Oh, for crying out loud. I'll read and you check. Did we turn off the milkman? Telephone? Furnace? Utilities? Newspaper? Garbage? Mail?"

"Check."

"Did we defrost the refrigerator? Unplug the washer? Disconnect the Avon lady?"

"Check."

"Did we change our address on magazine subscriptions, insurance policies and credit cards?"

"Check."

"Do we have all of our valuables including jewelry, stocks, checks, cash, and important papers in one place?"

"They're in my shirt pocket," he said dryly.

"Can you drive with the tropical fish on your lap and a pot-bound philodendron at your feet?"

"I think so."

"Did we ever find the front door key?"

"Did we ever have one?"

"I guess that's it," I said, smiling. "I have the checkerboard and the beach ball. All we have to do is find the car keys and the kids and. . . ."

We both looked at each other at the same time. Then we started ripping cardboard boxes open.

"Could they be packed in a Number Two box with the cocktail olives and used razor blades?"

"Try the Number Five box marked 'Faded Towels and Shirt Cardboards for Finger-painting. . . .' "

Actually, this wasn't the first time we had ignored the children in the whole operation. When we made plans to move, it never occurred to us to discuss it with our children. We knew our older son would follow the refrigerator into combat if he had to. Our daughter makes her residence behind the wheel of a compact, so it was just a matter of finding a home for her mouthwash. And we had raised our younger son with a two-word philosophy, "Trust us."

Then, a woman at the dry cleaners said, "I cannot believe you did not call a family council and discuss it with your children. Moving a child against his will often makes a psychological imprint that is difficult to heal."

"I don't know about you," I said, as we gathered around the dining room table, "but I feel like Ozzie and Harriet voting on whether or not to have the fruit punch or the Shirley Temple fizzie at the fraternity sock hop."

My husband cleared his throat. "I suppose you wonder why I have gathered you all together. We are moving in a few weeks and wanted to encourage some discussion on it."

My son ate an apple noisily (core and all) and said it was all right with him and left. My daughter asked us to leave the new address in the sun visor of the car and made her exit. Our youngest son said simply, "I'm not going."

"WHATYA MEAN YOU'RE NOT GOING!" we shouted.

"I've thought it over," he said, "and I've got too much going for me here. My friends . . . my school . . . my paper route."

"But where would you live?" we asked.

"I could get an apartment."

"A twelve-year-old in an apartment. You can't even ride your bike across the highway."

"I thought family councils were supposed to be democratic," he said.

"They are," barked his father, "and if you still have relatives living in town you want to see again, be quiet."

"You and your crummy democratic way," I said, "I told you it wouldn't work."

His father took a deep breath and steadied himself against the table. "As council president, I move to motion that discussion on the matter of moving be closed and any objections must be submitted in writing before the next council meeting which has been indefinitely suspended. The family council is adjourned."

We both sat there. "Wonder what a psychological imprint looks like?" I asked my husband.

"I don't know," he said. "The only thing I can remember from my father is a hand imprint on my hindside that stayed red for a year and a half. It's probably the same thing."

We spent all of our time being apprehensive about traveling across country with three hostile children. We should have given more time to thinking about traveling with a dog.

I've read about people who simply will not travel unless they can take their animals with them.

But then, I've also read about monks who flog themselves with chains for penance, and a native tribe in New Zealand that inflicts pain by wearing spears through their tongues.

I am as crazy about animals as the next one, but face it, following a moving van 3,000 miles with a dog's rump in your face, and his ears whipping your face as they flap in the no-draft is no way to travel. We were not on the road with our dog eight hours before we realized he placed certain restrictions on everyone in the car.

1. He demanded a seat of his own. In the front. Next to the window. With his own safety belt.

2. When another car passed with a dog in it, he declared the car open range and sprang from the front to the back seat, gouging everyone with his toenails and obstructing everyone's view. (My husband remembers the entire state of Texas as a hairy tail.)

3. There would be none of this crack-the-window-and-leave-the-dog-in-the-car-while-we-eat routine. The first time we tried it his screams were picked up by a Russian satellite. From then

on, he ate hamburgers, fries, chicken, pizza, and tacos with the rest of the people.

4. He was quite selective about his rest-rooms, rejecting the barren strips along the roadside, open field, and secluded forests. He preferred the intimacy of a lawn chair at poolside, a potted plant in the motel lobby or the leg of a hotel manager.

"The problem," said my husband one night at the motel, "is the dog has nothing to do."

"He chewed up the last three coloring books I bought him," I said dryly, "and he doesn't sing well."

"Don't be cute," he said. "I feel sorry for him. I think the answer is to stop more often and let him run and be with other dogs."

The next afternoon we pulled up to a roadside park and followed the signs to a section marked, DOG AREA. The grass was so tall we could barely find the picnic table. Delicately, we made our way through where we found ourselves surrounded by dogs.

"This is great," said my husband. "Just what he needs. Now where's the dog?"

We looked around to discover him in the well-manicured lawn section sitting on a bench eating fried chicken with an older couple.

I shook my head. "I know he's a dog. You know he's a dog. Do you want to tell him and break his heart?"

We had three thousand miles to talk about the house we wanted. A friend who is an Air Force wife says there is nothing to reading ads in the newspapers. You just have to speak the language. Once you break the language code salesmen use in selling houses, it's no sweat. For example:

"A Handyman's Dream." If you're married to a contractor, buy it. If not, forget it. Chances are the last major repair on the house was a new chain for the john.

"Spacious Grounds and Green Grass." This means the septic tank is gone. To be sure, check out the house during a drought. If there is an oasis, pass it by.

"Tenants Leaving City—Immediate Occupancy." They don't tell you the former occupants were a motorcycle gang who left skid marks on the living room floor and used the dumbwaiter for beer cans.

"No Children." Show me a landlord who will not accept children and I'll show you a landlord who doesn't permit squeaky rockers, asthmatic coffeepots, heel plates on your loafers, or flushing after 5 P.M.

"You've got to see it to believe it." You do and you won't.

"Priced for quick sale." Watch out for these, especially if the owners wish to be paid in pesos.

"Southern Charmer. Built in 1732." The plumbing was built in 1732. The rest was patched up with defense-cabin leftovers.

"Country Living." Yes, but which one? We once lived in a house so far out of town, we had to get malaria shots.

"Convenient to Stores." It's usually over one.

Another pitfall we had to watch out for was neighborhoods. I guess there are some naïve women who think that when you buy a home you consider only its physical features, its distance from good schools, and its convenience to shopping centers.

Rarely do they interview their prospective neighbors until they have an unpleasant experience. When I was first married, I fell into a "bad neighborhood." I discovered one of my neighbors baked bread. Another was a size three who did not go into maternity clothes until she was 8½ months. (My stomach was larger than hers when I coughed.) And she dusted her mailbox.

Four years ago I hit it lucky. We bought a house between two cemeteries. But then, how often do those opportunities come along?

That's why I think it's a good idea to do a "home study" on a neighborhood before you find yourself in a nest of thin, intelligent, talented, organized mothers, who are also athletic. (If the good Lord had meant for me to play tennis, he would have divided my legs from the hips to the knees.)

Before I buy I always ask them to answer true or false to the following: Ovens with see-through doors should be banned.

Surplus kids should be recycled in the name of ecology.

Christmas tinsel in the rug is a lived-in home.

A small waist makes you tire easily.

A well-balanced meal is boring.

Eliminate clutter. Get rid of your sweeper attachments.

If you have checked true to each of these, I wish you lived in my neighborhood.

We looked at one house and I saw a neighbor out of doors. As we were talking, one of her children came up and asked, "Mom, did you iron my plaid skirt?"

"Of course," smiled the mother patiently, "it's hanging in your closet, dear."

"But are you sure you ironed it?" insisted the child. Her mother nodded. "Okay," said her daughter. "It's just that I'm not used to a cold zipper."

Now there's a neighbor I could love.

It's hard to believe that we bought the new house in three days.

Unless your marriage was made in heaven, I do not recommend it. We have always adhered to a theory that the union of two people was never meant to withstand the punishment of (1) hanging wallpaper together, (2) pruning shrubbery side by side, (3) working as a team on the checkbook, (4) sharing an electric blanket with a single control, (5) spending three rainy days in a camper, or (6) having children ten and a half months apart.

We have just added to this list (7) buying a house. Being extremely efficient, my husband kept a notebook of the dozen or so houses we viewed and at the end of the day in our hotel room, we would go over the day's crop.

"The one with the woman cleaning the pool was well built," said my husband.

"The house?"

"No, the woman."

"Personally," I said, "I like the house with the meatloaf in the oven. There's something about onions. . . ."

"Was that the one where the owner kept following us around and pointing, 'This is the bathroom'?"

"Yes, and you were rude to keep shouting, '*Right.*' I loved the decorator's house, but it was too small. How old is Junior now?"

"Forget it. He's only twelve and isn't even engaged."

"I liked the one with the basketball hoop," said a voice.

"Who's he?" I asked tiredly.

"Our twelve-year-old," said my husband.

"We've got to start narrowing it down," I sighed.

"Okay, I vote for the house on that deserted dirt road," he grinned.

My eyes flashed. "You won't be happy until I have to organize a garbage car pool, will you? Why don't we get that long ranch house from that adorable woman who had my book on her coffee table?"

"Our furniture wouldn't fit into that house."

"Since when does Early Poverty fit *any* house?" I snarled. "Did the house with the vicious dog do anything for you?"

"I couldn't see much from the car with the windows rolled up," he said. "Besides I'm thinking we had better give up buying and look for a rental."

"That tears it," I snarled. "We look at thirty-one houses in three days, count bathrooms, check out plumbing, interrupt dinners, make pages of notes, and you suggest renting. That's what you can expect, I guess, from a man whose mother wore a navy blue dress to our wedding."

"We'll buy the one with your book on the coffee table."

I threw my arms around him. "Wonderful. You may have to sleep with the storm windows for a while until we can figure out storage, and if it doesn't work out, we can always shop for another house. . . ."

# She Has
# a Cold.
# Shoot Her.

When women's lib comes out for Equal Colds, I will join it.

I never minded dancing backward . . . or having buttons on the wrong side of my blouse, or having to ask for a key every time I want to go to a service-station rest-room. But just once I would like to have my cold given the same respect as a man's cold.

A few weeks ago when my husband had the sniffles, he took his cold to his bed, summoned three medical opinions, insisted I mail the children out of the state, installed a dumbwaiter in his bedroom (me!) and wrote to ABC insisting he would make a great two-part series for "Marcus Welby, M.D."

Two days ago, I awoke to pain. My head was feverish, my lips cracked. My throat was dry. I was nauseated. Every bone in my body begged to be put to rest. "I do not feel well," I said to my husband. "In fact, I don't mean to be dramatic, but think I am dying."

"Does that mean you're not going to get dressed?" he asked impatiently, looking at his watch.

"You don't understand," I said, "it is pure penance to breathe. My head aches. My eyes feel like round razor blades, and it's only a matter of minutes before I go to that big utility room in the sky."

"I feel the same way when I sleep too long in the mornings," he said.

"But it's only six-thirty," I said huskily.

"So, eat a little bacon, hash browns covered with catsup . . . and where are you going?"

You've heard it sisters, now what are we going to do about it?

I propose we initiate federal legislation to make women's colds legal in all of the fifty states to be protected under a new law called: Bombeck's Equal Cold Opportunity Bill.

The bill would provide that women would receive more than fifteen minutes to get over a twenty-four-hour virus.

Under Equal Opportunity, her cold would be granted the right to stay in bed and would be exempt from car pools, kitchen duty, laundry, bowling, and visiting the sick.

Any husband who degrades and taunts his wife's cold with such remarks as "Maybe it was the pot roast," or "You're just bored," or "If it hangs on till spring you'd better see a doctor," or "Get on your feet, you're scaring the children," will be liable to a fine.

Any husband who mentions bacon and hash brown potatoes to a dying woman would be put away for fifty years . . . without benefit of trial.

I would also like to see women protected from well-meaning families when you are flat on your back. There is nothing any worse than to lie there looking as sexy as open garbage and have your family get along beautifully.

As Grandma says, "I've never seen your house so immaculate. The children are doing a fantastic job. You really should get help when you get home. (The implications being exactly what you think they are.)

Or a husband who says, "Don't worry about a thing. Your daughter is an amazing cook. I don't know where she gets it. Last night we had steak, potatoes, and green beans. Tonight, she's going to surprise me."

Or a daughter who chirps, "I love keeping house. Did all the laundry today in an hour. I made the boys clean their own rooms. All you have to do is sit on them."

Or a son who smiles, "Wow, did we have a day. I had the gang over and they didn't have to be quiet like when you're home writing. We really had a blast. We helped Dad clean out your kitchen cabinets."

Just when it sounds as though you could be replaced by a recording, your small son whispers, "The dog wet on the bedroom carpet, the hamster died, we spilled beets all over the refrigerator, argued all day Monday, and the green beans were so tough we fed them to the meal worms."

You know, I'm going to live with that kid in my old age.

I make old age sound like a certainty. I don't mean to. What

with the doctor shortage, you are lucky to get an appointment . . .
especially if you're new in town.

"Hello," I said over the phone, "I have just moved into the
community and wonder if the doctor could. . . ."

"I'm sorry," interrupted the nurse, "but the doctor does not accept any new patients."

"I'm not really new," I giggled. "I'm forty-four years old. Some
of the parts you can't even get any more."

"You do not understand," she said, without glee in her voice.
"The doctor does not take on any more patients."

I called the Medical Society in the area and in calling the
list of numbers she gave me discovered Dr. Frizbee did not work
on weekends . . . or the Friday preceding them; Dr. Coldiron
had a phone that was unlisted; Dr. Shuxley could not see me
until two days before Thanksgiving, unless I was bleeding profusely and in that event could work me in as an emergency
sometime the week of October 10; and Dr. Dlux was home with a
cold he couldn't seem to shake for the last six weeks.

I became as frustrated as Martha Mitchell facing a telephone
strike. The idea of getting a doctor became an obsession with
me . . . a game, so to speak.

"Hello there," I said huskily to one doctor. "This is Joey
Heatherton. I have a chest cold." (Click)

"Hi there. This is Mrs. Arnold Palmer. If you could see me for
five minutes, I could take five strokes off your game." (Click)

"Hi. I wasn't feeling too well and wondered if you would
consider seeing me if I told you I made house calls." (Click)

"Hello. I'm an old, rich person and want to leave my fortune
to someone to whom I am grateful and has shown me some kind
act." (Click)

"Doctor? Are you wearing your stethoscope? Fine. You're
invited to a come-as-you-are party." (Click)

Doctors often work sixty hours a week. The golf on Wednes-
days is a myth. They are bogged down by paper work and
hypochondriacs. Few of them want their sons to walk in their
shoes.

But the fact remains, I had to lie to get a doctor to see me.

I told him I was well and felt wonderful, but just needed a physical for camp.

When I talked with a doctor about the shortage, he said they could possibly alleviate the shortage by releasing medical students into the community. But the real problem was that so many doctors were specializing, it cut down on the number of general practitioners.

I found this to be quite true when I took my cold to Dr. Weazel last week.

"Is it a summer or winter cold?" he asked.

"Summer."

"Then you'll want to see my colleague, Dr. Stamp, on the third floor."

Dr. Stamp's nurse got out a form and asked, "Where is the location of your summer cold? Head, nose, or chest?"

"Mostly in the nose," I said. "I can't seem to breathe."

"That would be Dr. Alvenaz on the eighth floor."

"Which nostril," said Dr. Alvenaz's nurse.

"Mostly my left."

"That's too bad," she said, "Dr. Flack is out of town. His calls are being handled by a wonderful right-nostril man, Dr. Riggs. He's down on the fifth floor."

Dr. Riggs took a look at my left nostril and said, "Do you sneeze a lot?"

"Oh yes," I said.

"I thought so. We have a great sneeze specialist in the building. Just joined forces with a top fever-blister consultant. They're on the main floor off the lobby. I think perhaps he can help you."

Dr. Hack was quite reticent to infringe on Dr. Flack's left nostril, but he did say he thought he could prescribe a box of nose tissue and a Berlitz record of a German saying, "Gesundheit."

"I could venture one step further," he said, "and suggest two aspirins and bed."

"What kind of bed?" I asked. "Double, rollaway, single, twin, bunk, or trundle."

"It doesn't really matter," he fidgeted.

"And what about the mattress?" I insisted. "Firm, hard, semi-firm, downy soft, or orthopedic?"

"I really don't think. . . ."

"And what about the sheets? Cotton, percale, satin, contour, fitted, patterned, floral, pastel, or white. Let's talk about pillows while I'm here. Should it be duck, down, goose, swan, diseased chicken, what?"

"Really, madam," he said, "I am only a sneeze doctor. Don't make trouble."

How insulting could you be to a doctor whose stethoscope is made out of tinker toys?

Besides, these experiences in a doctor's office are vignettes compared to the drama of a hospital visit.

After every hospital stay, I experience a gnawing sensation that sends giddy tingles up and down my spine.

I have the feeling it is only a matter of time until hospitals go the way of zoos: they will lock up all the visitors and let the patients/or animals roam free.

I base this on a recent experience in the hospital, at which time there were more tourists roaming around my room than there were in Rome during Easter week.

Just for the record, I made note of the people ministering to my needs:

A fledgling pathology worker who kept thrusting a hypodermic needle into an orange and mumbling to himself, "I think I got the hang of it now."

A farsighted candy-striper who was arranging two rosebuds in a specimen vial.

A visiting clergyman who wanted to pray with me.

A dietitian engaging in an in-depth dialogue with me on why I did not eat the Tomato Surprise.

Three neighbors who were having a heated discussion on who was legally responsible for my expiration if I should fall out of bed.

An intern who was lost.

And an assortment of workers who were specialists in their respective fields: window-sill wiper, under-the-bed duster, sheet smoother, mail deliverer, pillow fluffer, bed-raiser supervisor, water-pitcher captain, boy paper carrier, milk-and-cracker foreman, and pulse-and-temperature recorder.

Any minute I expected to hear Ben Grauer announce that in sixty seconds, the big ball would fall from the New York *Times* building and it would indeed be another New Year.

The Woodstock atmosphere not only slows down a patient's recovery, it often turns the "sickee" into a totally different personality. I have seen shy, introverted women enter a hospital who were too embarrassed to say the word pregnant (when they were). Two weeks of hospital routine and they were whipping up and down the halls like wood nymphs dressed only in a table napkin and an ID bracelet. (I once discovered myself discussing my irregularity with a TV repairman I had never seen before in my life.)

The very idea of locking up the help and the visitors and letting the patients run the hospital captures my imagination. I get some kind of a thrill just thinking about standing in front of the cage occupied by my night nurse, Mrs. Needles. I would wait until I saw signs of her deep breathing. Then I would rattle the cage vigorously. When that didn't rouse her, I would thrust my flashlight into her face, put my arm inside, grab her by the throat and shout into her exposed ear, "Mrs. Needles! *Mrs. Needles!* Will you need something tonight to help you sleep?"

In my imagination, I have dreamed of an entire section devoted to visiting birds. I know a lot of strange birds who deserve to be visited back.

The Good News Warbler:

She's the gem who sits at your sickbed and informs you that while you are flat on your back your children are under the close scrutiny of the welfare department, your dog wandered off, possibly to die, she hasn't seen your car since they towed it home, and your husband is finding solace with a person who is well. (She will mention how your hair reminds her of Elliott Gould.)

The Long-Winded Mean-Mouth Thrush:

This is the well-meaning visitor who can't make it to the hospital in person, so she calls you on the telephone and talks . . . and talks . . . and talks. There is no way to get her off the line.

"As I was telling Frank just the other day. . . ." she rambles.

"I am having labor pains three minutes apart, Delores," I venture, "I have to hang up now."

"Wait a minute," she says, "did I tell you what Leroy brought home from camp. This'll tear out your stitches."

"The doctor is here now, Delores. He wants to take out something."

"Hang on a minute," she says irritably, covering the mouthpiece. Later she returns and says, "Leroy is bugging me. He wants to know if he can have a soft drink. I swear all that sugar is going to rot his teeth."

"Can I call you back, Delores?" I ask feebly. "I'm beginning to black out now."

"Well, don't," she commanded, "until I tell you about Bernice's garage sale."

The Bungling Loony Bird:

I can hardly wait to call on this rare species when she's in custody. She's the wrongo who can't do anything right. She never comes to the hospital empty-handed. There's a bag of caramels for the toothless; cookies for the diabetic; pizza for the gall-bladder recoverer; roses for the allergy sufferer, and a book on ice hockey for the new mother.

The AMA Crested Warbler:

Whatever you've got, the AMA Crested Warbler knew someone on a soap opera with the same thing who had to be .written out of the script.

A civilian, she is virtually in love with the drama of the hospital and will perch for hours on your bed taking your pulse and quoting from old aspirin bottles.

The Loitering Bedside Hawk:

This is the bird who arrives in time for hospital breakfast and never knows when to go home. She is usually someone you have known for about two weeks. Once you have ascertained you look rotten, you pursue such breathless-making subjects as What outdoor scene are you going to pick for your next checkbook? Does Tom Jones wear lifts in his shoes and should the government control the sale of fireworks?

The Swift-Tailed "Caught Cha":

This is the species that swoops through your door in moments that would at the very least be called "inopportune."

When you are lying flat on your back with your sheet off, trying to pull your gown over your hipbone, the door will crash open—and it's Caught Cha.

When you have a compact mirror trained on your backside to see if the last shot administered left a crater in your skin, a draft of air will herald the Caught Cha.

The Bluebird of Happiness:

For obvious reasons, I have saved my visit to my doctor until last, as timing is of the essence.

I would visit my doctor only when he is bathing in a saucepan with one arm balancing the soap and washcloth and the other clutching a wet sheet to his body.

Then I would hover over his breakfast tray and with a look of horror point to a mound of white and gasp, "What is that?" Finally, I would fight my way through the crowds of people around his bed and before parting toss a humorous little one-liner over my shoulder like, "Get some rest."

# Happy
## Mother's
## Day,
## Colonel Sanders

Looking back, I realized now that I married too young, but when you're forty-three and in love, who can tell you anything?

The transition from typewriter to toilet bowls is never an easy one. I always wondered if someone ran an ad in the New York *Times*: WANTED: Household drudge, 140 hour week, no retirement, no sick leave, no room of own, no Sundays off. Must be good with animals, kids and hamburger. Must share bath, would 42 million women still apply?

Every day my husband returns to his lair and asks mechanically, "What kind of a day did you have today?"

Resentment caused me to turn on him the other day and ask, "What kind of a day did you think I had?"

He grabbed a pencil and began to write. The result was headed:

### ERMA'S DAY

8 A.M.: Get everyone out of the house and make a fresh pot of coffee. Leave just enough in pot to spoon out a cup for husband at dinner and a piece to chip off for his breakfast.

8:30 A.M.: Separate husband's socks . . . from one another. Make sure there is not a pair that matches.

9 A.M.: Lint socks. Gathering up small pieces of thread and dust is tedious, but it is worth it to see him bite his necktie in half, out of rage.

10:00 A.M.: Go through his jewelry box and take out all the large cuff links with B on them and put them on your blouses.

10:30 A.M.: Take tucks in all of his underwear and slacks to make him think he is gaining weight.

11:00 A.M.: Borrow his razor blades to take the hem out of the living room draperies.

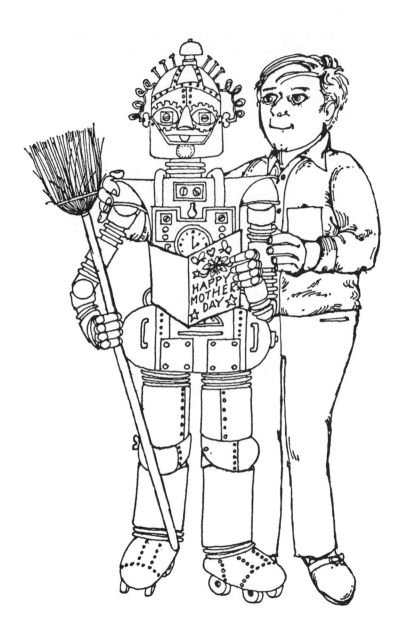

Break for lunch, followed by "As The World Turns."

3 P.M.: Wash good white tennis sweater in hot water with red blanket.

4 P.M.: Invite small neighborhood children into the garage to play with husband's power tools.

5 P.M.: Put an onion into the oven to make husband think dinner is on.

6–11 P.M.: Tell husband what a hard day you had.

"Well," he said triumphantly, "did I miss anything?"

"Yes," I said, "when you are asleep, I run out and move the car seat up under the steering wheel so your legs will cramp."

"You know," he said, "the more I think about it, the more I'm convinced that someday women will be replaced by automation."

On that thought I went to bed only to dream that my husband ran away with my modern kitchen and was living in sin with it in an apartment in New Jersey.

"What kind of wife is this?" I asked, storming into his room without knocking.

"The best kind," he said. "When I come home, Phyllis, the electric cocktail stirrer, has a drink for me; Iris, the oven, has hot hors d'oeuvres on her shelf; Evelyn, the broiler, has a steak going; Margaret, the electric percolator, has fresh, hot coffee brewing; Roberta, the stereo, has soft music going; and when I am finished, Bertha, the disposer does away with my leftovers neat and tidy."

"You're not being fair," I sobbed.

"Oh, but I am. Elsa, the dishwasher, never grabs my plate out from under me before I am finished. And Toni, the refrigerator, works day and night to keep me in ice cubes."

"You're pretty cute, aren't you?" I said. "But what about your laundry?"

"Meet the twins, Shirley and Selma. Shirley washes my clothes to perfection. Never have I had to wear pink underwear or use faded peach handkerchiefs. And Selma, God love her, dries my clothes smooth and knows enough to keep her lint trap shut when I am tired."

"What's that dinging?" I asked.

"It's Iris, reminding me my Baked Alaska is ready. Isn't she a treasure?"

"So were the Dead Sea Scrolls," I said dryly.

"You're jealous," he smiled.

"Who me? Ridiculous. I just wondered who is going to warm your feet on a cold winter night and pick up after you?"

"No sweat," he said. "Meet Caroline, my electric blanket, and Jeanine, my electric broom."

"But who listens to your problems and laughs at your jokes?"

"I've got Sophie, a portable tape recorder, and Bunny, a cassette of warm, soft laughter. Really, my dear, you are wasting your time here. What could I possibly have with a real, live wife that my girls cannot do with maddening efficiency?"

I shook him suddenly out of a sound sleep.

"If you wanted a girl with a clock in her navel, why didn't you marry one?" I shouted.

See what I mean? Not for a minute do men appreciate the frustrations . . . the futility . . . the loneliness . . . the decisions we make in a single day.

To begin with, there is no such thing as a simple household chore. All of them have built-in aggravations.

Take the laundry. I wish you would.

My washer is on a new tack.

For years, it has seen fit to eat one sock out of every pair I have fed into it. Oh, I questioned it at first, but after a while everyone adjusted. They would put a cast on one leg, or a bicycle clamp around their trouser cuff or laugh nervously and say, "Good heavens, one sock *is* brown and the other one pale blue, isn't it?"

Three weeks ago, my washer did a reversal. It gave birth to a pair of men's briefs. They did not look familiar to me, but then, I get a little behind sometimes and have been known to stumble onto navel bands in pre-soak. (The baby is thirteen.)

For starters, I put the briefs on my thirteen-year-old's stack of laundry. He came down early the next morning and asked, "Where's a belt? My shorts keep falling down."

"Don't be funny," I said. "Put them in your brother's drawer."

The sixteen-year-old came out the next morning and said, "Where's a belt?"

"Give them to your father," I said dryly.

My husband said, "They aren't mine. They've got elastic in them. I haven't owned a pair with new elastic in years."

I figured out they had to belong to a friend of my son's who had just spent a few weeks with us, so I put them in an envelope and mailed them to Ohio. We received them back within a week with a note attached. "These are wonderful for showing home movies on but somewhere there must be someone walking around who needs these. They aren't ours."

I sent them to my father who also spent a few weeks with us. He called long distance to say if this was his birthday present, would I please exchange them for the right size.

The shorts became an obsession with me. Where did they come from? Where had they been? Was there an anxious mother somewhere looking into her washer and saying, "Is that all there is?"

I asked the milkman if they looked familiar. (He has never gotten out of his truck since. He just sets the milk at the end of the drive.)

As a result of the handling, the briefs became soiled, so yesterday I put them back into the washer. After the spin cycle, I felt around for them and they were gone. In their place, I found a faded beach towel with little black footprints on it that I have never owned in my life.

I'm going to pretend I didn't see it. The headaches are coming back.

My second favorite household chore is ironing. My first being hitting my head on the top bunk bed until I faint.

An ad in a midwest newspaper read, a while back, "WANTED: Women to do ironing for housewife ten years behind in everything. Must have strong courage and sense of humor. Phone___."

I figured there was a woman I could live next door to in perfect harmony. I iron "By appointment only." I learned long ago that if I ironed and hung three dresses in my daughter's closet, she would change three times during dinner.

The other day my son wanted me to iron his jeans for a class play. "Which leg faces the audience?" I asked, with my iron poised in mid-air.

"Boy," he said, "you're sure not Mrs. Breck."

I hadn't thought about Mrs. Breck in years. She was an antiseptic old broad who used to live two houses down from me. She had an annoying habit of putting her ironing board up on Tuesdays and putting it away again at the end of the day. (What can you expect from a woman who ironed belt buckles?)

One afternoon I dropped in on her as she was pressing the tongues in her son's tennis shoes.

"You know what you are, Mrs. Breck?" I asked. "A drudge."

"Oh, I enjoy ironing," she grinned.

"You keep talking like that and someone is going to put you in a home."

"What's so bad about ironing?" she smiled.

"No one does it," I snapped. "Did you ever see the women on soap operas iron? They're just normal, American housewives. But do you ever see them in front of an ironing board? No! They're out having abortions, committing murder, blackmailing their boss, undergoing surgery, having fun! If you weren't chained to this ironing board, you could too be out doing all sorts of exciting things."

"Like what?" she chuckled, pressing the wrinkle out of a pair of sweat socks and folding them neatly.

"You could give Tupperware parties, learn to Scuba dive, learn hotel management while sitting under a hair dryer, sing along with Jack La Lanne, collect antique barbed wire, start chain letters. I don't know, woman, use your imagination!"

I read the newspaper ad again. It intrigued me, so I dialed the number and waited.

"Hello, Mrs. Breck speaking . . ."

Son of a gun. It sure makes you feel good when you had a part in someone's success, doesn't it?

That fact that housewives are a misunderstood group was evident recently at a cocktail party. A living room psychologist was analyzing women who move furniture every time they cleaned house.

"Basically," he announced, "they are women who hate men.

They cannot bear the thought of a man entering his home and walking across the floor without cracking his femur bone in three places. Rearranging furniture is a little more subtle than putting a cobra in a basket by the bed."

I took exception to his remarks. "Women who rearrange furniture have imagination. They have creativity. They have style. . . ."

"Don't forget hernias," he prompted. "Why is it a woman cannot pinch the clasp on her bracelet, yet can move a fifteen-hundred-pound freezer from the basement to the garage?"

Everyone laughed, but it occurred to me that men don't really know boredom as women do. If we had offices with secretaries with appointment books you could do our week with one original and six carbons. Same old egg on the plate, same old dustballs, same old rumpled beds, same old one-of-a-color socks in the wash.

An attack of monotony does strange things to a woman. Once, for no reason at all, after I finished cleaning the bathroom, I filled an apothecary jar full of popcorn and put it on the back of the commode.

Another time, I put an early American eagle on the doghouse. Usually when I clean, I will fill a brandy snifter with water and food coloring and float a zinnia in it which goes stagnant in ten minutes and hatches mosquito larvae by nightfall.

I will try anything to break the monotony . . . change a light bulb, paint a wall with an artist's brush, put the dining room furniture in the living room and the living room furniture in storage.

"When I clean tomorrow," I told my husband, "I am going to take out the tub in the bathroom and put the washer and dryer in its place. Then I'm going to cut out the front of the tub and make it into a campy sofa for the living room."

"If you want to change something, why don't you wash the draperies?" he mumbled.

"If you're going to use language like that, the least you could do is send the children out of the room," I said.

Two thing have always bothered me about my domesticity. One was when the children sent Colonel Sanders a Mother's

Day card, and the other was a remark made by my husband one evening who said, "Get out of the kitchen before you kill someone."

I have always felt cookbooks were fiction and the most beautiful words in the English language were "room service."

My insecurity at entertaining was compounded when I read an item in a social column recently about a bash for several hundred people where the host was quoted as saying, "We had a pig in our freezer and our neighbors had turkeys in theirs, so we just decided to have a turkey and swine party."

I opened my freezer. I had three snowballs left over from last winter, fourteen packages of chicken innards that were being saved until "garbage day," two radio batteries that someone said would recharge themselves if put in the freezer, a half-eaten piece of taffy with a retainer brace in it, and thirty pounds of hamburger.

I could just imagine myself picking up the phone and saying, "Hey gang, wanta come over Sunday? I'm roasting chicken necks in a pit and for dessert we are having fresh batteries over snowballs."

When I entertain, I do it with all the grace of a water buffalo with a migraine. To begin with, a spontaneous, impromptu, instant party takes me anywhere from three to four weeks to pull off.

First, I must amass enough glasses. This involves numerous trips to the gas station.

Then I must make the house look as though it has never been lived in by children. We must paint, plaster, buy pictures, remove the baby gate from the top of the basement stairway (we haven't had a baby in thirteen years), and replace all the dead house plants with fresh green ones.

Finally, I must pull together a menu.

"What should I serve?" I ask my husband, leafing through a stack of cookbooks.

"How about that wonderful pork Mary Lou made on her rotisserie?"

"How about Sloppy Joes?" I ask.

"Hey, I know. The Spanish dish we had at the Dodsons with the whole clams in it."

"How about Sloppy Joes with a lot of pepper?"

"Maybe we could have a luau and serve something from the pit?"

"How about Sloppy Joes buried in the sandbox?"

Our parties go well enough, I guess, but it's a little disconcerting to open up the paper the next day and read where your husband is quoted as saying, "We had 30 pounds of hamburger in our freezer that wasn't moving and our neighbors had 30 bottles of catsup without labels to unload, so we had a Sloppy Joe Party."

Of course, we've never given a party in our lives that something (or someone) didn't crawl inside our wall and die.

It's the price you pay for rustic, rural living.

In my mind, I visualize a group of mice meeting on a cornfield and one of them says to the other, "Bufford, you don't look too good."

"Oh, I'll be all right," says Bufford, "it's just a head cold."

"Nevertheless," says the leader, "why don't you check in at Bombeck's wall?"

The night of our last party, Bufford didn't make it to the wall. He staggered into our old pump organ and died.

My husband came into the house, sank to his knees and gasped, "Not again! Where this time?"

"In the pump organ," I said.

"Can't we get rid of the odor?"

"Only if you want to paint the living room."

"We mustn't panic," he said, patting his wrists with a deodorizer wick. "We're just going to have to make sure that no one plays the organ tonight." We both nodded.

The party was in high gear when Max Marx sat down to play the organ. I grabbed a can of deodorizer and followed him.

"What are you doing?" he asked, annoyed.

I turned the deodorizer on myself. "It's Skinny Dip," I said feebly, "to make me irresistible."

I watched in horror as he pulled out the stops on the organ and started to pump. As the bellows wheezed in and out, spreading misery throughout the house, three women fainted and one man put out his pipe.

"I say," he said, pausing, "do you have a dog?"

"We have three of them, but they're outside."

He began to play again, then stopped and sniffed. "Is someone in the house cooking sauerkraut? Or making sulfur with a junior chemistry set?"

"No."

"Is someone wearing old gym shoes?" he persisted.

His wife came over at that moment and leaned over his shoulder.

"Max, your music stinks!"

"Is that it?" he said, and moved on to the kitchen for a stronger drink.

# We Have
## Measles . . .
### It Must
### Be Christmas

The other day Brucie complained, "My head hurts and my nose is stuffy."

"Ridiculous," I said. "It's too early. Christmas is a whole week away."

Normal people can always predict when the holidays are near at hand. There is an air of excitement, the smell of holly, the ringing of bells, the singing of carols. At our house, if we have measles, it must be Christmas.

Down at the laundromat, I am known as Typhoid Mary.

"What are you having this year for Christmas?" they ask as I sort my clothes.

"Well, I've got one exposure to chicken pox, one who has only had mumps on his left side, and one who just threw up to keep things interesting."

It's never serious enough to be an emotional drag, but I've forgotten what real Christmases are like. I cornered my friend Donna Robust and begged, "Tell me again about Christmas at your house."

"Well," said Donna, "on Christmas morning I get up first and. . . ."

"Start going through the yellow pages to find a drugstore open," I said, my eyes glistening.

"No, no," she laughed. "I turn on all the lights around the Christmas tree. Then I ring the sleigh bells and. . . ."

"I know, I know," I said excitedly, "it's pill time. You give one a spoon of Coke Syrup, another an aspirin, and the baby a suppository for nausea."

She shook her head. "I summon them all around the tree to open up their presents. Then, after breakfast, we all get dressed. . . ."

"Can you imagine that?" I sighed. "Everybody dressed."

"Then we go to church and that afternoon we have fifteen or twenty people in for Christmas dinner."

"Once I saw my dad on Christmas. He slid two batteries under the door for a robot monster that didn't include them. We were contagious at the time."

"I bet that was nice," she said.

"Oh, and another time the doctor dropped by to check on us and brought in a bit of snow on his boots. The kids went wild."

"Maybe this year things will be different," said Donna, patting my hand.

"Maybe so," I sighed. "But tell me again about how you all get dressed and go out. . . ."

## The Twelve Days of Christmas

On the first day of Christmas my husband gave to me a car with a dead battery.

On the second day of Christmas my husband gave to me two suits for pressing, one dog for worming, and a car with a dead battery.

On the third day of Christmas my husband gave to me three names for drawing, fifty cards for sending, one gift for mailing, and a car that would take till Saturday.

On the fourth day of Christmas my husband gave to me one house for trimming, one tree for buying, one broken ladder, and a short trip to surgery.

On the fifth day of Christmas my husband gave to me three kids for shopping, walnuts for chopping, fruitcake for baking (with Mom's recipe), one house for cleaning, eight doorbells, one Avon call, and a paper route for delivery.

On the sixth day of Christmas my husband gave to me one garage attendant, one hostile doorman, two window washers, one errand boy, and three single secretaries.

On the seventh day of Christmas my husband gave to me one instant party, one broken punch bowl, one littered carpet, three pounds of chip dip, and three unemployed secretaries.

On the eighth day of Christmas my husband gave to me a driveway for snowing, red nose for blowing, long list for going, and a stinking home cold remedy.

On the ninth day of Christmas, my husband said to me, "I have a chipped tooth." "Did you get my rented suit?" "Hope you brought enough loot" for the annual Christmas charity.

On the tenth day of Christmas my husband gave to me a pageant by the wee tots, a gift of a flu shot, and a bird that looked better off than me.

On the eleventh day of Christmas my husband gave to me a bike for construction . . . where are the instructions? . . . these are for a wagon . . . my spirit is draggin', and besides it's a quarter past three.

On the twelfth day of Christmas my husband gave to me gifts of a steam iron, half a water heater, plunger for the bathroom, a blouse size 43, two scented soaps, one paperback, three hair nets, and a toothbrush with a dead battery.

## The Newsletter

I regard the family Christmas newsletter with a mixture of nausea and jealousy.

Nausea because I could never abide by anyone organized enough to chronicle a year of activities. Jealous because our family never does anything that I can talk about on a religious holiday.

For years, I have been assaulted with Frieda and Fred's camping adventures, Marcia and Willard's bright children (their three-year-old has a hit record), and Ginny and Jesse's kitchen-table version of "The Night Before Christmas."

"You know something?" I announced at dinner the other night. "We're a pretty exciting family. This year, instead of the traditional Christmas card, why don't we make up a newsletter?"

"What would we say on it?" asked a son.

"What everyone else says. We could put down all the interesting things we did last year. For instance, you kids tell me anything you did in school that was memorable. (Silence) This is no time for modesty. Just spit out any award or recognition you received throughout the school year."

Finally, after five minutes, one son said, "I passed my eye examination."

"See," I said excitedly, "I knew if we just thought about it a bit. Now, where have we been that's exciting?"

"We got lost that Sunday and went by the industrial school where you told us one of your relatives made license plates."

"I don't think our Christmas list wants to read about that," I said. "Let's see, have I been any place?"

"You went to that Sarah Coventry jewelry party last spring."

"How about that?" I said excitedly. "Now, keep it rolling. Anyone got promoted? Married? Divorced? Hospitalized? Retired? Give birth? (Silence)

"Anyone say anything clever last year? How about the year before that? Did anyone compose a song? Write a letter? Belch after dinner? (Silence)

"Anyone protest anything? Stop biting their nails? Scrape a chair in the Christian Science reading room? Get up in the morning before ten? (Silence)

"Anyone lick a stamp? Kick the dog? Wash their gym suit? Sit up straight in class? Replace a light bulb? Breathe in and out?"

They all sat there silently contemplating their year. Finally, I brought out a box of Christmas cards.

"What are you doing? We thought you were going to send out a family newsletter for Christmas."

"No sense antagonizing the poor devils who sit around and do nothing all year."


## "Are You Awake?"

I just signed a pact with the kids.

If they will sleep on Christmas morning until 3:30, I promise not to let my head fall in the gravy during dinner as I have done in previous years.

The "Christmasthon" has been a tradition at our house since the children were old enough to walk. They appear in our bedroom at some unreal hour and chant, "Mama."

"What?"

"It's Christmas."

"Christmas who?"

"Christmas morning. Are you awake?"

"No."

"Want me to turn on the light so you can see how late it is?"

"And blind your poor mother on . . . what day is it again?"

"Christmas."

"Tell Daddy. He'll be choked."

"Daddy."

"I gave at the office."

Minutes later, Daddy is out of bed, shouting, "For God's sake, do they have to sit around with a flashlight counting the hairs in my nose?"

Once on our feet, we are literally caught up in the ear-splitting pandemonium that is Christmas.

The numbing boom-boom of padded pajama feet on the carpeted stairway.

The deafening click of the switch as the lights illuminate the tree.

The crash of tissue in eager little hands.

The shattering roar of tongues licking peppermint.

The piercing scratch of the dog who wants outside.

The blatant blast of the fire as it crackles in the hearth.

The resounding clang of cereal detonating itself in a bowl.

What seems like days later my husband says, "You look like Dorian Gray. What time is it?"

"It is 3:15 A.M."

"Time flies when you're having fun," he says, yawning.

"Will you keep it down?" I say irritably.

## "Just What I Wanted"

Last year, in Macy's department store in New York, Santa Claus offered his knee to housewives. The results were interesting. As a group, housewives didn't make a lot of demands as to what they wanted so much as what they didn't want. They didn't want drudgery in a box with a ribbon tied around it, any more than their husbands wanted a rubber band organizer for his office.

Our image has become so distorted through television that men are often confused as to what really turns us on.

The other day I was on my hands and knees in the bathroom trying to scrape a piece of caramel off the seat (don't ask!). I was wearing a pair of slacks with the zipper pinned together, a sweatshirt belonging to my daughter. My hair looked like a $1.98 wig that had been reduced.

My husband peered in with a package under his arm and said, "I didn't know what to buy you for Christmas. You've got everything."

I sat back on my heels numbly.

He had that same look on his face the first Christmas we were married and he bought me a cemetery lot and explained, "I was eating your pot roast and this idea came to me like a flash."

He had that same look on his face the year he gave me an appointment card for a free yearly chest X ray/or 5,000-mile checkup—whichever came first.

He had that same look on his face last Christmas when he bought me a barber's kit so I could cut the boys' hair on the patio and save a few bucks. When I saw it, I ran from the room, crying.

"Well, what did you expect, for crying out loud," he said, "a jewel for your navel?"

"And why not?" I charged.

"I didn't know your size!" he shouted back.

"Just once," I said, "I would like you to look at me and not see a plastic person with sticky jelly on her elbow, oatmeal in her hair, and a diaper pin on her blouse. Once . . . just once . . . I'd like you to see me as I really am—a temptress!"

I felt sneaky, but I had to know what he had in mind for this Christmas. I went quickly to the shelf in his bedroom where he had just put the package. I prayed. Please not a garden hose, a cheese slicer, or a card of iron-on patches. Slowly, I felt inside the box and eased out the contents. It was a large, fake jewel with a note: "One size fits all, Nosey."


## The Ayes Have It

For years I've been telling educators they put school levies on the ballot at the wrong time of year. If they had mothers vote during the Christmas vacation, there isn't a levy in the country that would fail.

There is something about being trapped in the same house for a week with a kid with a bouncing ball that makes education important.

I don't know which is worse—the child with nothing to do or the child with something to do.

The kid with nothing to do wants to talk about it. The $200 worth of Christmas toys are all dependent on four Size C batteries that are available only at a Japanese discount house in Japan.

They cannot possibly invite anyone in because there would be a group of them with nothing to do.

They cannot go outside because they would meet someone else with nothing to do and be doubly bored.

They cannot do homework, make beds, empty garbage, or dry dishes because a vacation is when you're supposed to have nothing to do.

They cannot watch television because that is something to do when there is nothing else to do.

The kid with something to do drives you nuts because whatever he does it involves you.

"If you could run in and pick up Charlie and Tim and stop at the store on the way back and get some ice cream and chocolate syrup, we could make a mess in the kitchen."

"We're waiting for you to get down the sled that Daddy stored under the lawn furniture, then we'll get out of your hair."

"Could we have three mason jars, the wheels off your vacuum sweeper, a box of cotton, two pieces of foil, and a banana? We got an idea."

As I was telling my neighbor Maxine yesterday, "Kids today have no stimulant for imagination. The dolls eat and belch, toy cars go 70 miles an hour, their planes fly, their rockets launch, their stoves cook, their games light up, and TV takes them all over the world. They're bored."

"You're right," said Maxine. "Whatya wanta do today? Take a nap?"

"I'm getting too old," I said. "Wanta look for loose change in the chairs?"

"That's boring. We did that yesterday. We could hid from the kids."

"Na . . . It's no fun when they're not here."


## Clever and Creative

The holiday season brings to the surface a breed of women who is not to be believed.

As a matter of fact, I have spent a lifetime avoiding these congenital savers who appear from nowhere and ask, "You're not throwing away those old corn pads just because they're used, are you?"

Their entire life revolves around making something out of nothing—or is it the other way around?

I was at a luncheon the other afternoon when, heaven forbid, I found myself surrounded by not one, but three Junk Junkies. It was like being in a foreign country.

"Do you need any more popsicle sticks?" asked Dorothy.

"No, dear, but I'm short on piano keys."

"I've got some in my basement," said Karen, "unless you want to use up my Tabasco bottles and the arthritic chicken bones."

"We'll get the favors out of the way, then we'll start collecting glass from the rear windows of cars for our decanters," she said proudly. Then, noticing I was there, she turned to me and asked, "What are you making for Christmas?"

"I am making myself sick."

"No, no, I mean what creative things are you doing this year?"

I thought for a moment. "I am wrapping a bed sheet around the bottom of the Christmas tree to cover up the wooden stand." (There was silence.) "I am using a wet sponge to moisten the stamps before I put them on my Christmas cards." (No one moved.) "I replaced the light in the cellar stairway."

Finally, Dorothy spoke. "You mean to say you haven't saved your eggshells for Christmas ornaments? Your old apple cores for sachet or your potato peelings for centerpieces?"

"Oh, I saved all of that together," I said.

"What did you make out of it?" they asked excitedly.

"Garbage."

The women looked at me piteously . . . unbelieving. Suddenly, because I felt inadequate and spiteful, I wanted to shock them. "What would you say if I told you I throw out my old coat hangers by the carload?" (They winced.) "And another thing. I don't save my old milk cartons or my bleach bottles." (They gasped.) "And I don't dress my extra toilet tissue in a red suit for Christmas with a cotton beard. What do you think about that?" (They turned from me.)

They will feel more kindly toward me when they hear I paid fifteen dollars for a termite-ridden log painted gold and stuffed with eight hundred jelly beans on coat hangers with paper hats at the Christmas bazaar.

# Would
## You Believe,
### Love
#### Goddess?

On the occasion of my fortieth birthday, I went into the Bureau of Motor Vehicles to have my driver's license renewed.

The man behind the counter mechanically asked me my name, address, phone number, and finally, occupation.

"I am a housewife," I said.

He paused, his pencil lingering over the blank, looked at me intently and said, "Is that what you want on your license, lady?"

"Would you believe, Love Goddess?" I asked dryly.

If there is one hang-up that plagues every woman it is the "Who am I?" thing. How can we serve a husband, kids, an automatic washer, the Board of Health, and a cat who sits on top of the TV set and looks mad at you because you had her fixed and still have something left over for yourself?

In my lifetime, I have had many identities.

I have been referred to as the "Tuesday pickup with the hole in the muffler," the "10 A.M. standing in the beauty shop who wears Girl Scout anklets," and "the woman who used to work in the same building with the sister-in-law of Jonathan Winters."

Who am I?

*I'm the wife of the husband no one wants to swap with.*

The whole affair was humiliating.

We went to a neighborhood gathering and noted with some embarrassment and shock that they were wife-swapping. One by one a couple would slip off until finally there was only my husband playing "The World Is Waiting for the Sunrise" on a five-string ukelele and me eating the leftover canapés on everyone's paper plate. We went home without speaking a word to one another.

That night I had a dream in which my husband and I awoke in a world where everyone had entered a commune . . . and no one wanted us.

The two of us wandered from one group to another begging to join their free society only to be rejected for one reason or another.

At one commune, we almost made it. The leader looked at us closely and said, "In a commune, we all work in various capacities. Some women tend children, others cook, others clean house, others do laundry. In what capacity would you like to work?" she asked, turning to me.

"Do you have any openings for sex objects?" I asked.

"Hah!" snarled my husband. "With that line you could get the Nobel prize for humor."

Turning to my husband, the leader asked, "And you, sir, what are some of your talents that could be considered contributions to our group. Chopping wood? Building fires? Harvesting crops?"

"I can play 'The World Is Waiting for the Sunrise' on a five-string ukelele," he said.

"Don't be modest," I interrupted. "He can also watch two hundred televised football games in a single weekend without fainting. He can reseat a commode with Play Doh, and he can make himself invisible when it comes time to take out the garbage."

"We are a sharing society," said the leader in a soft voice.

"Did you hear that, Harlow?" I asked, nudging my husband. "A sharing society. That's not going to be easy for a man who sleeps with his car keys."

"You should talk," he barked. "We were married twelve years before you let me drink out of your Shirley Temple mug."

"Please," said the leader of the commune, holding up her hand in a sign of peace, "I don't think a commune is the place for you two. You are compatibly incompatible."

"Which means?" asked my husband.

"Which means you are too married to live in peace and harmony."

The rest of the dream was a nightmare. We are the last two married squares on the face of earth living in a swinging free-marriage-less society. When we check in at a hotel, bellhops snicker when they see we have luggage. Managers stiffen when we sign our names Mr. and Mrs. and say, "We don't want your kind in our hotel." Our children are taunted by cruel playmates who chant, "My Mommy says Your Mommy and Daddy are living in wedlock. Yeah yeah!"

I awoke suddenly from the dream to the voice of my husband who said, "For crying out loud, what's that car doing parked in our driveway? They're just sitting there looking."

"Well, who do you think they are?" I shouted. "They're tourists from the commune here to look at the married freaks."

*I'm the mother of no. 39's football pants.* A woman leaned over at the high school football game last week and said, "Hi, aren't you the mother of no. 39's football pants?"

"Yes," I said.

"You don't know me," she said, "but our sons share the same pants. You see, my Boyd sits on the bench while your son sits in the bleachers and the next week Boyd sits in the stands while your son gets to sit on the bench."

"I see," I nodded.

"What kind of bleach do you use for the stains?"

"Just a pre-soak," I said, "and then my regular detergent."

"I thought so," she said. "A few weeks ago, you overdid."

"Weren't the pants clean?" I asked.

"They were too clean, dear. The boys complained. When they're too white it looks like they never play."

"I'll watch it," I said.

"Have you met any of the other mothers yet?"

"No."

"Well, over there is the mother of 71. She has pants all to herself. He's the captain, you know. Beside her is the grandmother of 93's. He got the new stretch ones. They're trying them out. Wonderful woman. Comes to every game. And of course you know the mother of no. 15's pants. She's the quarterback's mother. Her pants take a beating. At the first away game, they were dragged in the mud twenty-three yards before they were finally ripped."

"Well I never," I said.

"Listen, don't worry about the red stains on the left knee this week."

"Blood?" I asked.

"Jelly bun," she said. Then she added, "You know when women like us have so much in common, we ought to get together more often. Why don't you call me, and we can chat over lunch."

"What's your name?" I called after her.

"Alternate bench mother of 39's pants. I'm in the book!"

*I'm an illegible name tag.* My husband and I are veterans of innumerable school functions (he being in education). That means something like a simple coffee after a flute concert is turned into a ceremony, second only to a national political convention.

Miss Prig is in charge of fashioning small name tags shaped like tulips out of colored construction paper which are pinned to your back. Then Mr. Flap, the football coach, announces that on one side is the name of a famous personality. You are to mingle throughout and by asking questions of each guest find out who you are . . . an ice breaker, so to speak. When the game is finished, you then turn the name tag to the other side, and *voilà!* you know who you are.

Invariably, Miss Toasty, who is in charge of straight pins, blows it, and seventy-five adults are circulating around a room with one arm behind their back asking painfully, "Am I living? Am I in politics?"

Actually, I question the value of name tags as an aid to future identification. I have approached too many people who have spent the entire evening talking to my left bosom. I always have the insane desire to name the other one. It is most disconcerting. Without ever looking at my face, they will say, "Hello there, so you are Edna Bondeck."

"No," I will say, smiling engagingly at their left bosom, "I am Erma Bombeck."

"Don't tell me," they say. "You are related to that tall man over there with a crick in his right arm from holding the name tag behind him."

"Right," I say, my eyes never leaving their tag for a moment, "and you are Fruit of the Loom."

"No, that's a label from my underwear that got stuck in my name tag while my arm was behind my back. Are you new in the area?"

"Yes I am. And it's wonderful meeting so many new chests . . . er, people."

"I'm sure it is. See you around."

The entire evening is a faceless one. At the end I say good-by to the blonde with the exceptional posture, the braless militant, the chest of hair under the body shirt and kcebmoB lliB.

"Oh, for crying out loud," says my husband. "It's me with my name tag upside down."

I looked carefully into his face. "Oh yeah. Let me see some identification."

*I'm Edna.* My mother-in-law and I have a great relationship. She calls me Edna and I call her on her birthday, Mother's Day, and Christmas.

At the wedding when she insisted they put a funeral flag on the fender of her car and drove with her lights on, I sensed somehow I was not what she would have chosen for her son.

But, God love her, she has a sense of humor and somehow we have all survived. She has accepted me for what I am. A mistake. And I have learned to live with her through the miracle of sedation.

One of her idiosyncrasies, however, I will never adjust to. I call it her Last Breath Performance.

Check this. I am driving the car and she is sitting beside me. Out of the clear blue sky, I hear her suck in her breath, moan slightly and slump, steadying her head with her hand. I wait, but she doesn't exhale.

The first time this happened I figured (a) She was leaving the car on a permanent basis; (b) I had closed the electric windows on a gas-station attendant and was towing him by his fingers; (c) We were being followed by a tornado funnel.

Instinctively, I jammed on the brakes of the car, nearly hurling her through the windshield, turned around, grabbed her by the shoulders, and shouted hysterically, "What's the matter?"

"Darn it," she said, "I just remembered I forgot to lock my back door."

During subsequent drives, I was to learn that she gasped and groaned at girls in shorts, roses in full bloom, a half stick of gum discovered in her raincoat, and the realization that tomorrow was her sister-in-law's birthday.

She didn't limit her Last Breath Performance to the car.

When she watched television or read the newspaper, she would inhale noisily, freeze, put her hand over her mouth, and say, "How do those poor people in Needles, California, stand the heat?"

I pride myself on being able to live in peace with my mother-in-law, and she puts up with me. The other day we were driving together, when she sucked in her breath, clutched her purse, and mumbled, "Oh my!"

Figuring she had just remembered her dental appointment, I kept moving and promptly smacked into a truck pulling out from the alley.

She shook her head and made a clicking noise with her tongue. "I tried to warn you, Edna, but you wouldn't listen."

*I'm the dog's mother.* As everyone knows I hold the record for the longest post-natal depression period ever. I could hardly wait for the Empty Nest Syndrome, at which time I was going to climb in it, eat bourbon balls before breakfast, watch soap operas, and eventually run away with a vacuum cleaner salesman.

On the day the Empty Nest became a reality, I found to my horror there was a dog in it—which the family explained would keep me company. I needed company the way a man reading *Playboy* needed his wife to turn the pages for him.

The dog was friendly enough, had fair manners, and was playful. He only had one hang-up. He had to be let in and out of the house 2,672 times a day.

Some dogs have a blade-of-grass complex. They can't seem to pass one without stopping and making it glisten. This beast never passed a door without scratching it, jumping up to the door handle and howling like he only had two seconds before he would no longer be responsible for what happened.

At the end of the first day I was near exhaustion. I had not gotten the breakfast dishes cleared off the table, the beds made, or the laundry started.

"I'll bet you were playing all day with that dog," teased my husband.

"What makes you think that?" I asked.

"Look at the way that little dickens is jumping up and down."

"He is aiming for your throat. He wants out."

"Don't be ridiculous. He just came in."

Finally, the dog let out a shriek that took off the tops of our heads and threw himself at the door.

Mechanically, I opened up the door and stood there with my hand on the knob.

He gave another yap and I opened up the door and he was in again.

"Why did he want in after you just let him out?" asked my husband.

"Why do fairies dance on the lawn? Why is the Pope always

a Catholic? Why indeed?" The dog yipped and I opened the door for him to leave again.

"You mean to tell me it's this way all day?"

I nodded, at the same time opening the door so he could bounce in again.

"I got it," said my husband snapping his fingers. "We'll go out when he goes in and when he comes out we'll go in. That way we'll confuse him into not knowing if he is in or out."

Standing there huddled in the darkness on the cold porch scratching with our paws to get in, I tried to figure where I went wrong. I think it was when my mother said, "Grab him. You're not getting any younger."

*I'm room service in tennis shoes.* "What in heaven's name is that hanging over your dirty-clothes hamper?" asked Mother. "It looks like a basketball hoop made out of a bent coat hanger."

"It's a basketball hoop made out of a bent coat hanger," I said.

"It looks terrible."

"That's easy for you to say," I said. "You don't have to run through dirty underwear in your bare feet or find the laundry before you can do it. When the boys improve on their hook shots, I'll have it made."

"What's this?" she scowled.

"You mean that bar across the door you just cracked your head on? It's an exercise bar so the boys can build up their muscles."

"And this ironing board," she persisted. "Don't you ever get tired of falling over it? Want me to take it down?"

"What for?" I asked. "We're not moving."

The trouble with Mother is she has forgotten what it is to live in a house furnished in Contemporary Children. I used to fight it too. At one time I was so naïve I thought only edible things belonged in the refrigerator, bicycles without wheels should be discarded, and if you had eight people to dinner, all the glasses had to match.

I went crazy trying to keep an antiseptic house in a wet shoe-string world. Then one day I was doing cafeteria duty with a mother of six children who said a curious thing. "I wonder how my kids will remember me. Will they remember me as a Mother who never had rings around the bathtub or will they remember the popcorn we ate in the living room?

"Will they remember how many committees I chaired, or will they remember the fresh doughnuts in the kitchen after school?

"Will they remember how cleverly I co-ordinated the blue in the sofa cushions with the pillows or will they remember I hung the outline of their hand in the living room like it was an original Renoir?

"It's funny," she said, "I came from a large family and I can't even remember what color my bedroom was or if there was mud in the hallway or fingerprints around the light switches. All I can remember is the laughter, the love, and a crazy basketball hoop my mother made out of bent coat hangers and put over the clothes hamper and how my mother was always there to talk to."

Well, I can't begin to tell you how that story brought tears to my eyes. I wanted to be that kind of mother.

Yesterday, I stacked my cookies in pyramids and waited for the kids to come home from school. The phone rang. "Mom? I went home on Greg's bus. We're going to shoot baskets and mess around."

"But . . . when are you coming home?" I asked soulfully.

"I don't know. His brother will bring me."

"Wanta know what I did today?" I asked excitedly.

"Not now, Mom. You can tell me when I get there."

"But I'll forget it by then."

"Write it down." (Click)

I ate a cookie and watched the clock. The door opened and I greeted our daughter.

"Hi, guess what I got on sale today?" I said, following her to her bedroom.

"Tell me while I change," she said.

"Change for what? You going out again?"

"I'm going to the library. They're holding a couple of books I have to pick up today."

"Don't you have time for milk and cookies and talk with a mother who is always here?"

"I'm on a diet. You eat 'em, but don't ruin your dinner."

"It's no fun eating by yourself. Can I go with you?"

"You'd be out of place in the library. No adults go there in the afternoon."

I ate another cookie and awaited the arrival of my other son.

"Did I get any mail?" he asked.

"A thing that looks like a picture from Baltimore. Did I tell you the funny thing the butcher said today?"

"Hey, that's Jim O'Brien's autograph I sent for. I'm gonna call Brian. Why don't you run along and watch TV."

I sat there deflated. That's the trouble with mothers today. No wonder we're rotten. There's no one to communicate with us. No one to share our day after school. No one to give us a sense of importance. Small wonder we hang around the beauty shops in gangs, join organizations, have long lunches with fattening desserts. There's no one to care. I stood outside of the bathroom door and called in to my son. "I forgot to tell you something. Are you in there?"

"Who is it?" he asked.

"It's Mother."

"Mother who?"

*I'm a household word.* A neighbor of mine suggested that since I have been writing a column for the newspaper, I have become a household word.

"You mean like bleach, leftovers, and grease-clogged sinks?"

"Of course not," she said. "I mean like Flip Wilson, Carol Burnett, and Martha Mitchell."

"Oh really now," I said, "you do run on. If you asked someone what a Bombeck was, they'd think it was a nearly extinct bird in the Everglades who eats mosquito eggs."

"My dear, you are wrong," she insisted, "you have quite a following."

With some immodesty, I decided to test her theory one afternoon when I called home from an airport in Philadelphia.

"Hello, operator. This is Erma Bombeck calling. I'm a household word and. . . ."

"Is Household the party's first name or last?" she asked.

"Neither, I was being funny. This is Erma Bombeck and I. . . ."

"Steinbeck?"

"No, Bombeck. That's B as in Boy O-M-B-E-C-K."

"Mary Household Bondack. Do you have an area code?"

"No, I don't want to talk to Mary Household Bondack."

"Then you wish to call station-to-station. If you do not know the number in that city, you may hang up and call the area operator and 555-1212."

"Operator. Don't hang up! OPERATOR! (redial) Operator, I wish to call collect to . . . my name is Erma Bombeck. Not Ernie. Erma, E as in Edna r-m-a Bombeck."

"Bomberg? Bromfield? Brombreck? Brickbat? Would you spell that again, Miss Beckbomb?"

"Look, you're pretty warm with Brombeck. Let's ride with that one. I am trying to call home collect and this is my number."

The operator speaks. "I have a collect call from Mrs. Edna Brombecker."

My son answers. "That's my mom and she isn't home now. She is in Philadelphia."

"Dear heart," I yelled, "it's Mama. Accept the charges."

"My mama isn't home now. Can I take a message?"

"Yeah," I shouted. "Call *Mrs.* Erma Bombeck at. . . ."

"How do you spell the last name?" he asked slowly.

I hung up and sat there awhile, numb. I can't believe this is how Martha Mitchell made it as a household word.


*Joan of Arc?* A friend confided to me the other day that whenever an unpleasant situation arises, she resorts to play-acting. She pretends she is a character living out a scene.

"You are some kind of nut," I said.

"We all do it," she replied. "I've seen you when your husband goes out of town for a few days. I don't know who you are, but you're certainly not yourself."

She was right, of course. Actually, I am several characters when my husband goes out of town. As I stand in the driveway, clutching my shawl and drawing my children close to me to stave off the harsh winds, I am Marmee March, the brave young mother in *Little Women.* Upon my frail shoulders rests the responsibility of the family. I play it to the hilt. "Prithee have a good trip," I yell. Then to the children, "Come, let us go in and pop corn and sing 'Rock of Ages.'"

By the second day, being alone with the kids, I am not so gallant. I am Stella Dallas who is cast aside by society to serve and suffer without friends, family, or love. I am forgotten by the world (Mother didn't even call) and sentenced to a life of loneliness, pain, and "Let's Make a Deal."

By the third day, as I visualize that bum living it up in a Holiday Inn Motel, I go into my Belle Watling routine. She's the woman of pleasure in *Gone With the Wind*. I tell myself I was just a passing diversion to bear his three children, but now he has abandoned me and gone on to brighter lights in tinsel town. Is it my imagination? Or did I really get the cold shoulder at the meat counter?

My St. Joan is probably my best effort. I perform it my fourth day alone. It's a consumptive performance where I clomp around in my robe and slippers until noon and when the washer repairman says, "I found a pair of training pants in your pump. That's thirty-four dollars," I just cough and say, "It doesn't matter any more, really."

By the fifth day, the kids have me on the run and they know it. Discipline and reasoning are gone. Play-acting has lost its fascination. As my husband pulls into the driveway, I approach him with a band of plastic daisies around my head while I shred my apron into small pieces.

"Who are you today?" he asks.

"Ophelia," I snap.

"That bad?" he asks.

"That bad."

# But
## Seriously,
### Folks . . .

*Time.*

Time.

It hangs heavy for the bored, eludes the busy, flies by for the young, and runs out for the aged.

Time.

We talk about it as though it's a manufactured commodity that some can afford, others can't; some can reproduce, others waste.

We crave it. We curse it. We kill it. We abuse it. Is it a friend? Or an enemy? I suspect we know very little about it. To know it at all and its potential, perhaps we should view it through a child's eyes.

"When I was young, Daddy was going to throw me up in the air and catch me and I would giggle until I couldn't giggle any more, but he had to change the furnace filter and there wasn't time."

"When I was young, Mama was going to read me a story and I was going to turn the pages and pretend I could read, but she had to wax the bathroom and there wasn't time."

"When I was young, Daddy was going to come to school and watch me in a play. I was the fourth Wise Man (in case one of the three got sick), but he had an appointment to have his car tuned up and it took longer than he thought and there was no time."

"When I was young, Grandma and Granddad were going to come for Christmas to see the expression on my face when I got my first bike, but Grandma didn't know who she could get to feed the dogs and Granddad didn't like the cold weather, and besides, they didn't have the time."

"When I was young, Mama was going to listen to me read my

essay on 'What I Want to Be When I Grow Up,' but she was in the middle of the 'Monday Night Movie' and Gregory Peck was always one of her favorites and there wasn't time."

"When I was older, Dad and I were going fishing one weekend, just the two of us, and we were going to pitch a tent and fry fish with the heads on them like they do in the flashlight ads, but at the last minute he had to fertilize the grass and there wasn't time."

"When I was older, the whole family was always going to pose together for our Christmas card, but my brother had ball practice, my sister had her hair up, Dad was watching the Colts, and Mom had to wax the bathroom. There wasn't time."

"When I grew up and left home to be married, I was going to sit down with Mom and Dad and tell them I loved them and I would miss them. But Hank (he's my best man and a real clown) was honking the horn in front of the house, so there wasn't time."


## *"I've Always Loved You Best"*

It is normal for children to want assurance that they are loved. I have always admired women who can reach out to pat their children and not have them flinch.

Feeling more comfortable on paper, I wrote the following to put on the pages of their baby books.

### To the Firstborn

I've always loved you best because you were our first miracle. You were the genesis of a marriage, the fulfillment of young love, the promise of our infinity.

You sustained us through the hamburger years. The first apartment furnished in Early Poverty . . . our first mode of transportation (1955 feet) . . . the seven-inch TV set we paid on for thirty-six months.

You wore new, had unused grandparents, and had more clothes than a Barbie doll. You were the "original model" for unsure parents trying to work the bugs out. You got the strained lamb, open pins, and three-hour naps.

You were the beginning.

### To the Middle Child

I've always loved you best because you drew a dumb spot in the family and it made you stronger for it.

You cried less, had more patience, wore faded, and never in your life did anything "first," but it only made you more special. You are the one we relaxed with and realized a dog could kiss you and you wouldn't get sick. You could cross a street by yourself long before you were old enough to get married, and the world wouldn't come to an end if you went to bed with dirty feet.

You were the child of our busy, ambitious years. Without you we would never have survived the job changes, the house we couldn't afford, and the tedium and the routine that is marriage.

You were the continuance.

### To the Baby

I've always loved you best because endings are generally sad and you are such joy. You readily accepted the milk-stained bibs. The lower bunk. The cracked baseball bat. The baby book, barren but for a recipe for graham cracker pie crust that someone jammed between the pages.

You are the one we held onto so tightly. For you see, you are the link with a past that gives a reason to tomorrow. You darken our hair, quicken out steps, square our shoulders, restore our vision, and give us humor that security, maturity, and endurity can't give us.

When your hairline takes on the shape of Lake Erie and your children tower over you, you will still be "The Baby."

You were the culmination.

## The Lost Christmas

There is nothing sadder in this world than to awake Christmas morning and not be a child.

Not to feel the cold on your bare feet as you rush to the Christmas tree in the living room. Not to have your eyes sparkle at the wonderment of discovery. Not to rip the ribbons off the shiny boxes with such abandon.

What happened?

When did the cold, bare feet give way to reason and a pair of sensible bedroom slippers? When did the sparkle and the wonderment give way to the depression of a long day? When did a box with a shiny ribbon mean an item on the "charge"?

A child of Christmas doesn't have to be a toddler or a teen. A child of Christmas is anyone who believes that Kings have birthdays.

The Christmases you loved so well are gone. What happened?

Maybe they diminished the year you decided to have your Christmas cards printed to send to 1,500 of your "closest friends and dearest obligations." You got too busy to sign your own name.

Maybe it was the year you discovered the traditional Christmas tree was a fire hazard and the needles had to be vacuumed every three hours and you traded its holiday aroma for a silver one that revolved, changed colors, played "Silent Night" and snowed on itself.

Or the year it got to be too much trouble to sit around the table and put popcorn and cranberries on a string. Possibly you lost your childhood the year you solved your gift problems neatly and coldly with a checkbook.

Think about it. It might have been the year you were too rushed to bake and resorted to slice-and-bake with no nonsense. Who needs a bowl to clean—or lick?

Most likely it was the year you were so efficient in paying back all of your party obligations. A wonderful little caterer did it for you at three dollars per person.

Children of Christmas are givers. That's what the day is for. They give thanks, love, gratitude, joy, and themselves to one another.

It doesn't necessarily mean you have to have children around a tree. It's rather like lighting a candle you've been saving, caroling when your feet are cold, building a fire in a clean grate, grinding tinsel deep into the rug, licking frosting off a beater, giving something you made yourself.

It's laughter, being with people you like, and at some time falling to your knees and saying, "Thank you for coming to my birthday party."

How sad indeed to awake on Christmas and not be a child.

Time, self-pity, apathy, bitterness, and exhaustion can take the Christmas out of the child, but you cannot take the child out of Christmas.

## I Love You, Edith Bunker

Bigots may be all right in their places, but would you want your daughter to marry one?

Edith Bunker did the day she said, "I do, I will, and I'll keep doing it until I get it right" to Archie Bunker, the Irish Godfather of TV's "All in the Family."

Personally, I love Edith Bunker. She hasn't read anything current since a cereal box offered an African violet to people with irregularities. She regards the six o'clock news as a filler between "As the World Turns" and "Roller Derby." She fills up her husband's plate at picnics and apologizes because the baked beans oozed over his chicken. If Gloria Steinem asked her to make a contribution to her sex she'd say, "Honey, Archie gives at the plant."

What's to envy about Edith? She's a giver and God knows there are few of them left in the world. Edith is at the end of every line, whether it be at the bank, the check-out, or the clinic. She would drive Archie to the hospital for a paper cut. But she would refuse anesthetic for her own surgery if it cost extra. She would hang a picture over her living room sofa that the milkman's wife painted by number.

She would lend you her new Christmas sweater and wouldn't complain if you sweat in it. She is one of the last of the vanishing breed of listeners—remember them? They are people who sit quietly and look at you in the face when you talk and when you're finished there is a silence. They haven't been thinking of a story they could tell.

Edith has a tolerance toward humanity and unconsciously looks for the bright side. She would find humor in Jane Fonda's acceptance speech for the Oscar.

Actually, Edith is not too complex. What you see is what she is. Edith has never learned about the plastic veneer or sophistication that people cover themselves with. If it were suggested to her that she not refer to Phase II as a bar of soap, she'd say, "Am I pronouncing it wrong?"

It is a sad commentary on my life, but I don't know many Edith Bunkers. The people I know still wear dark glasses indoors even though they fall over things. They refuse to have people in for dinner until all their dishes match. They are bored, miserable, depressed, and unfulfilled because in 1965 Betty Friedan told them they were. (Would Betty lie?)

I have a theory if anything is ever to be resolved with mankind it won't be the Archie Bunkers with the wall-to-wall mouth who will do it. And it probably won't be Meathead and his wife Gloria (who put the IN in "All in the Family"). It will be the Edith Bunkers. Their unselfishness, their regard for human feelings, their patience, their caring, and their love of everyone will bring it about.


## Flag

On television the other week a group of students were talking about their confrontation with New York construction workers. "We made a mistake," said one of the students. "We attacked their symbol—their flag. We shouldn't have done that. It's important to them."

The phrase stuck in my mind. *"Their* flag. *Their* symbol." I thought it was theirs too. Or is it? As a parent, I guess I always thought respect for the flag was congenital. Is it possible I was so busy teaching the basics, I never took the time to teach "flag."

"Oh say can you see by the dawn's early light. . . ."

("Don't slouch. Pick up your feet. Don't talk with food in your mouth. Stop squinting. Turn that radio down. Get off the phone. Tie that shoestring before you trip on it.")

"Shoot if you must this old gray head but spare your country's flag. . . ."

("Don't snap your gum. Stop eating all that junk before dinner. Sit up straight. Look at me when I talk to you. Your eyes are going to stay crossed someday. Get your homework done. Wear boots.")

"I pledge allegiance to the flag of the United States of America. . . ."

("Shut that door behind you. Get the mud off your shoes. Quit rustling that bag. Go to sleep. Don't slam the door. Leave your sweater on. Get a haircut.")

"If anyone attempts to haul down the American flag, shoot him on the spot."

("Stop fidgeting. Keep your feet on the floor where they belong. Don't talk back. What do you say to the nice lady? Wash your hands. You're letting in flies. Pick up that mess.")

"We came in peace for all mankind."

("You're going to be late. Eat something. Bring me the change. Hang that up. Brush your teeth. Apologize. Get your elbows off that table. Got a clean handkerchief? Tuck your shirt in. Be home early.")

Did I forget to tell them it was their flag they hoisted over Mount Suribachi? Their flag that flies over champions at the Olympics? Their flag that draped the coffin of John F. Kennedy? Their flag that was planted in the windless atmosphere of the moon? It's pride. It's love. It's goose bumps. It's tears. It's determination. It's a torch that is passed from one generation to another.

I defy you to look at it and tell me you feel nothing.


## X-Rated World

I got some flack on a column I once did on horror movies. Some readers felt I was condoning violence and bad taste for letting my youngsters see them.

There was a time when I probably would have agreed with them. That's when the world had a GP rating and horror movies were rated X.

Maybe it's time we stopped flapping about the world of make-believe ("Did Tarzan marry the girl or not? And was the chimp illegitimate?") and zero in on the big problem: reality.

We are shocked when our children see rats, snakes, and frogs devouring humans. We can turn our backs when they are live-ins in most slums around the country.

We scream censorship when there is murder committed before our children's eyes on the tube. We can endure it when it appears on the six o'clock news with a dateline: Vietnam.

My children in their short span on earth have seen Watts in flames, mothers with clubs and rocks protesting schools, college students slain by national guardsmen, mass slaughter in California, and political conventions that defy anything they have seen on a movie screen.

They have heard language from congressmen that curls their hair. They have seen animals slain to extinction by humans with clubs and shot at from moving cars. They have flinched from gunshots that fell leaders of countries because they hold views that are different from those who slew them.

I challenge you to protect a generation from violence that has seen the horrors of Kent, Dallas, and Attica.

If it doesn't, it should bother someone that our children are short on laughter. We are giving birth to the most educated, bright, intelligent, serious, dedicated group of adults who ever sat in a playpen. Where is the little mouse who used to outsmart the cat in the cartoons? Where is the newspaperman who used to dress in a phone booth and wear wrinkled underwear with a cape? Where indeed?

*Bonnie and Clyde* was a joke to young movie-goers . . . a gas. So was *Butch Cassidy and the Sundance Kid.* So was *Willard.* To them, the violence was exaggerated, absurd, unreal.

It's the reality that frightens them and gives them nightmares. God help us. It does me too.